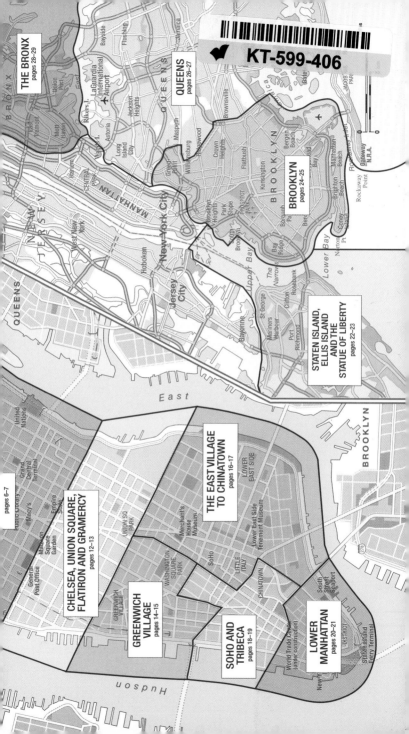

KT-599-406

THE BRONX
pages 28–29

QUEENS
pages 26–27

BROOKLYN
pages 24–25

STATEN ISLAND, ELLIS ISLAND, AND THE STATUE OF LIBERTY
pages 22–23

THE EAST VILLAGE TO CHINATOWN
pages 16–17

CHELSEA, UNION SQUARE, FLATIRON AND GRAMERCY
pages 12–13

GREENWICH VILLAGE
pages 14–15

SOHO AND TRIBECA
pages 18–19

LOWER MANHATTAN
pages 20–21

pages 6–7

INSIGHT GUIDES

NEW YORK

smart guide

APA PUBLICATIONS

Part of the Langenscheidt Publishing Group

Contents

Areas

Below: the Guggenheim
Museum on Fifth Avenue.

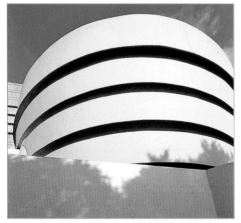

A–Z

Left: New York from the Top of the Rock at Rockefeller Center.

Atlas

Below: after hours in the city that never sleeps.

New York

'I Love New York' has been the city's catchphrase since the 1970s. And, truly, there is a lot to love about this modern-day Colossus that holds top rank in business, the arts, and international clout. Sure, there've been critics – 'I'm sick o' New York City' the Irish-born poet James B. Dollard once wrote. But forward-looking New Yorkers, native-born and adopted, shrug and move on.

New York Facts and Figures

Total population: 8.31 million
Population density: 27,608 per sq mile
(71,505 per sq km)
Population of Manhattan: 1.6 million
Total area: 301 sq miles (780 sq km)
Area of Manhattan: 23.7 sq miles (61.4 sq km)
Annual visitors: 46 million
No. of hotel rooms: 76,000
Average daily hotel room rate: $312
No. of restaurants: 18,696
Average cost of dinner: $40.78
No. of Broadway theatres: 39
Average cost of a Broadway ticket: $76.43

New York State of Mind

First-time visitors to New York usually come with wide eyes and high expectations. And the city generally doesn't disappoint, even if it frustrates. No matter what you're after, you'll find it here: great theater, museums, luxurious hotels, history, nightlife, sumptuous dining. The only thing that's difficult to find is peace and quiet. But if you stay in a high-rise hotel far above the teeming streets, or venture into Central Park, you can find some of that, too.

At first it can all be a little overwhelming: 12,800 taxis, 6,000 buses, 6,400 miles of streets, 578 miles of waterfront, more than 18,000 restaurants, and 76,000 hotel rooms. But once you get over the crowded streets, the wailing sirens, and the multitude of hawkers, you can start to see that there is more to New York than its tourist attractions.

A City Transformed

If anything characterizes New York today, it's how much the city has raised itself up from the dark days of the 1970s and 1980s. Crime is now at low levels New Yorkers have not seen since the 1960s, and the city is generally cleaner and more efficient. The upshot is that both tourists and businesspeople are flocking here in unprecedented numbers. Alongside the flourishing hotel trade, good new restaurants are also opening up right and left, which is great news for visitors and residents alike.

If you want to see an example of how the city can reinvent itself, just look at Times Square. A few years ago, the area was filled with porn theaters and pickpockets. Today Times Square is still choked, but with new office buildings and hotels, refurbished Broadway theaters, media giants like MTV, a new, iconic TKTS booth, and thousands of tourists.

Not that the story is uniformly positive. The New York area has some of the highest unemployment rates in the US. The disparity between the rich and the poor is great; most new housing is affordable only to the wealthy.

Below: the New York skyline inspires both awe and affection in visitors and locals alike.

A Heady Mix

Tension is inevitable in such a complicated, crowded and expensive place, but everyone gets along pretty well. The five boroughs of New York City have a total population of approximately 8 million, with immigrants from all corners of the world. There are more Italians than in Venice, more Irish than in Dublin, more Jews than in Jerusalem. The former mayor David Dinkins was fond of calling New York a 'gorgeous mosaic.'

Getting Around

By the end of their first trip, most visitors are hooked. It is exhilarating walking the crowded streets, or seeing the Statue of Liberty looming over the harbor. Getting your bearings is easy. The cigarette-shaped island of Manhattan is divided into three areas: Midtown, Uptown, and Downtown. Midtown is the busy, pulsating heart of the city, with most of New York's major attractions: Times Square, the Empire State Building, Rockefeller Center, and MoMA. Uptown is the area around the northern part of Central Park – the Upper East Side, the Upper West Side, and Harlem. Downtown is not only the oldest part of Manhattan, but also the place for the newest hotspots: if it's hip and trendy, then it's probably happening Downtown. Surrounding Manhattan are the four other boroughs of New York City – Staten Island, Brooklyn, Queens, and the Bronx.

Highlights

▲ **Central Park** encompasses more than 843 acres (337 hectares) of woodlands, lawns, and lakes – a masterpiece of landscape architecture.

▶ **Statue of Liberty** Lady Liberty has welcomed millions to the city.

▶ **The Big Five** The Met, MoMA, the Guggenheim, the Whitney, and the American Museum of Natural History are treasure houses of world art, science, and culture.

▲ **Empire State Building** After 9/11, this Art Deco landmark once again has the city's highest observation deck.

▶ **Times Square** Gotham's neon heart is brighter than ever.

◀ **Culinary Capital** Hot new chefs serve up a never-ending feast.

Midtown

Starting above 34th Street and running up to Central Park, Midtown is what most people have in mind when they think of the Big Apple: the bright lights of Times Square, the soaring frame of the Empire State Building, the grand sweep of Fifth Avenue. This is where billboards vie with world-class art, where power lunching and power shopping are a way of life, and where, as the old saying goes, there's a broken heart for every light on Broadway. From the Museum of Modern Art to the United Nations, the Chrysler Building to Grand Central Terminal, this is New York at its most iconic.

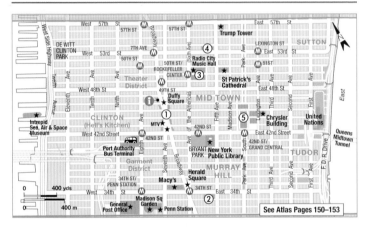

Times Square ①

Times Square lies at the intersection of Broadway and Seventh Avenue, at the heart of Manhattan's theater district. The most recent renovation is Duffy Square, which has a new glass **TKTS** booth located under the red translucent steps. Same-day discounted theater tickets for Broadway shows are available here.

At the corner of 44th Street is the MTV studio. On the east side of Duffy Square is the studio of Good Morning America. The **Times Square Information Center** is in the Embassy Theater on Seventh Avenue between 46th and 47th.
SEE ALSO ESSENTIALS, P.49; THEATER, P.146

Fifth Avenue

Few streets evoke the essence of the city as powerfully as Fifth Avenue. It's all here – the audacity of the Empire State Building, the ambition of Rockefeller Center, the old-world Gothicness of St Patrick's.

The **Empire State Building** ② rises like a rocket from 34th Street. Completed in 1931, it was for many years the tallest structure in the world. The observation deck has stunning views, among the most iconic in the US. Farther Uptown, the

New York Public Library is a 1911 Beaux Arts monument and one of the world's finest research facilities, with some 88 miles (142km) of bookshelves. To the rear of the library is **Bryant Park** and the delightful **Bryant Park Grill**. At East 50th Street is the International Building, with Lee Lawrie's monumental *Atlas* at its entrance. The statue is over 25ft (8m) tall, but it is dwarfed by the Gothic spires of **St Patrick's Cathedral**, the largest Catholic church in the country. At 57th Street, fashionistas browse Louis Vuitton, Dior, and the expensive emporia of Trump Tower.
SEE ALSO ARCHITECTURE, P.32, 33;

Left: Radio City Music Hall.

weathervanes.
SEE ALSO MUSEUMS, P.90, 91

East 42nd Street

From Fifth Avenue, stroll east on 42nd Street to **Grand Central Terminal** ⑤, a Beaux Arts masterpiece completed in 1913. The concourse accommodates hundreds of thousands of commuters daily, while the **Oyster Bar** is a favorite of power lunchers. To the east is the **Chrysler Building**, an Art Deco spire completed in 1930 and, for a few months, the world's tallest structure. The United Nations Headquarters occupy the eastern end of 42nd Street. Tours depart every half-hour.
SEE ALSO ARCHITECTURE, P.32; RESTAURANTS, P.120

Midtown West

The west side is rougher around the edges than the east, encompassing the garment district, diamond district, and Hell's Kitchen (known nowadays as Clinton), as well as Penn Station and the Port Authority Bus Terminal. You'll find acres of retail space at **Macy's** in Herald Square; the Circle Line boat tour by the Hudson River; and basketball, hockey, music, and more at **Madison Square Garden**.
SEE ALSO MUSIC, P.107; SHOPPING, P.137; SPORTS, P.144

CHURCHES, P.44; FASHION, P.50–1; RESTAURANTS, P.120

Rockefeller Center ③

Enter this Art Deco city within a city from Fifth Avenue via the Channel Gardens, a sloping walkway that leads to the base of the soaring G.E. Building. A gilded statue of Prometheus rises above a sunken plaza, which, in winter, is the site of an ice-skating rink and a giant Christmas tree. Tours of the **NBC Studios** depart regularly (www.nbcuniversalstore.com). Atop the G.E. Building is the Rainbow Room restaurant, and the more affordable **Rainbow Grill**, while the Top of The Rock observation deck provides stunning views of the city. Across 50th Street is **Radio City Music Hall**, the famous Art Deco theater.
SEE ALSO ARCHITECTURE, P.33; BARS, P.34; MUSIC, P.107

Museum of Modern Art

One of Midtown's most important cultural centers is the Museum of Modern Art ④, or MoMA, on 53rd Street between Fifth and Sixth avenues. Devoted to works of art created after 1880, the collection includes such masterpieces as Van Gogh's *Starry Night* and Dali's *The Persistence of Memory*. Also on 53rd Street is the **American Folk Art Museum**, which features everything from quilts to

Right: Grand Central Terminal.

7

Upper East and West Sides and Central Park

The Uptown neighborhoods on either side of Central Park are similar in appearance but different in attitude. The Upper East Side is traditionally a home of the genteel rich. The Upper West Side tends to be scruffier, younger, and more liberal in outlook, although, in this age of astronomical rents, hardly less moneyed. Between them is Central Park, a leafy oasis of lakes and lawns that, for many New Yorkers, is the calm at the eye of the urban storm.

See Atlas Pages 150–151

Museum Mile

Nine museums occupy this stretch of Fifth Avenue between 82nd and 105th streets. Most prominent is the **Metropolitan Museum of Art** ①, a Gothic behemoth with the largest art collection in the United States, ranging from ancient works to modern masterpieces.

The other heavy hitter is the **Solomon R. Guggenheim Museum** ② (at 89th Street), housed in Frank Lloyd Wright's distinctive funnel-shaped building. Among the other museums on this strip are the **Neue Galerie**, **National Academy Museum and School of Fine Arts**, **Cooper-Hewitt National Design Museum**, **Jewish Museum**, **Museum of the City of New York**, and **El Museo del Barrio**. SEE ALSO MUSEUMS, P.94, 95, 97, 98

Madison Avenue

Madison Avenue is a block from Fifth but a world apart. Wave goodbye to the prim and proper salons of the Four Hundred, because Madison is the land of ritz and glitz – a slick marketplace for the hyperactive consumer. At 75th Street, the **Whitney Museum of American Art** ③ represents the full range of 20th- and 21st-century American art, including the work of such luminaries as Edward Hopper, Georgia O'Keeffe, Willem de Kooning, and Jackson Pollock.

From the Whitney to 59th Street, Madison is all about conspicuous consumption. The names on the storefronts read like a roster of the fashion elite: Ralph Lauren, Yves Saint Laurent, Giorgio Armani, Prada, Ungaro. One of the city's quintessential shopping scenes is **Barneys New York** on 61st Street. Another Manhattan favorite is **Bloomingdale's** on 59th Street (and Lexington). SEE ALSO FASHION, P.51; MUSEUMS, P.98; SHOPPING, P.138

Park Avenue

Compared to flashy Madison Avenue, Park is like a noisy version of a Parisian boulevard. A highlight is the Regency Hotel, a favorite for power breakfasts among media big-wheels. Another is the Colony Club at 62nd Street, which has a stately brick facade befitting the soci-

Left: the incomparable Metropolitan Museum.

Central Park West

Central Park West is the Upper West Side's most affluent residential district. The most famous apartment building is The Dakota (1 W. 72nd Street), which has had tenants such as Lauren Bacall. Strawberry Fields, a popular knoll dedicated to John Lennon, who lived at The Dakota and was shot outside in 1980, is across the street, in Central Park. It's a short walk uptown to the 79th Street entrance of the **American Museum of Natural History** ⑤, which sprawls over four blocks and is known for its collection of dinosaur fossils and the Rose Center for Earth and Space. SEE ALSO MUSEUMS, P.93

Central Park ⑥

Separating the Upper East and West sides is Central Park, an expansive green space designed in the 1850s by Frederick Law Olmsted and Calvert Vaux. Highlights include the **Central Park Zoo**, pretty Bethesda Terrace and Fountain, and, at 104th Street, the Conservatory Garden. There is a year-round schedule of events. SEE ALSO CHILDREN, P.42; PARKS AND GARDENS, P.116

The **Frick Collection** at Fifth and 70th is housed in the mansion of steel magnate Henry Clay Frick and features mainly European works of the 16th to 19th centuries, *see p.95.*

---

ety women on its membership list. Nearby are two fine cultural sites: the **Museum of American Illustration** (128 E. 63rd Street) and the excellent **China Institute** (125 E. 65th Street). The large, medieval-style **Seventh Regiment Armory**, built in the 1870s, is at 66th Street. At 70th Street, the **Asia Society** houses the well-regarded Rockefeller collection of Asian art. SEE ALSO MUSEUMS, P.94

Columbus Circle to Lincoln Center

Columbus Circle, at the southwest corner of Central Park, has undergone big changes in recent years. The glass towers of the Time Warner Center are

home to **Jazz at Lincoln Center**, the CNN Studios and nearly 50 high-end shops and restaurants. A new addition, the **Museum of Arts and Design**, has transformed a long-vacant building at 2 Columbus Circle. About four blocks up Broadway, flanked by the prestigious Juilliard School and Fordham University, is **Lincoln Center for the Performing Arts** ④. About 5 million people a year attend performances at the center, which encompasses the **Metropolitan Opera**, **New York City Ballet**, and other organizations. Lincoln Center is in the midst of a vast overhaul and modernization of its 1960 campus.

Running alongside, Columbus Avenue has a relaxed vibe and more opportunities for dining or shopping. SEE ALSO DANCE, P.47; MUSEUMS, P.91; MUSIC, P.106, 108

Right: Central Park West.

9

Harlem and Beyond

A second Harlem Renaissance is under way. Associated with urban decay for many years, much of the neighborhood has been spruced up and is attracting new residents, including ex-President Bill Clinton, who maintains offices on 125th Street. Dubbed Nieuw Haarlem by Dutch settlers in the 17th century, the area later served as a country seat for Alexander Hamilton and other notable New Yorkers of the early American period. An influx of African-Americans in the early 20th century gave rise to a blossoming of black culture that nurtured the talents of such luminaries as Langston Hughes, Zora Neale Hurston, and Duke Ellington.

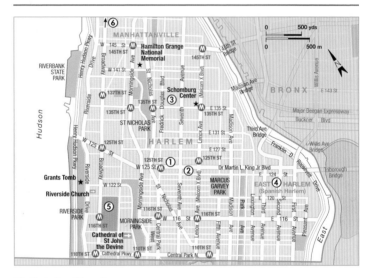

Martin Luther King, Jr Boulevard

Also known as 125th Street, Martin Luther King, Jr Boulevard is Harlem's vibrant main drag, with throngs of passersby and street vendors, and music blaring from nearby shops. You'll find several landmarks on this river-to-river strip, including the **Apollo Theater** ①, where Billie Holiday, Ella Fitzgerald, and James Brown launched their careers. Amateur Night has been a weekly tradition since 1934. A few blocks away, the **Studio Museum** ② in Harlem features paintings and sculpture and also houses an official NYC Information Center.

SEE ALSO MUSEUMS, P.99; MUSIC, P.106

Historic District

Situated around 138th Street between Adam Clayton Powell, Jr, and Frederick Douglass boulevards, the St Nicholas Historic District encompasses an area of 19th-century townhouses known as **Strivers Row** ③, in honor of the black professionals who moved there in the 1920s. There are several cultural institutions in the area. At Lenox Avenue and 135th Street, the Schomburg Center for Research in Black Culture contains one of the world's most important collections of African-American art and artifacts. On St Nicholas Park is Hamilton Grange National Memorial, which was the 19th-century home of Founding Father Alexander Hamilton.

Left: Martin Luther King, Jr Boulevard (125th Street).

the world's largest bell carillon atop its 22-story tower. Both churches host special events throughout the year. Grant's Tomb at 122nd Street is the final resting place of Civil War general and former president Ulysses S. Grant and his wife, Julia. The grave, the largest tomb in North America, was dedicated in 1897 as a national memorial and is said to be inspired by Les Invalides in Paris, which holds Napoleon's tomb. It is operated by the National Park Service.
SEE ALSO CHURCHES, P.44

The Cloisters ⑥

Perched on a rocky bluff overlooking the Hudson River at Manhattan's northern tip, this branch of the Metropolitan Museum of Art is dedicated to medieval art and architecture. The exhibits are integrated into the building, much of it reconstructed from pieces of 12th-century monasteries. The driving force behind the institution was John D. Rockefeller, Jr. But the man who really got it started was George Grey Barnard, a sculptor and collector who scoured the French countryside for church sculpture and architectural fragments.
SEE ALSO MUSEUMS, P.98

Join **Harlem Spirituals Gospel and Jazz Tours** (www.harlemspirituals.com) for a gospel service at a Harlem church and a bountiful soul food brunch.

East Harlem

Known as **Spanish Harlem** ④ due to its large Puerto Rican population, East Harlem also has a big Haitian community and remnants of an old Italian neighborhood on First and Pleasant avenues above 114th Street. One of the most colorful spots is **La Marqueta**, set under the elevated rail line on Park Avenue between 111th and 116th streets. The marketplace sells mangoes, papayas, cassavas, tamarinds, exotic herbs, and other tropical staples. While the number and variety of stalls have decreased in recent years, there is strong community and city support for its revi-

talization. To learn more about Latino culture, visit Uptown's **El Museo del Barrio** at Fifth Avenue and 104th Street.
SEE ALSO MUSEUMS, P.94

Morningside Heights

Schools and churches dominate this neighborhood, which includes **Columbia University** ⑤ (with its lengthy list of Pulitzer Prize winners) and Barnard College, as well as the Jewish Theological and Union Theological seminaries. At 112th Street and Amsterdam Avenue, the **Cathedral of St John the Divine** is home to the city's largest Episcopal congregation. It's also said to be the world's second-largest Gothic cathedral; construction began in 1892 and is still unfinished. At Riverside Drive and 120th Street, Riverside Church has

Right: Strivers Row.

11

Chelsea, Union Square, Flatiron, and Gramercy

Wedged between Midtown and Greenwich Village is a cluster of neighborhoods with surprisingly varied personalities. Chelsea is a former industrial area with a vibrant gallery scene and thriving gay community. Union Square and the Flatiron District are home to a variety of media-related businesses as well as some of the city's most notable chefs. Gramercy Park is a relatively quiet residential enclave known for its stately townhouses and well-heeled residents.

See Atlas Pages 152–155

Gallery Scene and the Meatpacking District

Former industrial buildings west of Tenth Avenue house the Chelsea gallery scene. The **Chelsea Art Museum** ①, a light, airy showplace for contemporary artists, sets the stage on W. 22nd Street between Tenth and Eleventh avenues. Nearby are high-profile galleries such as **Matthew Marks** and **Mary Boone**. The Meatpacking District comprises the blocks around the far west end of 14th Street, now one of the most fashionable neighborhoods in the city. Be sure to check out the designer boutiques on West 14th. One of the main reasons for venturing this far west is to dine and socialize, even if many of the stylish patrons here look as if they haven't eaten for days. **Chelsea Market**, at Ninth Avenue and 15th Street, is a paradise for food lovers with a dozen or so bakeries, delis, and other stores.
SEE ALSO FOOD AND DRINK, P.61; GALLERIES, P.65, 66; MUSEUMS, P.99

Chelsea Piers ②

During the gilded age of ocean travel, this stretch of the Manhattan waterfront served luxury liners. Today, after decades of neglect,

Chelsea Piers has been reborn as a sports and entertainment complex. Cruises are available at the marina.
SEE ALSO SPORTS, P.145

Historic Chelsea

At the turn of the 20th century the stretch of Sixth Avenue between 14th and 23rd streets was lined with fashionable department stores; these huge emporia now house chain stores. West of Eighth Avenue along 20th or 21st streets is an enclave of row houses around the precincts of the 19th-century General Theological Seminary. The tree-lined quadrangle can be visited most afternoons, and provides a calm oasis. The **Chelsea Hotel**, on 23rd Street between Seventh and Eighth avenues,

Left: meeting up in the Meatpacking District.

Left: the Flatiron Building.

Little India

Known affectionately as Curry Hill, this enclave around 28th Street between Broadway and Lexington is peppered with Indian and Pakistani restaurants and grocery stores. Among the best is Kalustyan's at 123 Lexington – two floors of Indian and Middle Eastern spices, grains and prepared foods.

Flower District

Under pressure from the booming real estate market the once large district has shrunk. Wholesalers are now clustered on two blocks of West 28th between Seventh Avenue and Broadway. It's a good place for a morning stroll.

Gramercy Park ⑥

East of the Flatiron District is Gramercy Park, a well-heeled area built in the mid-1800s. At the center of the neighborhood is Gramercy Park itself, a gated patch of green open only to guests at the glamorous **Gramercy Park Hotel**. South of the Park, Irving Place is lined with brownstones and several restaurants.
SEE ALSO HOTELS, P.79

is a landmark of bohemian decadence. The transformation of the **High Line** ③, a 22-block long-abandoned elevated rail line, into a much desired greenway and public park will further revitalize the far west side neighbourhoods.
SEE ALSO HOTELS, P.79

Union Square ④

Union Square was a stylish prospect in the mid-1850s but was abandoned by the genteel. The square gained notoriety in the years before World War I as a platform for political demonstrations. Rallies drew crowds through the 1930s, but the lure of radicalism dwindled. Today, Union Square brims with life, a resurgence attributable to the **Greenmarket**, a farmers' market.
SEE ALSO FOOD AND DRINK, P.61

Flatiron District

The Flatiron District north of Union Square is named after

> Dylan Thomas and Bob Dylan are just two of the luminaries who stayed at the Chelsea Hotel. Here Andy Warhol shot the film *Chelsea Girls*, Jack Kerouac wrote much of *On the Road*, and punk rocker Sid Vicious allegedly killed his girlfriend Nancy Spungen.

the **Flatiron Building** ⑤, erected in 1902 at the intersection of Fifth Avenue, Broadway, and 23rd Street. The surrounding buildings were built in the 19th century for industrial use. The regeneration of the area owes a lot to these cast-iron buildings, with their vast interiors. Just east of here at 28 East 20th Street is the small **Theodore Roosevelt Birthplace** museum, a replica of the president's place of birth.
SEE ALSO ARCHITECTURE, P.32

Right: taking art to the streets.

13

Greenwich Village

The Village has a long history of being a neighborhood on the edge. An outpost of the city's wealthiest families during the mid-1800s, the area later served as a hotbed of bohemian culture, where, in various periods, practitioners of free love, Beat poetry, gay rights, and the hippie lifestyle found themselves in like-minded company. Such illustrious inhabitants as Theodore Dreiser, Eugene O'Neill, Jackson Pollock, Jack Kerouac, and Bob Dylan drank and fought in the bars here, wrote and painted in the apartments. The bohemian days are gone, but the Village remains a haven for colorful people and a lively community spirit.

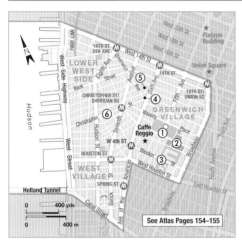

Above: walking the dog in the West Village.

Washington Square Park

On sunny days and balmy evenings, all the colorful life of the Village is on display at Washington Square Park ①. Folk singers strum guitars; kids zip around on skateboards; chess players face off against each other. Originally a potter's field and place for public hangings, and later the epicenter of the fashionable New Yorkers in Henry James's novel *Washington Square*, this little park was a stomping ground of Beat poets in the late 1950s and folk singers and hippies in the 1960s. It's in the midst of a multi-phase reconstruction, but some areas still remain accessible.

The first houses were built in the 1820s, and Washington Square soon became a highly desirable place to live. Several of these fine houses can still be seen along the north side of the square. Their 19th-century elegance is at odds with **New York University** ②, which dominates the area. There is an interesting view down Washington Mews, a small cobbled street where the wealthy kept their stables, now converted into residences. Stables have also been turned into attractive row houses on Macdougal Alley, accessible from Washington Square West.

The **marble arch** dominating the square was planned as a temporary addition. The first version was made of wood and stood here between 1889 and 1892 to commemorate the centennial of President George Washington's inauguration. No one wanted to part with it after the celebration, so Stanford White was commissioned to build a marble version. White also designed

Left: the Village was and is the site of gay rights events.

loween Parade, a fun spectacle of wild costumes and giant puppets that passes through the Village on Sixth Avenue.

Start exploring the neighborhood at the striking **Jefferson Market Library** ④ at 10th Street and Sixth Avenue. Originally part of a complex that included the Women's House of Detention, it was built as a courthouse in 1877 and is where, in 1906, Harry Thaw went on trial for shooting architect Stanford White, whom he suspected (correctly) of having an affair with his wife. On 10th Street is **Patchin Place** ⑤, a mews where playwright Eugene O'Neill, journalist John Reed and poet e.e. cummings lived. **Christopher Street** runs through the heart of the neighborhood and is the symbolic center of the gay community, which, in recent years, has expanded north to **Chelsea** ⑥. The original Stonewall Inn stood at 57 Christopher Street near Seventh Avenue. Today, a bar with the same name is next door.

SEE ALSO FESTIVALS AND EVENTS, P.59; GAY AND LESBIAN, P.69

Take a break and watch the amateur basketball players in **The Cage**, the public basketball courts at West Fourth Street and Sixth Avenue. The play here is a bit more physical because of the smaller, non-regulation-size court.

Judson Memorial Church on the south side of the square. It was designed in Italian Renaissance style and completed in 1892.

Farther east, on the corner of La Guardia Place, is New York University's **Kimmel Center for University Life**. It stands on the site of Marie Branchard's boarding house, known as the 'house of genius' because of her illustrious guests, including writers Eugene O'Neill, Theodore Dreiser, and Stephen Crane. The studio of painter John Sloan, a member of the group known as The Eight, was a few houses farther on.

Bleecker ③ and MacDougal Streets

On weekends students and tourists pile into the bars and restaurants here. This was hippie heaven in the 1960s, when musicians such as Dylan, the Mamas and the Papas, and Jimi Hendrix played the clubs and lived in walk-up apartments. For a taste of those times, visit Matt Umanov's guitar shop, or go to **Caffè Reggio** on MacDougal.

SEE ALSO CAFÉS, P.40

West Village

This tangle of streets west of Sixth Avenue was the site of the 1969 Stonewall riots, a violent clash between gay men and police that became a defining moment in the gay rights movement. Nowadays, the area is better known for the annual **Hal-**

Right: the marble arch in Washington Square Park.

The East Village to Chinatown

The East Village is a place that stays up late, where fashion and politics tend to be radical, and whose residents have included Beat icons like Allen Ginsberg as well as Yippies and Hell's Angels. Beneath its scruffy avant-garde surface, the East Village and surrounding neighborhoods have long been a sanctuary for immigrants, with Puerto Rican social clubs next to tiny boutiques, Jewish delis near nightclubs. Like many Downtown neighborhoods, old and new lie cheek by jowl.

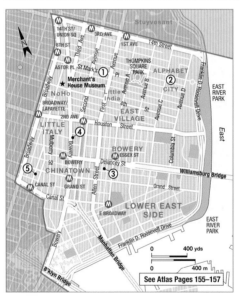

See Atlas Pages 155–157

NoHo and NoLita

In the early 20th century, lower Broadway around 9th Street was part of the 'Ladies' Mile' of department stores. Later it was a dingy pause between SoHo and the East Village. All that changed in the mid-1980s, when hip retailers moved into the area north of Houston (NoHo) and north of Little Italy (NoLita) between Broadway and the Bowery and gave it a gritty,

postindustrial cachet reminiscent of TriBeCa in the early days. This area also has some small, interesting museums, such as the **Merchant's House Museum** and an off-beat theater scene that includes the excellent **Public Theater**.
SEE ALSO MUSEUMS, P.100; THEATER, P.147

Little India

Not to be confused with the

other Little India on 28th Street (see p.13), this strip of Indian restaurants on 6th Street between First and Second avenues is an excellent choice for a cheap tasty meal.

St Mark's Place ①

In the 1960s, St Mark's Place was the East Coast's counter culture center, where Andy Warhol presented Velvet Underground "happenings" and, later, barefoot freaks tripped out at the Electric Circus. Although it has become increasingly gentrified, St Mark's is still one of the city's liveliest thoroughfares, lined with cafés, tattoo parlors and little shops. The graffiti gets thicker as you approach Tompkins Square Park, once a tent city for the homeless, now cleaned up and used by local families.

Alphabet City ②

For decades the very name was synonymous with crime and poverty, but, in parts of the neighborhood, slums and graffiti-covered walls have been supplanted by bars and restaurants with a young, hip clientele. Parks have been divested of drug dealers, while former bodegas have metamorphosed into fashion boutiques. As in other cutting-

St Mark's-in-the-Bowery at 10th Street and Second Avenue is the second-oldest church in Manhattan, built in 1799 on land owned by colonial governor Peter Stuyvesant, *see p.45.*

edge neighborhoods, it's wise to exercise caution.

The Lower East Side

This neighborhood south of Houston Street was once the most densely populated place in the US. Hundreds of thousands of immigrants — mostly Jewish and Italian but also German, Irish, and others — were packed into tenements such as those preserved at the **Lower East Side Tenement Museum** ③ on Orchard Street. These days you'll see stores with Jewish names and Chinese or Hispanic owners, a

Right: the Lower East Side is good for vintage fashion.

reminder that this neighborhood still attracts new arrivals, including the bohemian pioneers who have opened cool bars, boutiques, and designer hotels, such as **The Hotel on Rivington**. Many of the businesses that gave the area its character have been forced out by soaring rents; **Guss' Pickles** is a stalwart, while the Sunday bazaar on Orchard Street is still the place for clothing bargains.
SEE ALSO FOOD AND DRINK, P.63; HOTELS, P.81; MUSEUMS, P.100

Left: wide-eyed in Chinatown.

Little Italy

The heart of this neighborhood is Mulberry Street, where the sidewalks are lined with cafés, restaurants, and social clubs. A shadow of its former self, Little Italy comes alive during the **Feast of St Anthony** in June and the Feast of San Gennaro in September. Also in this neighborhood, on the Bowery, is the striking **New Museum** ④ with a focus on contemporary art.
SEE ALSO FESTIVALS AND EVENTS, P.58; MUSEUMS, P.100

Chinatown

One of the largest Chinese-American settlements as well as one of Manhattan's most vibrant neighborhoods, Chinatown started in the 1870s, when Chinese railroad workers drifted east from California. Once squeezed into a three-block area bordered by Mott, Pell, and the Bowery, today it encompasses around 40 blocks. A great place to learn about the neighborhood and the Chinese-American experience is the recently moved and expanded **Museum of the Chinese in America (MOCA)** ⑤. Food is one of Chinatown's main attractions. There are hundreds of restaurants here, as well as lively markets.
SEE ALSO MUSEUMS, P.100

SoHo and TriBeCa

In the late 19th century, SoHo (south of Houston) was known as Hell's Hundred Acres because of the wretched working conditions in its factories and warehouses. A century later, the very same buildings – many with ornate cast-iron facades – lured artists and other urban pioneers to the neighborhood, sowing the seeds of a cutting-edge gallery scene and, by the 1980s, a real estate boom that soon spilled over into TriBeCa. The starving artists and guerrilla galleries have long since been priced out of the market. What remains is an urban playground for the famous, fabulous, and wealthy known for loft living, tiny boutiques, and stylish restaurants.

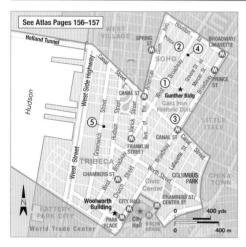

Above: SoHo shopping.

West Broadway ①

SoHo's main drag is lined with stores offering everything from jewelry to quirky household wares. On Saturdays it's packed with tourists loaded with shopping bags. From Houston to Canal, you'll find a clutch of designer boutiques, interspersed with tempting restaurants, bars, and cafés, and the effortlessly stylish **Soho Grand Hotel**. Separating SoHo from TriBeCa, Canal Street is frantic with street vendors selling everything from electrical goods to designer knockoffs.

SEE ALSO HOTELS, P.81

Prince Street ②

Prince Street has all but forsaken galleries and turned into prime shopping territory, although you will still find an intriguing trompe l'œil mural at the corner of Greene Street. Nearby, you can shop for quirky dresses at **Anna Sui**, or take a coffee break at any one of a number of espresso bars. **The Apple Store** (103 Prince Street) is a slick shop dedicated to iPods and everything Apple. The Romanesque Revival-style building on the next corner has been transformed into the small, luxurious **Mercer Hotel**. Beneath the hotel is the highly acclaimed restaurant, the **Mercer Kitchen**.

SEE ALSO FASHION, P.56; HOTELS, P.81; RESTAURANTS, P.129

Greene Street

In the late 19th century, Greene Street was the center of New York's most notorious red-light district, where brothels with names like Flora's and Miss Lizzie's flourished behind shuttered windows. This is also the heart of the SoHo **Cast Iron Historic District** ③. On five cobblestone blocks are 50 cast-iron buildings, the

Left: enjoy the view from your terrace at the Tribeca Grand.

Hudson River. Called Washington Market in the days when the city's major produce businesses operated here, this is one of Manhattan's most pleasant Downtown neighborhoods. An eclectic blend of renovated warehouses, the area sports Corinthian columns, condominium towers, and celebrity restaurants. Its largely residential atmosphere makes a pleasant change of pace from SoHo's tourist-packed streets.

Greenwich Street is where much of TriBeCa's new development is centered, although you can still find some early remnants like the 19th-century lantern factory between Laight and Vestry streets that now houses million-dollar lofts. The corner of Greenwich and Franklin streets is where actor Robert De Niro transformed the old Martinson Coffee Factory into the **Tribeca Film Center** ⑤. On the first floor is the **Tribeca Grill**. Many come here in the hope of seeing De Niro or film biz luminaries from the upstairs offices, although this rarely happens. SEE ALSO MOVIES, P.89; RESTAURANTS, P.130

Two conceptual artworks by Walter De Maria recall SoHo's days at the cutting edge of the art scene. The **Broken Kilometer** is composed of 500 brass rods on the floor of a loft at 393 West Broadway. **New York Earth Room**, at 141 Wooster Street, is a room filled with soil.

highest concentration in the world. At the corner of Broome Street, the 1872 Gunther Building is particularly interesting, as is the splendid cast iron structure at 72–76 Greene Street opposite.

Broadway

Once home to the city's most elegant stores, and later to textile outlets and discount shops, the stately cast-iron buildings on Broadway above Canal Street acquired cachet in the 1980s, first as museums, then as galleries, and then as stores like Crate and Barrel and Eddie Bauer. A new Bloomingdale's has added traffic to Downtown's busy sidewalks, and recent imports H&M, Topshop, and Uniqlo are also proving popular.

A 1904 cast-iron confection called the **Little Singer Building** stands across Broadway from **Dean & DeLuca** ④, the latter a luxurious cornucopia of fruits, vegetables, and imported gourmet specialties. The coffee bar is a good place for a quick, gourmand snack. A few galleries are located on the upper floors along this part of Broadway. SEE ALSO FOOD AND DRINK, P.63; GALLERIES, P.67; SHOPPING, P.139

TriBeCa

In the late 1970s, artists in search of lower rents migrated south from SoHo to TriBeCa – the Triangle Below Canal – which lies south of Canal Street to Chambers Street between Broadway and the

Right: stylish living in SoHo.

Lower Manhattan

Though poignant memories linger, New York's financial district is back on its feet and as bullish as ever. This is the place where a scrappy Dutch village grew into a world-class seaport, where George Washington took the oath of office, and where a group of traders started the country's first stock market in the shade of a buttonwood tree. Today, it's an area of varied charms, with an assortment of museums, parks, and historic sites. Visitors can stride the corporate canyons of Wall Street, stroll across the Brooklyn Bridge, cruise the harbor in a historic ship, and watch the new Freedom Tower rise from Ground Zero.

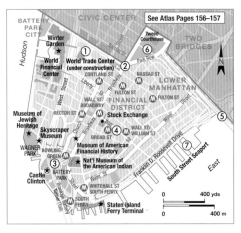

Above: Bowling Green's 7,000lb (3,200kg) bull.

Ground Zero

The grounds of the former World Trade Center are now a construction site, as work continues on the **Freedom Tower** ① (1 World Trade Center), a 1,776ft (541m) skyscraper slated to open in 2013. At the southern end of the site is the Tribute WTC Visitor Center. Five themed galleries chronicle the events of September 11, 2001, and honor the lives lost. There is another 9/11 exhibit at **St Paul's Chapel** ② about a block away on Broadway. Built in 1766, this landmark is the only church left from the Federal period, when luminaries like George Washington and Lord Cornwallis worshipped here.

SEE ALSO CHURCHES, P.45

Battery Park City

Built partially on earth dug from the World Trade Center's foundation, Battery Park City is an office and apartment complex on the Hudson waterfront. The World Financial Center has been repaired and is back in business. Also restored is the Winter Garden, a cavernous glass vault where you can take in a concert under a grove of palm trees. Stroll the riverfront Esplanade to the **Museum of Jewish Heritage**, a memorial to the Holocaust. Beyond the museum, pathways wind through Robert F. Wagner Jr Park. Those with an interest in architecture may enjoy the nearby **Skyscraper Museum** on Battery Place.

SEE ALSO MUSEUMS, P.101, 102

Battery Park ③

Named for a cannon battery that once stood here, this park at the tip of Manhattan encompasses **Castle Clinton**, a stone fort built in the early 1800s. An Icon of Hope, a sculpture that once stood in the World Trade Center Plaza, was moved to the park as a memorial. Ferries depart for the Statue of Liberty and Ellis Island.

A short walk away, on Bowling Green, is the **National Museum of the**

Left: the New York Stock Exchange; make money here.

city's main governmental buildings. The centerpiece is **City Hall** ⑥, a grand French-American hybrid completed in 1812. Behind is the former New York County Courthouse, better known as the Tweed Courthouse because Boss Tweed and his Tammany Hall cronies skimmed millions off the construction costs. For great views, walk down Park Row to the Brooklyn Bridge. SEE ALSO ARCHITECTURE, P.32

South Street Seaport

On the East River south of the Brooklyn Bridge, this 12-block 'museum without walls' was New York's main port until the late 1900s, when steamships found more suitable berths on the Hudson River. Renovation in the 1980s produced a historic district mixing ships and shops. Old ships are the chief attraction. Shoppers gravitate to the Pier 17 Pavilion, which has stores, cafés, and a food court. Schermerhorn Row has the last surviving Federal-style buildings. The **South Street Seaport Museum** ⑦ offers tickets for tours, cruises, and gallery exhibitions. SEE ALSO MUSEUMS, P.102

In 1783 George Washington bid his troops an emotional farewell at **Fraunces Tavern** at Broad and Pearl streets. A reconstruction of the tavern (and modest museum) is open for business, *see p.101*.

American Indian, housed in the former US Customs House, a Beaux Arts masterpiece built in 1907. A couple of blocks away, at Broadway and Beaver Street, is the **Museum of American Finance**. SEE ALSO STATEN AND ELLIS ISLANDS, P.22; MUSEUMS, P.101, 102

Wall Street ④

A world financial center, Wall Street took its name from a wooden stockade built by the Dutch against Indian and English attacks. The country's first stock exchange began just in front of 60 Wall Street in 1792, when 24 brokers gathered

beneath a buttonwood tree. Built in 1903, the **New York Stock Exchange** stands behind an impressive facade of Corinthian columns at Wall and Broad. Sadly, the visitor gallery is no longer open. The Greek Revival temple across the street is **Federal Hall**, where, in 1789, George Washington was sworn in as US President. Today it's a museum and memorial.

On the west end of Wall Street is **Trinity Church**, built in 1846. A cemetery out back is the final resting place of Alexander Hamilton, the Republic's first Secretary of the Treasury, killed in a duel with rival Aaron Burr. SEE ALSO CHURCHES, P.45

City Hall and the Brooklyn Bridge

Near the entrance to the **Brooklyn Bridge** ⑤ are the

Right: a rare cobbled street surrounded by skyscrapers.

21

Staten and Ellis Islands and the Statue of Liberty

A trio of islands round out the Manhattan experience. The smallest is the best known – Liberty Island, site of the iconic statue that towers over New York Harbor. Nearby Ellis Island isn't much bigger, but loomed large in the passage of some 12 million immigrants who arrived here in the late 19th and early 20th centuries. Staten Island is the least populated of the city's five boroughs, a mostly suburban area with a few unexpected attractions far off the usual tourist trails.

Statue of Liberty ①

Ferries to the Statue of Liberty and Ellis Island depart from Battery Park in Lower Manhattan. A limited number of timed tickets are available at Castle Clinton or can be reserved by phone (877-523-9849) or online (www.statuecruises.com). Some 10 years in the making, the statue was a gift from France to the United States and has served as a beacon for immigrants for more than a century. Sculptor Frédéric-Auguste Bartholdi's 151ft (46m)high structure was a wild dream that became a reality. Engineering expertise had to be harnessed to art, so Bartholdi called in Alexandre-Gustave Eiffel – creator of the Eiffel Tower – to design the truss-work supporting the copper

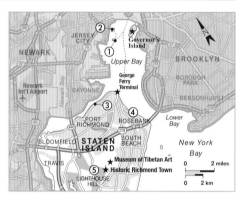

skin. Parisian workmen erected the statue in 1884. It was later dismantled and shipped for reassembly on Liberty Island. *Liberty Enlightening the World* was unveiled by President Grover Cleveland on October 28, 1886. Visitors had been allowed only as far as an observation deck at the top of the pedestal since 2001, but the crown is now reopened to the public.
SEE ALSO CHILDREN, P.43; MUSEUMS, P.103

Ellis Island ②

After the statue, the ferry continues to Ellis Island. The 'huddled masses yearning to

Left: enjoy great views of Lower Manhattan from here.

be free' – more than 12 million people who crossed the Atlantic during the great age of American immigration in the late 19th and early 20th centuries – could only complete their journey after first submitting to a rigorous screening process on this small island in New York Harbor. Designed to weed out the infirm, the mentally incompetent and the criminal, the screening allowed the vast majority to pass through; others were forced to sail back to their country of origin.

Today, more than 100 million Americans are descendants of those intrepid immigrants who landed at what was often called the 'Island of Tears'. Allowed to

Left: Lady Liberty was unveiled to the nation in 1886.

on Tompkins Avenue commemorates Antonio Meucci, who invented a telephone years before Alexander Graham Bell. Exhibits focus on Meucci's numerous inventions, as well as his friendship with Italian patriot Giuseppe Garibaldi, who stayed with Meucci during a visit to New York in 1850. This simple frame house was Meucci's home until his death in 1889. Nearby is the Alice Austen House Museum, which preserves the home and garden of the pioneering woman photographer who lived and worked here from 1866 to 1945.

SEE ALSO MUSEUMS, P.103

Lighthouse Hill ⑤

A cluster of hills rising from the center of Staten Island provides a suitable backdrop for the **Jacques Marchais Museum of Tibetan Art**, a collection of Buddhist art housed in a gallery built in the style of a Tibetan temple. Less than a mile away on Richmond Road is Historic Richmond Town, a restored 17th- and 18th-century village that recreates life in colonial New York.

SEE ALSO MUSEUMS, P.103

> The Statue of Liberty's copper skin is hammered to less than an eighth of an inch (3mm) thick but weighs more than 90 tons.

fall into ruin after it was closed in 1954, the main building on Ellis Island was restored with $156 million in private funds, and in 1990 it opened as the **Ellis Island Immigration Museum**, dedicated to chronicling the experience of the millions of immigrants who entered the United States through this facility.

SEE ALSO CHILDREN, P.43; MUSEUMS, P.103

Staten Island Ferry

If you're itching to get back out to sea, another 'cruise' is available from the tip of Manhattan – the Staten Island Ferry. The free, 20-minute trip offers excellent views of the Statue of Liberty and Manhattan skyline. The sight is especially splendid after

dark, when the city is illuminated for the night.

About 10 minutes by bus from Staten Island's St George Ferry Terminal is the **Snug Harbor Cultural Center and Botanical Garden** ③. The handsome visitor center is set in an 1831 home for retired seamen. In the **Botanical Garden**, visit the Chinese Scholars Garden and the White Garden inspired by Vita Sackville-West's English garden. Here, too, is the **Staten Island Children's Museum**, with interactive exhibits for kids.

SEE ALSO PARKS AND GARDENS, P.117

Rosebank ④

East of the ferry terminal is the Rosebank District, home of the borough's oldest Italian-American community. The **Garibaldi-Meucci Museum**

Right: the Ellis Island Immigration Museum.

23

Brooklyn

With a population of more than 2.5 million, Brooklyn would be the fourth-largest metropolis in the United States if it weren't a part of New York City. Though it is often overshadowed by Manhattan, the borough has a history and character all its own, not to mention world-class cultural institutions like the Brooklyn Museum of Art, a cutting-edge arts scene, and vibrant ethnic neighborhoods. As always in this city, change is never-ending, as the economy shifts, immigrant groups move in and out, artists colonize run-down neighborhoods, and gentrification sends real estate values through the roof.

Above: a winter's afternoon in Williamsburg.

DUMBO ①

The modern renaissance of Brooklyn began in classic New York style – by following the trail of artists. When SoHo became too expensive, they moved to DUMBO (Down Under Manhattan Bridge Overpass), now a thriving neighborhood that includes innovative theater at **St Ann's Warehouse** (38 Water Street). Nearby is **Bargemusic**, a converted coffee barge moored at Fulton Ferry Landing where you can hear live chamber music.

Red Hook

Continue south along the waterfront to Red Hook, one of the latest communities to break out of the old industrial mold, with art studios and performance spaces. Creative businesses as well as high-end retail complexes are putting down roots among restaurants and galleries.

Williamsburg

This neighborhood is packed at the weekend but quieter at other times. Bedford Avenue is the main drag, with clothing stores and funky cafés. **Berry Street**, a block west, attracts a hip crowd, too.

Brooklyn Heights ②

This area of historic row houses is among the most desirable in the city. Along the waterfront is the Promenade, a walkway with sweeping views of Lower Manhattan and the Brooklyn Bridge. Before the Civil War, **Plymouth Church** on Orange Street was a link in the Underground Railroad, while Henry Ward Beecher preached abolitionism to the congregation. The **Brooklyn Historical Society** is in a landmark building on Pierrepont Street and has a collection of historic Brooklyn maps, early copies of Walt Whitman's *Leaves of Grass* (printed in Brooklyn), and more. At the foot of Brooklyn Heights is the Civic Center. From here, it's a short walk down Boerum Place to the **New York Transit Museum**, housed in a classic 1930s subway station.

SEE ALSO MUSEUMS, P.104

Left: the Brooklyn Bridge.

The traffic circle at the western end of Eastern Parkway is **Grand Army Plaza**, where the Soldiers' and Sailors' Memorial Arch leads to **Prospect Park**. Designed by Frederick Law Olmsted and Calvert Vaux, the park rivals the ambition of the duo's better-known masterpiece, Central Park. In a corner of the park is the **Lefferts Homestead Children's Museum**, a colonial farmhouse portraying life in the 19th century.
SEE ALSO CHILDREN, P.43; MUSEUMS, P.104; PARKS AND GARDENS, P.117

Coney Island ⑤

On Brooklyn's southern waterfront is Coney Island. Among the bright spots at this faded seaside getaway is the **New York Aquarium**. For a taste of old-time Coney Island, visit the **Coney Island Circus Sideshow**, ride on the Cyclone, a classic wood-frame roller coaster, and stop for a bite at Nathan's famous hot dog stand at Surf and Stillwell. Farther east is Brighton Beach, and an enclave of Russian and Ukrainian immigrants – Little Odessa.
SEE ALSO CHILDREN, P.43

Eastern Parkway is the site of the **West Indian Labor Day** carnival, a festival of food and music, with costumed revelers, *see p.59*.

Flatbush

Where Atlantic meets Flatbush is the **Williamsburg Savings Bank**, the tallest building in Brooklyn. Nearby, on Lafayette Avenue, is the **Brooklyn Academy of Music**, a performance and cinema arts center, where cutting-edge performers such as Laurie Anderson and Philip Glass have appeared. Home to the Next Wave Festival since 1982, it includes the **Harvey Theater**.
SEE ALSO MUSIC, P.106

Eastern Parkway

Eastern Parkway runs from Bedford-Stuyvesant to Prospect Park and leads to some of the borough's most distinguished cultural institutions. Founded in 1899, the **Brooklyn Children's Museum** is the oldest children's museum in America and has recently undergone an exciting expansion. The **Brooklyn Museum of Art** ③ includes an Egyptian collection ranked among the best outside Cairo and London. The museum displays an array of world-class exhibits, period rooms, and a sculpture garden of artifacts salvaged from demolished buildings. Nearby, at **Brooklyn Botanic Garden** ④, the Japanese gardens alone are worth a visit, especially at cherry blossom time. The neighborhood of Park Slope runs along the park's western border and is filled with Victorian row houses. Seventh Avenue and Fifth Avenue, wall to wall with shops and restaurants, are just blocks from the park.

Right: Coney Island – be sure to eat a Nathan's hot dog here.

25

Queens

Visitors taking taxis from JFK or LaGuardia International Airport into Manhattan pass as swiftly as traffic allows through the largest and most diverse of the city's five boroughs. Named for Catherine of Braganza, the wife of England's Charles II, Queens is a sprawling patchwork of ethnic communities, ranging from established Greek and Italian neighborhoods in Astoria and a burgeoning Asian population in Flushing to dozens of small and emerging immigrant enclaves. At the heart of the borough is the former site of two World's Fairs, now a complex of museums, sports facilities, and parkland.

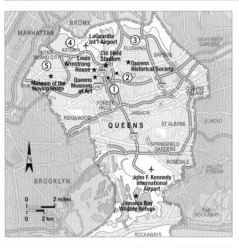

Flushing Meadows Corona Park ①

Developed for the 1939 and 1964 World's Fairs, the park encompasses more than 1,200 acres (480 hectares) between Northern Boulevard and Grand Central Parkway, with museums, sports facilities, and botanical gardens. On display in the **Queens Museum of Art** is the Panorama of the City of New York, a scale model of the city built for the 1964 World's Fair and renovated in 1994 to reflect the changes in the city. The New York Hall of Science, near the park's 111th Street entrance, is well known for its high-tech exhibits.

Another leftover from the World's Fairs is the gigantic steel globe, **Unisphere**, near the **National Tennis Center**, site of the annual US Open. Next door is **Citi Field**, the new home of the New York Mets baseball team. Nearby, the **Queens Botanical Garden** ② has the largest rose garden in the Northeast and is a popular spot for outdoor weddings. Jazz legend Louis Armstrong lived in Corona, and his former home has

Left: the Unisphere was a symbol of the 1964 World's Fair.

Left: ride a trolley in Flushing Meadows Corona Park.

Image chronicles the 'material culture' of the film and television industry. Astoria has one of the largest Greek communities outside Athens. Along main drags like Steinway Street and Broadway are Greek delis, Italian bakeries, and Asian markets.
SEE ALSO MUSEUMS, P.105

Long Island City ⑤

Artists discovered this aging industrial district in the early 1980s, and it's been attracting museums and galleries ever since. **MoMA** opened a branch here while awaiting the completion of its expanded venue in Manhattan. The **P.S. 1 Contemporary Art Center** is dedicated to the work of emerging artists. Its popular summer music series, Warm Up, draws music and art fans alike.

Perhaps the most beautiful exhibition space in Queens is the **Isamu Noguchi Garden Museum**. The brainchild of the late Japanese-American sculptor Isamu Noguchi, this converted factory houses nearly 250 works in 13 galleries. Outside, the Japanese-inspired sculpture garden is an oasis of calm. Just up Vernon Boulevard at Broadway, more outdoor art can be enjoyed at **Socrates Sculpture Park**. The view of Manhattan is terrific.
SEE ALSO MUSEUMS, P.104, 105

Along the southernmost strip of Queens, the **Rockaways** claim the biggest municipal beach in the country. To the east is Far Rockaway, to the west Neponsit, where mansions recall the days when wealthy New Yorkers vacationed here.

been turned into a museum: the **Louis Armstrong House Museum** (34–56 107th Street).
SEE ALSO MUSEUMS, P.105; PARKS AND GARDENS, P.119; SPORT, P.144, 145

Flushing ③

Sometimes referred to as Little Asia, this neighborhood bordering the park has enclaves of Korean, Japanese, Chinese, Indian, and Southeast Asian immigrants. The **Quaker Meeting House** on Northern Boulevard was built in 1694 and is the oldest house of worship in New York City. An excellent place to learn more about local history

is the **Queens Historical Society** (14335 37th Avenue). South of Kennedy Airport is **Jamaica Bay Wildlife Refuge**, a sanctuary for more than 300 bird species and offering birding workshops.
SEE ALSO PARKS AND GARDENS, P.118

Astoria ④

This neighborhood of modest apartment buildings and semi-detached houses seems an unlikely place for movie stars, but it's become a hub of New York's film industry. The film business dates back to the 1920s, when the Marx Brothers and Gloria Swanson were among the stars working for Famous Players-Lasky Studios. Kaufman Astoria Studios now occupies the site. The cameras are rolling again here and at the Silvercup Studios in neighboring Long Island City. The worthwhile **Museum of the Moving**

A 19th-century law encouraged the opening of cemeteries in Queens in order to reduce the demand for burial sites in Manhattan. As a result, Queens is a veritable city of the dead. In fact, the dead outnumber the living by more than two to one.

The Bronx

Named after Scandinavian pioneer Jonas Bronck, who settled here in the 1640s, the Bronx – particularly the South Bronx – suffered through urban decline, especially during the 1960s, '70s, and '80s. Much has changed since then. Beleaguered communities have been stabilized and are showing signs of vitality. You'll also find more than a few unexpected pleasures, including two of the city's largest parks, a vibrant Italian neighborhood, a beautiful arts center on the Hudson River, and, of course, the Bronx Zoo and New York Botanical Garden. Even Manhattanites make the trek to Yankee Stadium, which is saying something.

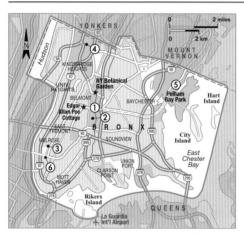

Above: the WCS headquarters is based at the Bronx Zoo.

Bronx Park ①

Idyllic woods seem unimaginable in this urban landscape, but a fragment of the area's original hemlock forest remains untouched at the **New York Botanical Garden**. The 1902 Enid A. Haupt Conservatory is the grandest structure on the grounds, a crystal palace that includes a central Palm Court and connecting greenhouses.

Also in Bronx Park is the **Bronx Zoo** ②, the country's largest urban zoo. Some of the most popular exhibits include the World of Darkness (nocturnal animals), Madagascar! and the Butter-

fly Zone. There's a Children's Zoo, a monorail through Wild Asia, and a Himalayan habitat. The Congo Gorilla Forest houses a troop of lowland gorillas in a rainforest habitat.
SEE ALSO CHILDREN, P.43; PARKS AND GARDENS, P.119

Grand Concourse

The zoo is at the geographic heart of the Bronx, but its architectural heart is the Grand Concourse. This Champs Elysées-inspired boulevard began as a speedway through rural hills and later attracted wealthy residents to elegant apartment buildings. North of the Grand

Concourse, Edgar Allan Poe's humble cottage is set among high rises on Kingsbridge Road. Poe moved here in 1846, hoping the country air would be good for his consumptive young wife and cousin, Virginia. On the Grand Concourse itself, at 165th Street, the **Bronx Museum of the Arts** ③ specializes in contemporary art. The building was originally a synagogue. It's encased in a pleated glass and metallic facade that suits its latter-day function.
SEE ALSO MUSEUMS, P.105

Belmont

Just east of the Bronx Zoo is the borough's Little Italy. Arthur Avenue, near the fork of Crescent Avenue and East 187th Street, teems with Italian restaurants, delis, and

Left: Van Cortlandt House Museum.

Yorkers, including Herman Melville, Duke Ellington, and five former mayors.
SEE ALSO PARKS AND GARDENS, P.119

Pelham Bay Park ⑤

On the borough's eastern shore, where the East River meets Long Island Sound, is Pelham Bay Park, the largest in the city, with more than 2,700 acres (1,080 hectares) of woodland, salt marshes, and nature trails, as well as a golf course, horseback riding facility, and public beach (Orchard Beach). A bridge leads from the park to City Island, a seaside community reminiscent of a New England village.
SEE ALSO PARKS AND GARDENS, P.119

Artists are finding cheap industrial spaces in Hunts Point, at the southernmost tip of the Bronx; this is also home to the Terminal Market and New Fulton Fish Market, part of the country's largest food distribution center.

---

bakeries. Stop in at the Belmont Library, at East 186th Street and Hughes Avenue, and visit the Enrico Fermi Cultural Center.

University Heights to Van Cortlandt Park

West of the Grand Concourse is University Heights, where, on the grounds of Bronx Community College, is the Hall of Fame of Great Americans, a neoclassical shrine designed by celebrated architect Stanford White. Above University Heights is Riverdale, a largely suburban neighborhood

Right: Belmont is the Little Italy of the Bronx.

known for Tudor-style mansions. Set on a picturesque headland of the Hudson River is Wave Hill, a public garden and cultural center with summer concerts, dance performances, and exhibitions.

East of Riverdale is **Van Cortlandt Park**. The fine **Van Cortlandt House Museum** ④ overlooks the park's lake from a perch at Broadway and 242nd Street. Built in 1748 by Frederick Van Cortlandt, son of a Dutch merchant, its rooms are filled with original furnishings. On the park's other side, **Woodlawn Cemetery** is permanent home to about 300,000 New

The South Bronx

At the opposite end of the borough – in both spirit and location – is the South Bronx, an area that suffered decline in the '70s and '80s, although conditions have improved in the last decade or so. **Yankee Stadium** ⑥, a brand new fan-friendly stadium opened in 2009, is the big attraction here – the home field of baseball legends such as Babe Ruth and Joe DiMaggio. Yankee fans proudly point out that more championship pennants have flown over Yankee Stadium than any other ballpark in the country.
SEE ALSO SPORTS, P.144

A–Z

In the following section the city's attractions and services are organized by theme, under alphabetical headings. Items that link to another theme are cross-referenced. All sights that are plotted on the atlas section at the end of the book are given a page number and grid reference.

Architecture

N ew York's builders had only one place to go to accommodate the hordes that were over-running this narrow strip of land: upwards. Hence New Yorkers seized on the skyscraper – a Chicago invention – to create the startling Manhattan skyline. Through the 20th century the city rose higher and higher, as records were left behind and one landmark structure followed another. After every setback – the 1930s Depression, 9/11 – New York has responded with yet more original, yet more spectacular new buildings. They represent the city's ambition, and its sense of fantasy and adventure.

Brooklyn Bridge

Subway: Brooklyn Bridge-City Hall; map p.156 C2

An engineering marvel built in 1870–83, this suspension bridge spanning the East River was designed by John A. Roebling, who died of tetanus after an accident at the site. An inspiration to artists and writers, the bridge's monumental proportions moved painter Joseph Stella to liken it to 'a shrine containing all the efforts of the new civilization of America.' Views of the bridge are excellent from Pier 17 at South Street Seaport and Brooklyn Heights Promenade.

Chrysler Building

Lexington Avenue/East 42nd Street; subway: Grand Central/42nd St; map p.153 D3

William Van Alen's 1930 masterpiece was briefly the world's tallest building. The 1,048ft (319m) structure, with automotive motifs such as gargoyles inspired by radiator caps, reaches a pinnacle of narrowing crowns topped by a rapier-like spire – an immense piece of Art Deco jewelry. Although not open to the pub-

The SoHo Cast Iron Historic District encompasses dozens of mid-19th-century buildings with ornate iron facades. Designed as warehouses and factories, they were later transformed into art studios and, today, residential lofts.

lic, visitors are allowed into the bronze-and-marble lobby.

Empire State Building

Fifth Avenue/West 34th Street; tel: 212-736 3100; www.esbnyc.com; daily 8am–2am; entrance charge; subway: 34th St/Herald Square; map p.153 C2

The 1,454ft (443m) structure, which took the 'world's tallest' title from the Chrysler in 1931, toned down the Art Deco vocabulary but still managed, with its sleek capstone tower and soaring marble lobby, to incorporate the geometry of aspiration that was a hallmark of the style.

Elevators in the lobby take you up to the observation deck on the 86th floor, and fantastic panoramic views of Manhattan. On a clear day you can see as far as 80

miles (129 km). For an additional fee, you can ascend to the smaller observatory way up on the 102nd floor.

Flatiron Building

175 Fifth Avenue/East 23rd Street; subway: 23rd St; map p.155 C4

Many steel-frame buildings went up in New York in the 1890s. People called them skyscrapers, but the first real breakout from 8–10 stories was Daniel Burnham's 1902 Fuller Building, known as the Flatiron. Rising 22 stories in the shape of a clothes iron, it owes its appeal not only to its height, but to the impression it gives of sailing up Broadway like the prow of a ship.

IAC Building

555 West 18th Street/West Street; subway:14th St/8th Ave; map p.152 A1

The curvy white-glass skin of this 2007 Frank Gehry creation, designed to evoke the sails of a ship beside the Hudson River waterfront, stands in counterpoint to the sharp angles of the city's anonymous glass boxes.

Left: Lower Manhattan's buildings dominate the skyline.

New York Public Library

Fifth Avenue/West 42nd Street; tel: 917-275-6975; www.nypl.org; Mon 11am–6pm, Tue–Wed 11am–7.30pm, Thur–Sat 11am–6pm, Sun 1–5pm; subway: 42nd St/5th Ave; map p.153 D3

Carrère & Hastings's 1911 library is one of several grand buildings in the Beaux Arts style, a French import that drew on classical, Renaissance, and Baroque traditions. Other examples are Richard Morris Hunt's 1902 **Metropolitan Museum of Art** *(see p.95)* and Warren and Wetmore's 1913 **Grand Central Terminal** *(see p.7).*

The library is one of the world's finest research facilities and has a vast collection that includes the first book printed in the United States – the *Bay Psalm Book* from 1640. The biggest treasure may be the Reading Room, a vast gem with windows that overlook Bryant Park.

The New York Times Building

620 Eighth Avenue/West 40th and 41st streets; subway: Times Square; map p.152 C3

A significant and heralded contribution to the city's architecture, the building was completed in 2007. The first New York building for its architect, Renzo Piano, it features an innovative double-skinned curtain wall of clear glass veiled by ceramic tubes which reflect light and change color throughout the day.

Rockefeller Center

Sixth Avenue/West 50th Street; tel: 212-632 3975; www.rockefeller.com; daily 7am–midnight; entrance charge for observation deck; subway: 50th St/Rockefeller Center; map p.153 D4

Raymond Hood's 1934 RCA Building – now the GE Building – is the centerpiece of Rockefeller Center. A more muted version of the Art Deco genre than the towers of the early 1930s, the structure in some ways presaged the slab-like skyscrapers to come. The **Top of the Rock** observation deck provides spectacular views over Manhattan, and of the iconic Empire State Building.

Seagram Building

375 Park Avenue/East 52nd and 53rd streets; subway: Lexington Avenue; map p.153 E4

In the postwar era, the spare-lined International style ruled the day. Mies van der Rohe's 1958 Seagram Building set the pattern for many more.

Solomon R. Guggenheim Museum

1071 Fifth Avenue/East 89th Street; subway: 86th St; map p.151 E4

Frank Lloyd Wright's only New York City building is this 1956 museum. At the end of his 70-year career, Wright designed the Guggenheim to provide a spiraling exhibition gallery with no formal division of floors.

SEE ALSO MUSEUMS, P.98

Woolworth Building

233 Broadway/Barclay Street; subway: Park Place, City Hall; map p.156 B3

This neo-Gothic tower, designed by Cass Gilbert in 1913, was known as the 'cathedral of commerce'. It cost five-and-dime baron F.W. Woolworth $13 million.

Right: the Chrysler Building.

Bars

Thirsty? You've come to the right place. One of the world's great drinking towns, New York has a bar for every mood, occasion, and budget. On the low end, you'll find a working-man's tavern in just about every neighborhood. On the high end is an endless parade of ultra-hip watering holes where the thin and fabulous gather behind velvet ropes. In between is a raft of night spots for every taste – prim or punk, gay or straight, wine, beer, Martini. If you can drink it, New York's got it. For more after-dark options, *see Gay and Lesbian, p.68–9; Music, p.106–9; and Nightlife, p.110–13.*

Midtown

Bogarts
99 Park Avenue/East 39th Street; tel: 212-922-9244; Mon–Fri 11.30am–midnight, Sat 10pm–4am; map p.153 D2
Popular with a young after-work crowd and a stone's throw from the train.

Bull & Bear
Waldorf-Astoria, East 49th Street/Lexington Avenue; tel: 212-872-1775; Mon–Sun 4.30pm–11.30pm; map p.153 E3
A long mahogany bar and masculine atmosphere set a clubby and congenial tone at this bar in one of the city's storied hotels.
SEE ALSO HOTELS, P.76

The Campbell Apartments
Grand Central Terminal, 15 Vanderbilt Avenue; tel: 212-953-0409; Mon–Thur noon–1am, Fri noon–2am, Sat 3pm–2am, Sun 3pm–midnight; map p.153 D3
For drop-dead glamour, step into this secret lair in Grand Central Terminal, once the private digs of a business magnate.

The Ginger Man
11 East 36th Street/Madison and Fifth avenues; tel: 212-532-

Above: try a mojito at Calle Ocho on the Upper West Side.

3740; Mon–Thur 11.30am–2am, Sat 12.30pm–4am, Sun 3pm–midnight; map p.153 D2
More than 100 bottled beers, including potent varieties of Belgian beer, plus Irish whiskeys and 20 or so single malt scotches, attract crowds to this tiny but inviting watering hole.

King Cole Bar
St Regis Hotel, 2 East 55th Street/Fifth Avenue; tel: 212-753-4500; Mon–Thur 11.30am–1am, Fri–Sat 11.30am–2am, Sun noon–midnight; map p.153 D4
Experience a taste of the Gilded Age at the impeccably appointed St Regis Hotel. A gorgeous Maxfield Parrish mural serves as a backdrop.

Monkey Bar
Hotel Elysée, 60 East 54th Street/Madison and Park avenues; tel: 212-838-2600; Mon–Sun 5pm–midnight; map p.153 E4
A posh room with cute primate-themed decor and drink menu captures much of the glamor of yesteryear.

Morrell Wine Bar & Café
1 Rockefeller Plaza/Fifth and Sixth avenues; tel: 212-262-7700; Mon–Sat 11.30am–midnight, Sun noon–6pm; map p.153 D4
The cellar is stocked with 2,000 bottles at this wine bar. It attracts a noisy warm-weather crowd that spills over into a sidewalk café.

Rainbow Grill
30 Rockefeller Plaza; tel: 212-632-5100; Sun–Thur 5pm–midnight, Fri–Sat 5pm–1am; map p.153 D4
An iconic, if touristy, New York setting atop Rockefeller

Left: bourbons and whiskies lined up in a row.

Stone Rose

Time Warner Center, 10 Columbus Circle, 4th floor; tel: 212-823-9769; Mon–Sat 4pm–2am, Sun 4pm–midnight; map p.150 C2

A large, stylish lounge in the soaring Time Warner Center, with marble, polished wood, and leather, and intoxicating views of Central Park.

Chelsea to Gramercy

Black Door

127 West 26th Street/Sixth Avenue; tel: 212-645-0215; Mon–Fri 4pm–4am, Sat–Sun 7pm–4am; map p.152 B1

Keep an eye out for the black awning to find this low-key yet sophisticated neighborhood bar. You can enjoy a chilled cocktail, but you won't find any beers on tap.

Old Town Bar and Restaurant

45 East 18th Street/Broadway and Park Avenue; tel: 212-529-6732; Mon–Sat 11.30am–1.30am, Sun 1pm–midnight; map p.155 C4

This old-time saloon is a beloved neighborhood hangout. After-work crowds toss down drinks and tasty burgers at the long mahogany bar.

The 20-block stretch around Second Avenue between 72nd and 92nd streets has a conspicuous number of Irish pubs including **Kinsale Tavern** (1672 Third Avenue; tel: 212-348-4370) and **O'Flanagan's Ale House** (1215 First Avenue; tel: 2212-439-0660), frequented mostly by students who live in the vicinity. Most of them don't serve anything more complicated than beer, wine and a few home-style dishes.

Plaza offers glorious views of the city and classic Art Deco decor.

Rudy's Bar & Grill

627 Ninth Avenue/West 44th Street; tel: 212-974-9169; Mon–Sat 8am– 4am, Sun noon–4am; map p.152 C4

A scruffy Hell's Kitchen haunt with bags of atmosphere where drinks are cheap and the hot dogs free.

Uptown

Barcibo Enoteca

2020 Broadway/West 69th Street; tel: 212-595-28052; Mon–Thur 4.30pm–12.30am, Fri 4.30pm–2am, Sat 3.30pm–2am, Sun 3:30pm–12.30am; map p.150 C3

A relaxing, sophisticated wine bar with an all-Italian wine list.

Calle Ocho

446 Columbus Avenue/West 81st and 82nd streets; tel: 212-873-5025; Mon–Thur 6pm–11pm, Fri 6pm–midnight, Sat 5pm–midnight, Sun 5–10pm; map p.151 C4

Fans say the mojitos at this sexy Caribbean lounge and restaurant are the city's best. Soft multicolored lights create an alluring, grotto-like atmosphere in the bar, second home to many of the neighborhood's moneyed young professionals.

Dublin House

225 West 79th Street/Broadway and Amsterdam Avenue; tel: 212-874-9528; Mon–Sat 8am–4am, Sun noon–4am; map p.150 C4

This one is for the old guard – a mellow, friendly lair filled with neighborhood regulars, students and old timers.

Right: New York's cocktails can be potent, and expensive.

Pete's Tavern
129 East 18th Street/Irving Plaza; tel: 212-473-7676; daily 11am–2.30am; map p.155 D3
This is one of the city's most historic pubs and reputedly where O. Henry penned *Gift of the Magi*. It still draws an illustrious crowd, who come for the companionable if somewhat dingy atmosphere.

Rodeo Bar
375 Third Avenue/East 27th Street; tel: 212-683-6500; Mon–Sat 11.30am–4am, Sun 11.30am–2am; map p.153 D1
Great for honky-tonk, fiddlin' or alt-country sounds while munching on southwestern fare of ribs, catfish, enchiladas, or "cowboy kisses." The preferred libations are Mexican beers and killer margaritas.

Greenwich Village

Acme Bar and Grill
9 Great Jones Street/Broadway and Lafayette Street; tel: 212-420-1934; Mon–Thur 11.30am–11.30pm, Fri–Sat 11.30am–12.30am, Sun 11.30am–10pm; map p.154 C2
This NoHo bar and restaurant has the look and feel of a Louisiana roadhouse. The customers are friendly, the margaritas generously proportioned, and the Cajun cooking tangy.

Brass Monkey
55 Little West 12th Street; tel: 212-675-6686; daily 11.30am–4am; map p.154 A4
Patrons have a choice of more than 50 beers in a laidback pub-style atmosphere. Irish-inspired food helps the drinks go down.

The Ear Inn
326 Spring Street/Greenwich and Washington streets; tel: 212-226-9060; daily noon–4am; map p.154 A2
Established in 1812, The Ear Inn is one of the select coterie that make up the oldest bars in Manhattan. The decor is dark, the atmosphere welcoming and relaxed. The clientele, an unholy mix of dockers and artists, has changed little

If the **Mulberry Street Bar** (176½ Mulberry Street between Broome and Grand streets) in Little Italy seems familiar, you may have seen it on the big screen. This *molto Italiano* bar has served as a setting for several scenes in the *Godfather* films, *Donnie Brasco* and *The Sopranos*.

over the years. Food is simple and hearty – think massive burgers and surprisingly good seafood.

White Horse Tavern
567 Hudson Street/West 11th Street; tel: 212-243-9260; Sun–Thur 11am–1.30am, Fri–Sat 1am–4am; map p.154 A3
No bar tour of Greenwich Village is complete without visiting this historic tavern, where Welsh poet Dylan Thomas knocked back one too many whiskeys before passing away at nearby St Vincent's Hospital.

Wilfie & Nell
228 West 4th Street/7th Avenue S.; tel: 212-242-2990; Mon–Wed 4pm–2am, Thur–Fri 4pm–4am, Sat 1pm–4am, Sun 1pm–2am; map p.154 B3
Small candlelit room with a flirty and friendly atmosphere. The snacks alone, simple and satisfying, are worth the visit.

East Village to Chinatown

Arlene's Grocery
95 Stanton Street/Ludlow Street; tel: 212-995-1652; daily 6pm–4am; map p.157 D4
This pioneer of the Lower East Side's alternative music scene still packs in hipsters eager to hear a wide variety of cutting-edge music or take the stage themselves for a go at hard-rock karaoke.

Left: shaken but not stirred in SoHo.

Above: the Lower East Side has a number of good bars.

A rowdy rocker-art bar on the Lower East Side with pinball machines and a pool table, paintings on the walls, and a regular gang of cool locals.

SoHo and TriBeCa

Fanelli Café
94 Prince Street/Mercer Street; tel: 212-226-9412; Mon–Thur 10am–2am, Fri–Sat 10am–3am, Sun 11am–2am; map p.154 B1

Want to know what SoHo was like before it was SoHo? Come to Fanelli. The service can be crotchety, but that adds to the sense of character in this handsome pub, which has been serving food continuously since 1874 (it was a speakeasy during Prohibition). The kitchen knocks out a great burger, reasonable pasta and good sandwiches. Photographs on the walls reflect the Fanelli family's obsession with boxing.

MercBar
151 Mercer Street/Prince Street; tel: 212-966-2727; Sun–Wed 5pm–2am, Fri–Sat 5pm–4am; map p.154 B1

This quintessential SoHo survivor sports contemporary (though inexplicable) western decor, with a canoe over the bar and antlers on the wall. Though supermodels don't hang out here much anymore, the crowd still tends to be sharp and upscale. In summer, when the doors are open, it's a great place to watch the designer-clad world slink by.

Vig Bar
12 Spring Street/Elizabeth Street; tel: 212-625-0011; daily 5pm–4am; map p.154 C1

A sleek candlelit bar with a relaxed atmosphere and well-

stocked bar. The perfect place for a chat away from the masses.

Walker's
16 North Moore Street/Varick Street; tel: 212-941-0142; Mon–Sat 11.45am–4am; map p.154 A1

This three-room pub in TriBeCa has been a vital part of the neighborhood since 1890 – a refuge during riots, fiscal crises, blackouts and, most recently, the World Trade Center disaster, when folks gathered to hear the latest news, comfort each other, and forget their troubles a while. The American diner fare is heartening.

Lower Manhattan

Ulysses
95 Pearl Street/Hanover Square; tel: 212-482-0400; daily 11am–4am; map p.156 B1

This Irish pub in the Financial District attracts brokers and bankers for after-work libations. The pub grub is nothing to write home about, but there's an interesting selection of brews.

Back Room
102 Norfolk Street/Delancey and Rivington streets; tel: 212-228-5098; Tue–Sun 7.30pm–4am; map p.157 D4

Everyone knows the coolest bars are hard to find at least that's the concept at Back Room, whose premises are marked by a sign to the 'Lower East Side Toy Company.' The speakeasy vibe continues inside with drinks served in teacups and a sliding bookcase door.

Happy Ending
302 Broome Street/Forsyth and Eldridge streets; tel: 212-334-9676; Tue 10pm–4am, Wed–Sat 7pm–4am; map p.157 D4

Fans of the film *25th Hour* can have a drink where Edward Norton sank a few the night before his departure to an upstate prison. Rumor has it that this Lower East Side basement was once a Chinese massage parlor and takes its name from one of their unadvertised practices.

Max Fish
178 Ludlow Street/East Houston and Stanton streets; tel: 212-529-3959; daily 5.30pm–4am; map p.157 D4

Right: The Ear Inn dates back to the early 19th-century.

Cafés

There are no fewer than 90 Starbucks in Midtown Manhattan, but none appear in the listings below. Instead, we focus mainly on independent shops, places as quirky and colorful as the patrons themselves. In New York, 'café' refers to a wide variety of places. Some are full-fledged restaurants; others are little more than a take-out counter and a table or two. Some have European flair; others are inspired by traditional American diners. But they all have one thing in common: coffee. They may sell bread or books or ice cream or groceries, but the key to their business is a good cup of joe.

Jamie Titus
Selected Works

Midtown

Beard Papa Sweets Café (inside Café Zaiya)
18 East 41st Street/Fifth and Madison avenues; tel: 212-779-0600; Mon–Fri 7am–8pm, Sat–Sun 10am–8pm; map p.153 D3
Cream puffs are the specialty at this chain, but the Belgian chocolate cake is equally enticing. There are better choices if you're fussy about coffee, but it's a good stop for something quick and sweet. (Also at: 2167 Broadway/West 76th Street, tel: 212-799-3770; 740 Broadway/Astor Place, tel: 212-353-8888; 5 Carmine Street/Sixth Avenue, tel: 212-255-4675.)

Cipriani Le Specialità
110 East 42nd Street/Lexington and Park avenues; tel: 212-557-5088; Mon–Fri 7am–7pm; map p.153 D2
This pretty little place is more akin to a deli or gourmet shop than a traditional café, but the espresso is excellent and the pastries, panini, and pasta rarely disappoint.

Juan Valdez Café
140 East 57th Street/Lexington Avenue; tel: 917-289-0981; Mon–Fri 7am–8pm, Sat–Sun 9am–7pm; map p.153 E4

Above: deciding where to have that important cup of joe.

About two blocks from Bloomingdale's, this little café is a pleasant and convenient spot for Colombian coffee and pastries.

Oren's Daily Roast
830 Third Avenue/East 51st Street; tel: 212-308-2148; Mon–Fri 7am–7pm, Fri 7am–6pm, Sat 9am–6pm, Sun 10am–5pm; map p.153 E3
Lines out the door indicate one thing: excellent, full-bodied coffee roasted daily and expertly brewed. There are eight more Oren's café-stores around Manhattan,

including one at Grand Central Station and another in Waverly Place, off Washington Square.

Uptown

Alice's Tea Cup
102 West 73rd Street/Columbus and Amsterdam avenues; tel: 212-799-3006; daily 8am–8pm; map p.150 C3
A hundred teas and a dash of whimsy make this an enchanting place for a light lunch and long, uninterrupted chats with a friend.

Café Lalo
201 West 83rd Street/Amsterdam Avenue; tel: 212-496-6031; Mon–Thur 8am–2am, Fri 8am–4am, Sat 9am–4am, Sun 9am–2am; map p.151 C4
You'll find a few salads and sandwiches on the menu, but they're little more than an afterthought to the dozens of heavenly cakes and pies.

Café Sabarsky
1048 Fifth Avenue/East 86th Street; tel: 212-288-0665; Mon and Wed 9am–6pm, Thur–Sun 9am–9pm; map p.151 E4
At this wood-paneled café on the ground floor of the

Left: the art-filled Arium Café in the Meatpacking District.

then you have come to the right place. This artisan bakery turns out a seductive array of muffins, tarts, croissants, cakes, and pastries, as well as several varieties of breads.

Chelsea to Gramercy

Arium Café and Gallery
31 Little West 12th
Street/Washington Street; tel:
212-463-8630; Tue 10am–6pm,
Wed 10am–8pm, Thur
10am–9pm, Fri 10am–8pm, Sat
10am–6pm, Sun 11am–6pm;
map p.154 A4

Part café, part art gallery, this tranquil spot in the Meatpacking District is a lovely choice for tea or a light lunch.

Joe, The Art of Coffee
9 East 13th Street/Fifth Avenue
and University Place; tel: 212-
924-7400; Mon–Fri 7am–
8pm, Sat–Sun 8am–8pm;
map p.155 C3

Forget the fancy decor and snooty baristas. The secret of Joe's success is a great cup of coffee and a pleasant set-

Below: the perfect afternoon: iced coffee and a paper.

If you ask for regular coffee, you'll most likely get brewed coffee. If you don't take anything in your coffee, ask for it black. Half and half – a mixture of cream and milk – is a popular addition.

Neue Galerie of German and Austrian Art, visitors can savor the dark coffee and excellent desserts of an old Viennese-style restaurant. Replicas of period banquettes and bentwood furniture, plus a Josef Hoffmann chandelier, provide a setting that is luxurious and distinctive. Cabaret and a *prix-fixe* dinner are presented at the café on select Fridays.

Edgar's Café
255 West 84th Street/Broadway
and West End Avenue; tel: 212-
496-6126; Sun–Thur 8am–1am,
Fri–Sat 8am–2am

The decor at this quirky but handsome place is inspired by Edgar Allan Poe, who once lived nearby. A good choice for light fare, tea, and coffee, including a creamy frappuccino and winning tiramisu.

French Roast
2340 Broadway/West 85th
Street; tel: 212-799-1533; daily
24 hours

This Parisian-style bistro and café is a lively, collegial spot for coffee, drinks, or a full meal. The sidewalk tables are pleasant on a fine day.

Payard Patisserie and Bistro
1032 Lexington Avenue/East
73rd Street; tel: 212-717-5252;
Mon–Thur noon–3pm, 5.45–
10.30pm, Fri–Sat noon–3pm,
5.45–11pm, Sun 11.30am–
3.30pm; map p.151 E2

You may not make it beyond the café-style tables in the front room, where glass cases are filled with delicate pastries, ice cream, and rich chocolates. But if you're hungry for something more substantial, press on to the back room for a full menu of dependable bistro classics.

Silver Moon Bakery
2740 Broadway/West 105th
Street; tel: 212-866-4717;
Mon–Fri 7.30am–8pm, Sat–Sun
8.30am–7pm

If you find it unthinkable to order coffee without something sweet to go with it,

ting modeled loosely on traditional Italian cafés. (Also at: 141 Waverly Place/Sixth Avenue, tel: 212-924-6750; 514 Columbus Avenue/West 85th Street, tel: 212-875-0100.)

Greenwich Village
Caffè Reggio
119 MacDougal Street/Bleecker and West 3rd streets; tel: 212-475-9557; Sun–Thur 9am–2.30am, Fri–Sat 9am–4am; map p.154 B2
In business since 1927, this is the best of the Village's Italian coffeehouses.
Cornelia Street Café
29 Cornelia Street/Bleecker and West 4th Streets; tel: 212-989-9319; daily 10am–1am; map p.155 B3
This still-bohemian Village café and restaurant holds regular poetry readings and music performances in the basement downstairs.
Sant Ambroeus
259 West 4th Street/Perry Street; tel: 212-604-9254; Mon–Sat 9am–11pm, Sun 10am–11pm; map p.154 B3
Elegant espresso, marzipan and more – all is heavenly (if pricey) at this Village newcomer. The original, much

plusher, location is on the Upper East Side (1000 Madison Avenue/East 77th Street, tel: 212-570-2211).
Tanti Baci
163 West 10th Street/Waverly Place; tel: 212-647-9651; daily 11am–11pm; map p.154 B3
More of a café than a restaurant, but regulars like its coziness and simple but reliable pasta and salads. The front patio is open in good weather.

East Village to Chinatown
Abraço
86 East 7th Street/First Avenue; tel: 212-388-9731; Tue–Sat 8am–6pm, Sun 9am–6pm; map p.155 D2
Despite the very tiny storefront, they still deliver an excellent cup of joe and wonderful house-made semi-sweets and savories.
De Robertis
176 First Avenue/East 10th and 11th streets; tel: 212-674-7137; Sun–Mon 9am–10pm, Tue–Sat 9am–11pm; map p.155 D2
Established more than a century ago, De Robertis remains an old-fashioned Italian *pasticceria* and café.

Below: meeting up with a friend and setting the world to rights in an East Village eatery.

Earthmatters
177 Ludlow Street/East Houston Street; tel: 212-475-4180; daily 8am–midnight; map p.157 D4
You get three in one at this East Village spot: a café, a reading library, and a vegan grocery store.
Jules Bistro
65 St Mark's Place/First Avenue; tel: 212-477-5560; Mon–Thur noon–4pm, 5.30pm–1am, Fri to 2am, Sat 11am–4pm, 5.30pm–2am, Sun 5.30pm–1am; map p.155 D2
A neighborhood bistro and café, with ever-satisfying traditional French fare, where live jazz can be heard at Sunday brunch.
Lucien
14 First Avenue/East 1st Street; tel: 212-260-6481; daily 11am–2am; map p.155 C1
This snug place is a slice of Parisian café society.

SoHo and TriBeCa
Bread
20 Spring Street/Elizabeth and Mott streets; tel: 212-334-1015; Sun–Thur 10.30am–midnight, Fri–Sat 10.30am–1am; map p.154 C1
This tiny café and wine bar is devoted to bread and all that can go between it. Hot panini are filled with everything from pesto chicken, avocado, and goat cheese to shiitakes, fresh sardines, and tomatoes, as well as the more traditional Parma ham, mozzarella, and *taleggio*. Bread also has an interesting antipasti plate and some tasty pasta dishes.
Café Borgia II
161 Prince Street/Thompson Street; tel: 212-677-1850; hours vary; map p.154 B2
Perk up a SoHo shopping spree with espresso and cannoli at this small place with bare-brick walls.
Café Gitane
242 Mott Street/Prince Street; tel: 212-334-9552; Sun–Thur

Cafés

Above: having a snack in MacDougal Street, Greenwich Village.

9am–midnight, Fri–Sat 9am–12.30am; map p.154 C1
The onset of Mayor Bloomberg's cigarette-free world was a blow to Le Gitane (named after a French cigarette brand), which somehow looked, if not smelt, better shrouded in smoke. However, the young, hip crowd still piles in for coffee, fresh salads, and light meals. They just take their smokes outside, in the shadow of old St Patrick's Cathedral.

Cupping Room Café
359 West Broadway/Broome Street; tel: 212-925-2898; Sun–Thur 8am–midnight, Fri–Sat 8am–2am; map p.154 B1
A quintessential SoHo café and restaurant, with bare-brick walls, pressed tin ceilings, and the work of local artists on the walls. Burgers and brunch are equally popular. Live music several nights a week.

Housing Works Used Book Café
126 Crosby Street/Jersey Street; tel: 212-334-3324; Mon–Fri 10am–9pm, Sat–Sun noon–7pm; map p.154 C1
Sip lattes in the company of penurious writers nibbling cakes and scribbling furiously in battered notebooks. Well-known writers and poets visit frequently, too, for readings and discussions with a loyal following of local artists, academics, and students.
SEE ALSO SHOPPING, P.136

Lower Manhattan

The Financier
62 Stone Street/Mill Lane; tel: 212-344-5600; Mon–Fri 7am–8pm, Sat 8.30am–6.30pm; map p.156 B1
This classy little café and eatery is a breath of fresh air among the Financial District's otherwise stale offerings. The menu includes pastry, panini, soups, and salads. (Also at two other downtown locations, both of which are open Sundays: 35 Cedar Street/Pearl and William streets, tel: 212-952-3838; World Financial Center, tel: 212-786-3220.)

Jack's Stir Brew Coffee
222 Front Street/Beekman Street and Peck Slip; tel: 212-227-7631; Mon–Fri 7am–7pm, Sat–Sun 8am–7pm; map p.156 B2
A very welcome outpost of the popular West Village coffee shop offering delicious, organic drip coffee. (Also at: 138 West 10th Street/Greenwich Avenue, tel: 212-929-0821.)

Right: the stronger and blacker, the better.

Brooklyn

Almondine
85 Water Street/Main Street; tel: 718-797-5026; Mon–Sat 7am–7pm, Sun 10am–6pm; map p.157 D1
Freshly baked breads and pastries are the highlight of this lovely spot in trendy DUMBO.

Bliss
191 Bedford Avenue/6th and 7th streets; tel: 718-599-2547; Mon–Fri 9am–11pm, Sat–Sun 10am–11pm
This vegetarian café is a favorite hangout of Williamsburg bohos and the alfalfa set.

Gorilla Coffee
97 Fifth Avenue/Park Place; tel: 718-230-3244; Mon–Sat 7am–9pm, Sun 8am–9pm
There's nothing fancy here, just rich, aromatic java prepared by people who know what they're doing. Coffee lovers will be rewarded.

Juniors
386 Flatbush Avenue Extension/Dekalb Avenue; tel: 718-852-5257; Sun–Wed 6.30am–12.30am, Thur 6.30am–1am, Fri–Sat to 2am
Brooklynites line up for justly celebrated cheesecake at this old-time bakery and diner, but, if you're really hungry, you can also order homespun dishes like meatloaf, brisket, matzo soup, and breakfast all day.

Children

If you plan to travel to New York with children, be sure to do your homework. Preparation – and lots of patience – are the keys to a successful trip. In some ways, New York is the perfect family destination because there are so many activities that both adults and children will enjoy – a Broadway show, for example, or a trip to Central Park Zoo. For kids who aren't accustomed to big-city life, even mundane experiences will be an adventure. You may be smitten by the city's art and culture, but what your kids might remember most vividly is riding the subway, pressing elevator buttons, and buying hot dogs from a street vendor.

Midtown

Broadway Shows

Discount, same-day tickets; TKTS booth (under the red steps), 47th Street/Broadway; tel: 212-912-9770; www.tdf.org; for evening performances Mon–Sat 3–8pm, Sun 3–7.30pm, for matinee performances Wed, Sat 10am–2pm, Sun 11am–3pm; map p.153 C4

Disney's arrival in the Theater District guarantees a choice of family-friendly shows, including long-running hits like *The Lion King*.

Empire State Building

Map p.153 C2

The view from the observatory thrills young and old alike.

SEE ALSO ARCHITECTURE, P.32

FAO Schwarz

767 Fifth Avenue/East 58th Street; tel: 212-644-9400; map p.151 D1

Toys R Us

1514 Broadway/West 44th Street; tel: 646-366-8800; map p.153 C4

The next best thing to Santa's workshop. FAO Schwarz is the classier toy shop, but Toys R Us has an indoor Ferris wheel.

SEE ALSO SHOPPING, P.136

Intrepid Sea, Air & Space Museum

Map p.150 A1

The collection of warplanes on this World War II-era aircraft carrier makes for a whiz-bang history lesson. Visitors can ride in the A-6 Cockpit Simulator and tour inside the Concorde.

SEE ALSO MUSEUMS, P.90

NBC Studio Tour

NBC Experience Store, GE Building, 30 Rockefeller Plaza; tel: 212-664-3700; Mon–Thur 8.30am–4.30pm, Fri–Sat 9.30am–5.30pm, Sun 9.30am–4.30pm; entrance charge; subway: 50th St/Rockefeller Center; map p.153 D4

A behind-the-scenes look at

Below: SoHo Children's Museum of the Arts.

such popular TV shows as *Saturday Night Live*, *The Today Show*, and *Late Night with Jimmy Fallon*.

SEE ALSO MEDIA, P.85

Sony Wonder Technology Lab

550 Madison Avenue; tel: 212-833-8100; http://wondertechlab.sony.com; Tue–Sat 10am–5pm, Sun noon–5pm; free; subway: 59th St; map p.153 E4

Four floors of interactive exhibits that explore information technology and design (and pitch Sony products).

Uptown

American Museum of Natural History

Map p.151 D4

Make a beeline to the dinosaur collection, then head to the spectacular Rose Center for Earth and Space.

SEE ALSO MUSEUMS, P.93

Talk about sweet dreams, **Dylan's Candy Bar** (1011 Third Avenue at East 60th Street, tel: 646-735-0078) has two floors of fancy sweets plus an old-fashioned ice cream counter.

Left: even kids have fun at the Metropolitan Museum of Art.

Brooklyn

Brooklyn Children's Museum

145 Brooklyn Avenue; tel: 718-735-4400; www.brooklyn kids.org; Wed–Fri noon–5pm, Sat–Sun 10am–5pm; entrance charge; subway: Kingston Ave

Founded in 1899, this is the oldest children's museum in America and has thousands of artifacts to gaze at – and plenty of buttons to twiddle.

New York Aquarium

Surf Avenue/West 8th Street; tel: 718-265-3474; www.ny aquarium.com; May–Sept Mon–Fri 10am–6pm, Sat–Sun 10am–7pm, Oct–Apr daily 10am–4.30pm; entrance charge; subway: W. 8th St–NY Aquarium

This Coney Island aquarium has a sea-lion show, shark feeding, walrus pool, sea otters, and penguins.

The Bronx

Bronx Zoo

Bronx River Parkway; tel: 718-367-1010; www.bronxzoo.org

The country's largest urban zoo has gorillas, big cats, giraffes, and lots of pettable animals.

SEE ALSO PARKS AND GARDENS, P.119

Below: the Sony Wonder Technology Lab.

Central Park Zoo

830 Fifth Avenue/East 65th Street; tel: 212-439-6500; www.centralparkzoo.com; Apr–Oct Mon–Fri 10am–5pm, Sat–Sun 10am–5.30pm, Nov–Mar daily 10am–4.30pm; entrance charge; subway: 5th Ave/59th St; map p.151 D2

Much loved for its sea lions, penguins, and polar bears. A vintage carrousel is nearby.

SEE ALSO PARKS AND GARDENS, P.116

Children's Museum of Manhattan

Has five floors of lively interactive exhibits dealing with art, science and nature.

SEE ALSO MUSEUMS, P.94

Metropolitan Museum of Art

Map p.151 E4

Children will be fascinated by the collection of Egyptian mummies.

SEE ALSO MUSEUMS, P.95

Chelsea

Chelsea Piers

West 23rd Street/Hudson River; tel: 212-336-6666; www.chelsea piers.com; hours and entrance charges vary by venue; subway: 23rd St; map p.152 A2

Facilities at Manhattan's largest sports and entertainment complex include roller- and ice-skating rinks, bowling alleys, batting cages, and a climbing wall, and the many special programmes for kids include a 'toddlers' gym.'

SEE ALSO SPORTS, P.145

SoHo

Children's Museum of the Arts

182 Lafayette Street; tel: 212-274-0986; www.cmany.org; map p.156 C4

Little kids love this brightly colored, pint-sized arts studio the best, as under-7s can paint, sculpt, and dress up.

SEE ALSO MUSEUMS, P.101

Statue of Liberty and Ellis Island

Ferry tickets: Castle Clinton, Battery Park; tel: 212-363-3200; www.nps.gov/stli; 9am–5pm, extended summer hours; free, but a charge for the ferry; subway: South Ferry; map p.156 A1

Climbing to Lady Liberty's observation deck is a New York tradition. The ferry ticket includes a visit to Ellis Island, site of the immigration station.

SEE ALSO MUSEUMS, P.103

Churches, Synagogues and Mosques

People of many faiths have found a home in this city of immigrants. Listed below are just a few of the most notable houses of worship, many of them landmarks in their own right. Whether you are looking for a spiritual experience or interested only in history and architecture, New York's religious institutions are a vital part of the city's cultural heritage.

Midtown

Central Synagogue
123 East 55th Street/Lexington Avenue; tel: 212-838-5122; www.centralsynagogue.org; subway: Lexington Ave-53rd St; map p.153 E4
Built in 1872, this landmark adds a note of Moorish-style elegance to an ordinary block.

Church of the Incarnation
209 Madison Avenue/East 35th Street; tel: 212-689-6350; www.churchoftheincarnation.org; subway: 33rd St; map p.153 D2
Built in 1864 in neo-Gothic style, this Episcopal church has stained-glass windows by Tiffany, Paul LaFarge and many English glassmakers.

St Patrick's Cathedral
Fifth Avenue/50th and 51st streets; tel: 212-753-2261; www.saintpatrickscathedral.org; subway: 50th St-Rockefeller Center; map p.153 D4
St Patrick's is the largest Catholic church in the country. Its construction took 21 years, from 1858 to 1879, and though now dwarfed by the glass towers around it, James Renwick, Jr's neo-Gothic cathedral remains a cornerstone of Midtown.

Above: New York Gothic at Broadway's Grace Church.

Uptown

Islamic Cultural Center
1711 Third Avenue/East 96th Street; tel: 212-722-5234; subway: 96th St
The city's largest mosque is a modern interpretation of traditional Islamic architecture. Muslims and non-Muslims may attend prayer services.

Temple Emanu-El
1 East 65th Street/Fifth Avenue; tel: 212-744-1400; www.emanuelnyc.org; subway: 68th St-Hunter College; map p.151 D2
Some 2,500 worshippers can gather under one roof here, making this one of the world's largest reform synagogues.

Harlem

Abyssinian Baptist Church
132 West 138th Street/Malcolm X Boulevard; tel: 212-862-7474; www.abyssinian.org; subway: 135th St
Established in 1808 in Lower Manhattan by African-American congregants unwilling to accept segregation, the Abyssinian moved to its present site in 1922 under the leadership of Adam Clayton Powell, Sr. His son, the Rev. Adam Clayton Powell, Jr, took to the pulpit in 1937 and championed the causes of justice and equality as both a religious and a political leader.

Canaan Baptist Church
132 West 116th Street/St Nicholas Avenue; tel: 212-866-0301; subway: 116th St
The gospel service at this Harlem church is a rousing and joyful experience.

Cathedral of St John the Divine
1047 Amsterdam Avenue/West 112th Street; tel: 212-316-7490; www.stjohndivine.org; subway: Cathedral Parkway

Left: Trinity Church in Lower Manhattan dates from 1846.

This was the seat of the city's Catholic archdiocese from 1809 until 1879, when the "new" St Patrick's Cathedral was completed.

St Mark's-in-the-Bowery
131 East 10th Street/Second Avenue; tel: 212-674-6377; www.dioceseny.org; subway: Astor Place; map p.155 D2
The second-oldest church in Manhattan, built in 1799 on the site of a chapel built in 1660 by governor Peter Stuyvesant, who is buried here.

Lower Manhattan

St Paul's Chapel
209 Broadway/Fulton Street; tel: 212-233-4164; www.saintpauls chapel.org; subway: Fulton Street–Broadway-Nassau; map p.156 B3
This Georgian-style Episcopal chapel is Manhattan's only church left from the Colonial era. A block east of Ground Zero, it has a 9/11 exhibit.

Trinity Church
74 Trinity Place/Broadway and Wall Street; tel: 212-602-0800; www.trinitywallstreet.org; subway: Wall Street; map p.156 A2
The present church, from 1846, is the third on this site.

The seat of the Episcopal Diocese of New York, this cathedral – begun in 1892 but still unfinished – is said to be the world's second-largest Gothic cathedral.

Mother AME Zion Church
146 West 137th Street/Adam Clayton Powell Boulevard; tel: 212-234-1545; subway: 135th St
This 'Freedom Church' – the first African-American church in the state – was established in 1776 in Lower Manhattan, and was a critical link in the Underground Railroad. Members included Paul Robeson. Mother AME moved into this grand edifice in 1925.

Greenwich Village

Grace Church
802 Broadway/East 10th Street; tel: 212-254-2000; www.grace churchnyc.org; subway: 8th St; map p.155 C3
This 1843 Gothic-Revival Episcopal church was designed by James Renwick, Jr at the age of 25. He later designed St Patrick's Catholic Cathedral.

St-Luke-in-the-Fields
487 Hudson Street/Barrow and Christopher streets; tel: 212-924-0562; www.stlukeinthefields.org; subway: Christopher St; map p.154 A3
The city's third-oldest church was built in 1821.

East Village to Chinatown

Eastern States Buddhist Temple of America
64 Mott Street/Bayard Street; tel: 212-966-6229; subway: Canal St; map p.156 C3
The air is thick with incense at this tranquil and popular neighborhood temple.

Eldridge Street Synagogue
12 Eldridge Street/Division Street; tel: 212-219-0888; www. eldridgestreet.org; subway: East Broadway; map p.157 D3
This 1887 Moorish-style synagogue has been restored as a cultural center and still has a small congregation.

Old St Patrick's Cathedral
263 Mulberry Street/Prince Street; tel: 212-226-8075; www. oldcathedral.org; subway: Broadway-Lafayette; map p.154 C1

Right: St Paul's Chapel is NY's oldest publicly used building.

Dance

New York's ballet companies stand toe to toe with any in the world. But it's in the realm of modern dance where the city has really distinguished itself, nurturing the talents of such visionaries as Martha Graham, Alvin Ailey, Merce Cunningham, and Paul Taylor. Although some of these masters have passed away, their ideas – and dance companies – continue to enchant audiences. Here too is a long tradition of Broadway hoofing, emerging street styles in the spirit of break dancing and hip-hop, and numerous small companies dedicated to pushing the boundaries of modern dance.

Dance Companies

Alegrías Flamenco Theater

239 West 14th Street/Seventh Avenue; tel: 917-667-2695; www.alegrias.com; subway: 14th St-8th Ave; map p.154 B4

Traditional and contemporary flamenco, with guest dancers from Spain. There are performances every Saturday.

Alvin Ailey American Dance Theater

School and offices: 405 West 55th Street/Ninth Avenue; tel: 212-405-9000; www.alvin ailey.org; subway: 57th St; map p.150 B1

The company was formed in 1958 when Ailey and other African-American modern dancers performed at the 92nd Steet Y. Former company member Judith Jamison became artistic director after Ailey's death in 1989. It encompasses two dance companies, a dance school, and much else. Though often touring, the Ailey companies perform regularly at the **New York City Center** (see p.47) and their own **Citigroup Theater**, within the West 55th Street center.

Above: Martha Graham and Bertram Ross.

American Ballet Theater

School and offices: 890 Broadway/East 19th Street; tel: 212-477-3030; www.abt.org; map p.155 C4

One of the world's foremost ballet companies performs each spring at the **Metropolitan Opera** *(see p.106)* and in fall at **Lincoln Center's Avery Fisher Hall**. If you're in New York with children, look up ABT Kids, a one-hour show of repertoire highlights designed specially for children.

Dance Theatre of Harlem

School: 466 West 152nd Street/Amsterdam Avenue; tel: 212-690-2800; www.dancetheatre ofharlem.org

Though the company of this major African-American dance center has not performed for some time, it continues to run an education program, *Dancing Through Barriers*, and its young dancers still perform at different venues.

Martha Graham Dance Company

School and offices: 316 East 63rd Street/Second Avenue; tel: 212-521-3611; http://martha graham.org; map p.151 E1

One of the world's most celebrated modern dance companies was founded in 1926 by dance pioneer Martha Graham, and has trained such notable performers and choreographers as Alvin Ailey, Twyla Tharp, Paul Taylor, and Merce Cunningham. The company tours worldwide but performs often at venues, festivals, and special events in the New York area.

Merce Cunningham Dance Company

Offices: 55 Bethune Street/Washington Street; tel: 212-255-8240; www.merce.org; map p.154 A4

Left and below: the New York City Ballet.

Street; tel: 212-691-9740; www.joyce.org; subway: 14th St-8th Ave; map p.152 A1
A 472-seat Chelsea venue dedicated to dance, hosting innovative choreographers, international companies, and traditional forms. **Joyce SoHo** (155 Mercer Street/Prince Street; tel: 212-431-9233) is a studio-style venue specializing in emerging artists.

Lincoln Center
Broadway/West 62nd and 65th streets; tel: (NY State Theater) 212-870-5570; www.lincoln center.org; subway: 59th St-Columbus Circle; map p.150 B2
The arts powerhouse, in midst of major transformation and modernization of concert and dance halls and public spaces, includes two major dance venues: the **David H. Koch Theater**, home to the New York City Ballet and its much-loved *Nutcracker* each winter, and the **Metropolitan Opera**, which hosts visiting ballet companies.

New York City Center
131 West 55th Street/Sixth and Seventh avenues; tel: 212-581-1212; www.nycitycenter.org; subway: 57th St; map p.150 C1
Major New York and international companies play here.

Performance Space 122
150 First Avenue/East 9th Street; tel: 212-352-3101; www.ps122.org; subway: 1st Ave; map p.155 D2
A multi-disciplinary arts center used by emerging and experimental artists, with a strong focus on dance.

Influenced by Zen and Dadaism, and a long-time collaborator of avant-garde composer John Cage, Cunningham, now aged 90, is known for creating physically challenging dances with no narrative structure and often disconnected from the music. The company performs worldwide. Dance classes can be taken at Bethune Street.

New York City Ballet
David H. Koch Theater, 20 Lincoln Center; tel: 212-870-5570; www.nycballet.com; map p.150 B2
New York's longest-established classical ballet company was founded in 1948 by Lincoln Kirstein and choreographer George Balanchine. It has two bases: **David H. Koch Theater** at Lincoln Center and, in summer, the **Saratoga Performing Arts Center** in upstate New York.

Paul Taylor Dance Company
School and offices: 551 Grand Street; tel: 212-431-5562; www.ptdc.org
A former member of the Martha Graham Company, Taylor is celebrated for both his dancing and choreography. Two Taylor companies tour worldwide, and the main company always performs a short season at **New York City Center** each Feb–Mar.

Performance Venues

Brooklyn Academy of Music (BAM)
30 Lafayette Avenue: tel: 718-636-4100; www.bam.org; subway: Atlantic Ave
BAM features local and touring dance companies throughout the year and is host of the annual Next Wave Festival of new and innovative works.
SEE ALSO MUSIC, P.106

Joyce Theater
175 Eighth Avenue/West 19th

Catch up on the latest moves at the Hip Hop Theater Festival (tel: 718-497-4282; www.hhtf.org), which stages a series of events in the New York area. Contact the Festival for schedules.

Essentials

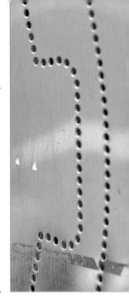

Even New Yorkers find the city a little bewildering sometimes. If you're an out-of-towner, it can be downright overwhelming. Here, then, is some practical information that will help you make sense of it all, from what to expect from the weather and what to do in an emergency, to where to mail a letter or where to find a tourist office. There are also details on health care, security and visas. For additional information, visit useful city websites such as http://nycgo.com, www.timessquarenyc.org and www.nycvisit.com. For the weather forecast, check www.weather.com.

Business Hours

New Yorkers work long and hard, in a city where this is generally regarded as a virtue. Normal business hours are 9am to 5pm, but stores tend to stay open much later and are often open on Sunday. Banking hours are nominally 9am to 3pm, but banks often open as early as 8am and don't close until early evening.

The **Port Authority Bus Terminal** (Eighth Avenue/West 42nd Street) and **Penn Station** (Seventh Avenue/West 32nd Street) open 24 hours a day; **Grand Central Terminal** closes at 1.30am.

Climate and Clothes

New York City has four distinct seasons, and is at its best in spring and fall. Summer temperatures hover in the mid-70s to mid-80s°F, but tempera-

Imperial to Metric Conversion	
ft–m	3.3 = 1
miles–km	0.62 = 1
acres–ha	2.47 = 1
lbs–kg	2.2 = 1
°F–°C	32° = 0° (subtract 30, divide by 2)

Above: a New York traffic cop.

tures in excess of 90°F are not uncommon. Expect uncomfortable humidity in July and August. September and October sometimes usher in a balmy, dry 'Indian summer' that fills parks and office plazas with sun worshippers.

Winter temperatures often drop below freezing and, with the wind chill factor, can feel much colder. The average temperature in January is 32°F (0°C). Average annual rainfall is 44in (112cm), snowfall 29in (7cm). Raincoats are handy year-round.

Crime and Safety

Manhattan is safer than it used to be, but crime remains a concern. With a few common-sense precautions you shouldn't run into serious trouble. Don't carry large sums of cash, or wear flashy or expensive jewelry. Keep a hold on your purse or shoulder bag and keep your wallet in a front pocket. Avoid traveling alone at night, and stay clear of deserted areas. Your best asset is knowing where you are and where you are going. With a little planning, you should be able to avoid dangerous parts of the city.

If you take the subway at night, look out for the off-peak waiting areas on platforms (marked in yellow), and stand near other people or, if possible, a ticket booth or transit police officer. Try and ride in the conductor's car in the middle of the train, and avoid riding in cars with only a few people in them. On buses, try to sit near the driver.

If you run into any trouble, call **911** or go to the nearest police station to report the crime. The police may not

Left: public telephones are easy to find in the city.

Tourist Information

New York has a 24-hour general information call line, 311. Operators can deal with enquiries on attractions, lost property, transportation and many other topics.

NYC Visitor Information Center

810 Seventh Avenue/West 52nd and 53rd streets; tel: 212-484-1222, 800-nyc-visit; http://nyc go.com; Mon–Fri 8.30am–6pm, Sat–Sun 9am–5pm; subway: 50th St-7th Ave; map p.150 B1

For maps and information on hotel packages and discounts at various attractions. There's also a center at City Hall Park (Broadway/Park Row) and in Harlem at the Studio Museum in Harlem (125th Street).

Times Square Information Center

1560 Broadway/West 46th and 47th streets; tel: 212-768-1560; www.timessquarenyc.org; Mon–Fri 9am–7pm, Sat–Sun 8am–8pm; subway: 42nd St-49th St; map p.153 C4

Citywide info, plus a ticket counter for shows.

Visa and Customs

For the latest information on US entry regulations, visit http://travel.state.gov; for customs, www.customs.gov.

Be prepared to pass through security checkpoints at airports and such tourist attractions as the Statue of Liberty and Empire State Building.

---

have much chance of finding an assailant, but they will do paperwork for insurance claims. If you are mugged, the safest bet is to give the mugger your money and leave the area as quickly as possible.

Disabled Travelers

Information on disability rights and facilities can be obtained from the Mayor's Office for People with Disabilities (tel: 212-788-2830; www.nyc.gov/mopd).

Emergency Telephone Numbers

For all emergencies: police, fire, ambulance, dial 911.
Australian Consulate
tel: 212-351-6500
British Consulate
tel: 212-745-0200
Irish Consulate
tel: 212-319-2555
Dental Emergencies
tel: 212-486-9458

Health and Insurance

Comprehensive health insurance is essential for all travelers to New York. Medical services are very expensive. **24-hour pharmacies** are plentiful, mainly in Midtown.

Money

ATMs are everywhere. Dollar travelers' checks can be used as cash in many places (with ID), so you don't need to change them at a bank.

Postal Services

The main post office (open 24 hours) is on Eighth Avenue between West 31st and 33rd streets. To find others, tel: 800-275-8777; www.usps.com.

Smoking

Smoking is banned in virtually all New York City bars, restaurants, and offices. If you want a smokers' room in a hotel, ask when booking.

Tipping

New York waiters and service workers expect tips of 15–20 percent as a right, not an extra. They can be very aggressive if you don't pay up.

Fashion

Paparazzi and publicity hounds swarm the city during New York's Fashion Weeks – held twice a year, in February and September – when the world's top designers unveil their new collections at shows and soirées. The main runways are set up under tents in Bryant Park, and attendance is by invitation only. But don't despair. The latest fashions are only as far away as the nearest boutique or department store. Prices are predictably steep, but you can often walk away with a steal if you shop during special sales or trawl the vintage shops for bargains. For department stores and other specialty stores, *see also Shopping, p.134–43.*

Midtown

CLOTHES AND SHOES

A/X Armani Exchange
645 Fifth Avenue/East 51st Street; tel: 212-980-3037; Mon–Sun 9am–9pm; map p.153 D4
Cheapest of the three tiers in Armani's empire: his mid-price range is Emporio Armani, and at the top is Giorgio Armani. (Also at: 568 Broadway/Prince Street, tel: 212-431-6000; 129 Fifth Avenue/West 20th Street, tel: 212-254-7230; 10 Columbus Circle, tel: 212-823-9321.)

Brooks Brothers
346 Madison Avenue/East 44th Street; tel: 212-261-9440; Mon–Fri 8am–8pm, Sat 9am–7pm, Sun 11am–7pm; map p.153 D3
This classic menswear firm stays commited to traditional style while offering updated trends to keep them in the marketplace. There are also lines for women and children. (Also at: 1934 Broadway/West 65th Street, tel: 212-362-2374; 1 Liberty Plaza, Broadway/Liberty Street, tel: 212-267-2400.)

Erès
621 Madison Avenue/East 58th Street; tel: 212-223-3550;

Above: a Fifth Avenue flagship with a 160-year history.

Mon–Wed Fri 10am–6.30pm, Thur 10pm–7pm; map p.151 D1
Women's bathing suits and lingerie, all in bright or pastel colors – and at high prices. (Also at: 98 Wooster Street/Prince Street, tel: 212-431-7300.)

Jay Kos
475 Park Avenue/East 58th Street; tel: 212-319-2770; Mon–Thur 10am–7pm, Fri–Sat 10am–6pm; map p.153 E4

This store exudes style and class, with beautifully cut shirts and suits of the finest fabrics. All very New England.

Niketown
6 East 57th Street/Fifth and Madison avenues; tel: 212-891-6453; Mon–Sat 10am–8pm, Sun 11am–7pm; map p.151 D1
This five-floor high-tech store is packed wall-to-wall with Nike products. Name your sport; they'll have the gear for it.

Syms
400 Park Avenue/East 54th Street; tel: 212-317-8200; Mon–Fri 8am–7.30pm, Sat 10am–6.30pm, Sun noon–5.30pm; map p.153 E4
Syms's 'I'm An Educated Consumer' shopping bag slogan is appropriate for the savvy male and female customers carrying away their discount designer clothes. (Also at: 42 Trinity Place/Thames Street, tel: 212-797-1199.)

JEWELRY AND ACCESSORIES
Michael C. Fina
545 Fifth Avenue/East 45th Street; tel: 212-557-2500;

Left: the best months for sales are February and August.

Betsey Johnson
248 Columbus Avenue/West 71st Street; tel: 212-362-3364; Mon–Sat 11am–7pm, Sun noon–7pm; map p.150 C3
Betsey Johnson makes clothes with attitude – bright animal prints, rhinestone-trim sweaters, and outrageously sexy dresses for the wild at heart. (Also at: 1060 Madison Avenue/East 80th Street, tel: 212-734-1257; 251 East 60th Street/Third Avenue, tel: 212-319-7699; 138 Wooster Street/Prince Street, tel: 212-995-5048.)

DKNY
655 Madison Avenue/East 60th Street; tel: 212-223-3569; Mon–Sat 10am–8pm, Sun 11am–6pm; map p.151 D1
This is Donna Karan's casual off-the-rack line. The higher-end Donna Karan line can be found further up Madison at no. 819, by East 68th Street. (Also at: 420 West Broadway/Spring Street, tel: 646-613-1100.)

Eileen Fisher
341 Columbus Avenue/West 76th Street; tel: 212-362-3000; Mon–Sat 10am–7pm, Sun 11am–6pm; map p.150 C4

Stylish fashions rule on Fifth Avenue, but there's certainly no dearth of jewelry, silver, or gift shops. Many of the world's top designers have their showpiece stores here – Cartier, Tiffany & Co., Prada, and the new Giorgio Armani flagship store among them.

Mon–Thur 11am–8pm, Fri 10am–7pm, Sat 10am–6pm, Sun 11am–6pm; map p.153 D3
Discounted jewelry, silver, and china make Fina a favorite among those registering bridal lists.

Tiffany & Co.
727 Fifth Avenue/East 57th Street; tel: 212-755-8000; Mon–Fri 10am–7pm, Sat 10am–7pm, Sun noon–6pm; map p.151 D1
Tiffany is in most major American cities, but this is the shop eternally glamorized by Audrey Hepburn in *Breakfast at Tiffany's*. Fabulous silver, jewelry, and china.

Uptown

CLOTHES AND SHOES
Allan & Suzi
416 Amsterdam Avenue/West 80th Street; tel: 212-724-7445;

Mon–Fri noon–7pm, Sat 11am–7pm, Sun noon–6pm; map p.151 C4
High-end vintage and second-hand clothes, from 1930s couture gowns and 1950s prom dresses to Gaultier, Westwood, Versace, and other discounted designer seconds.

Barneys New York
660 Madison Avenue/East 60th Street; tel: 212-826-8900; Mon–Fri 10am–8pm, Sat 10am–7pm, Sun 11am–6pm; map p.151 D1
The department store for style slaves of all ages, where you can blow a fortune on the latest lines of top designers from traditional to trashy to trendy. Bargain hunters love the huge warehouse sales in February and August at the Chelsea Barneys Co-op.

Betsey Bunky Nini
980 Lexington Avenue/East 71st Street; tel: 212-744-6716; Mon–Sat 10.30am–6pm, Thur 10.30am–7pm; map p.151 E2
This small boutique carries all the hip designers you'd expect in a big store, minus the crowds.

Below: Barneys has great sales.

51

Comfort and easy care are the main priorities of this designer, whose women's separates come in soft cottons and linens. This is their largest store, where they also have a plus-size selection; there are five more branches around Manhattan.

Emilio Pucci
24 East 64th Street/Madison Avenue; tel: 212-752-4777; Mon–Sat 10am–6pm; map p.151 D1

The 1960s master of psychedelic designs and bold graphic prints has made a big comeback. (Also at: 701 Fifth Avenue/East 55th Street, tel: 212-230-1135.)

Filene's Basement
2222 Broadway/West 79th Street; tel: 212-873-8000; Mon–Sat 9am–10pm, Sun 11am–8pm; map p.150 C4

Not the place to come if you're short on time as there are stacks of marked-down designer clothes and major brands. But if you have a nose for bargains, you'll be sure to sniff out some real finds. The shoe department is always worth a look. (Also at: 620 Sixth Avenue/West 18th Street, tel: 212-620-3100; 4 Union Square/East 14th Street, tel: 212-358-0169.)

Harry's Shoes
2299 Broadway/West 83rd Street; tel: 212-874-2035; Mon–Sat 10am–6.45pm, Mon and Thur 10am–7.45pm, Sun 11am–6pm

For decades this shoe shop has been a favorite of Upper West Side families.

The New York Look
30 Lincoln Center Plaza/West 62nd Street; tel: 212-245-6511; Mon–Thur 10am–9pm, Fri 10am–8pm, Sat 11am–9pm, Sun noon–7pm; map p.150 B2

Several locations throughout Manhattan, each carrying the same women's fashion lines, as well as shoes, handbags, and jewelry by a range of designers and in a range of prices. The name says it all. (Also at: 570 Seventh Avenue/West 40th Street, tel: 212-382-2760; 2030 Broadway/West 70th Street, tel: 212-362-8650; 468 West Broadway/West Houston Street, tel: 212-598-9988; 551 Fifth Avenue/East 45th Street, tel: 212-557-0903.)

Oilily
820 Madison Avenue/East 68th Street; tel: 212-772-8686; Mon–Sat 10am–6pm, Sun noon–5pm; map p.151 D2

Featuring clothes for small children and their mothers (and sisters), this store, with its bright, cheerful styles, brings out the kid in all of us. In a city specializing in black, these reds, pinks, blues, and oranges stand out.

Olive & Bette's
252 Columbus Avenue/West 72nd Street; tel: 212-579-2178; Mon–Sat 11am–7pm, Sun noon–6pm; map p.150 C3

Trendy women's clothes at reasonable prices, including T-shirts by Michael Streetars, Tote La Mode plastic bags and other hip streetwear. More Downtown than Uptown in attitude. (Also at: 1070 Madison Avenue/East 81st Street, tel: 212-717-9655; 384 Bleecker Street/Perry Street, tel: 212-206-0036; 158 Spring Street/West Broadway, tel: 646-613-8772.)

Patagonia
426 Columbus Avenue/West 81st Street; tel: 917-441-0011; Mon–Sat 11am–7pm, Sun 11am–6pm; map p.151 C4

When you are headed to the great outdoors, stop first at Patagonia. They can outfit you in waterproof jackets, fleece pants, thermal underwear, and other items to keep you snug and warm. (Also at: 101 Wooster Street/Spring Street, tel: 212-343-1776.)

Left: accessories hotter than a New York heatwave.

Polo Ralph Lauren
867 Madison Avenue/East 72nd Street; tel: 212-606-2100; Mon–Fri 10am–7pm, Thur 10am–8pm, Sat 10am–6pm, Sun noon–6pm; map p.151 D2

Housed in what is referred to as the Polo Mansion, this store covers the entire collection of Ralph Lauren's clean-cut Ivy League fashions for men and women. Blazers, tweed jackets, cable-knit sweaters, and evening wear, plus shoes, accessories, and household linens. The sports and children's departments are across the street.

Really Great Things
284-A Columbus Avenue/West 74th Street; tel: 212-787-5354; Mon–Sat 11am–7pm; map p.151 C3

New to the Upper West Side, this store carries fabulous women's fashion – clothes, bags, jewelry and shoes. It also carries unique items from brand-name designers.

R.M. Williams
46 East 59th Street/Madison Avenue; tel: 212-308-1808; hours vary; map p.151 D1

This Australian designer features oilskin coats, leather boots, and other rugged clothes worn down under.

Sean
224 Columbus Avenue/West 70th Street; tel: 212-769-1489; Mon–Sat 11am–8pm, Sun noon–7pm; map p.150 C3

A menswear collection for those who want something different from the usual khakis and collared shirts but are not ready for the hipness factor of Barneys or Prada. (Also at: 199 Prince Street/MacDougal Street, tel: 212-598-5980.)

Shanghai Tang
600 Madison Avenue/East 57th Street; tel: 212-888-0111; Mon–Sat 10.30am–7pm, Thur 10.30am–8pm, Sun noon–6pm; map p.151 D1

A wide range of fine-quality goods – silk dresses, pajamas, velvet pillows, photo albums, umbrellas, and purses – all made in China.

Theory
230 Columbus Avenue/West 71st Street; tel: 212-362-3676; Mon–Fri 10am–7pm, Sat 11am–7pm, Sun noon–6pm; map p.150 C3

Always on the cutting edge, Theory does moderately priced women's casual and business attire. (Also at: 40 Gansevoort Street/Hudson Street, tel: 212-524-6790; 151 Spring Street/West Broadway, tel: 212-226-3691.)

Town Shop
2273 Broadway/West 82nd Street; tel: 212-787-2762; Mon–Fri 10am–7pm, Sat 9.30am–6pm, Sun 11am–5pm

An old-school lingerie shop, where the assistants know your bra size just by looking. Though the clerks don't seem to have changed in 50 years, the shop keeps up with the times, and the range should satisfy any age or taste.

JEWELRY AND ACCESSORIES
David Yurman
729 Madison Avenue/East 64th Street; tel: 212-752-4255; Mon–Sat 10am–6pm; map p.151 D1

Yurman's distinctive gold and silver jewelry is regularly featured in fashion magazines; this place has his entire line.

Julie: Artisans' Gallery
762 Madison Avenue/East 65th and 66th streets; tel: 212-717-5959; daily 11am–6pm; map p.151 D2

Handmade jewelry and clothes made by different local and international artists that won't go unnoticed.

Longchamp
655 Madison Avenue/East 60th Street; tel: 212-223-1500; Mon–Sat 10am–7pm, Sun 11am–6pm; map p.151 D1

This French bag company has made a nice home for itself in New York. Its handbags and other leather goods are well made, practical, and chic.

Right: Betsey Johnson makes feminine clothes with attitude.

Left: trendy clothes at reasonable prices, *see p.52.*

Chelsea to Gramercy
CLOTHES AND SHOES
Anthropologie
85 Fifth Avenue/West 16th
Street; tel: 212-627-5885;
Mon–Sat 10.30am–8pm, Sun
11am–7pm; map p.154 C4
Funky and stylish women's
fashions and an assortment
of housewares, from Moroccan lamps and gardening
supplies to drawer pulls and
children's toys. (Also at: 50
Rockefeller Plaza, tel: 212-246-
0386; 375 West
Broadway/Broome Street, tel:
212-343-7070 and throughout
the city.)
Diesel
1 Union Square West/East 14th
Street; tel: 646-336-8552;
Mon–Sat 11am–9pm, Sun
11am–8pm; map p.155 C3
Considering youth fashions
usually have a shelf-life of
about a year or even less,
this high-concept denim and
sportswear manufacturer has
done well to stay at the forefront for so long. This vast
flagship store has plenty of
great choices for the artsy
and active. There are six
more Manhattan branches,
including the Diesel Superstore (770 Lexington Avenue/East
60th Street, tel: 212-308-0055.)
Jeffrey
449 West 14th Street/Tenth
Avenue; tel: 212-206-1272;

Mon–Fri 10am–8pm, Thur
10am–9pm, Sat 10am–7pm,
Sun 12.30–6pm; map p.152 A1
In the heart of the Meatpacking District, Jeffrey is
like a mini-Barneys, stocking high-end designers such
as Commes des Garçons,
Dries Van Noten, and Jill
Sander. Prices are equally
high end.
Loehmann's
101 Seventh Avenue/West 16th
Street; tel: 212-352-0856;
Mon–Sat 9am–9pm, Sun
11am–7pm; map p.154 B4
When all the department
stores in New York have had
their final sales and they still
have items to unload, they
send them over to
Loehmann's. The store
stocks designer clothes and
shoes at drastically reduced
prices.
Paul Smith
108 Fifth Avenue/East 16th
Street; tel: 212-627-9770;
Mon–Fri 11am–7pm, Thur
11am–8pm, Sat 11am–7pm,
Sun noon–6pm; map p.154 C4
British designer whose smart
suits, casual wear, and
accessories strike a perfect
balance between boldness
and elegance. His colored
pinstripes and velvet pants
may be too funky for some
men, but just the ticket for
others.

Zara
101 Fifth Avenue/East 17th
Street; tel: 212-741-0555;
Mon–Thur 10am–8pm, Fri–Sat
10am–9pm, Sun noon–8pm;
map p.155 C4
The Spanish store's success
lies in its ability to translate
catwalk collections into
affordable off-the-rack
clothes in record time. (Also at:
689 Fifth Avenue/East 54th Street,
tel: 212-371-2417; 750 Lexington
Avenue/East 59th Street, tel: 212-
754-1120; 39 West 34th Street/
Fifth Avenue, tel: 212-868-6551.)

JEWELRY AND
ACCESSORIES
Beads of Paradise
16 East 17th Street/Fifth
Avenue; tel: 212-620-0642;
Mon–Sat 11am–7.30pm, Sun
noon–6.30pm; map p.155 C4
You can string your own
necklaces with the first-rate
beads and gems on sale
here, or choose from the colorful range of already assembled imported jewelry.

Greenwich Village
CLOTHES AND SHOES
Darling
1 Horatio Street/Eighth Avenue;
tel: 212-367-3750; Mon–Sat
noon–8pm, Sun noon–6pm;
map p.154 B4
Cute dresses and lingerie,
many designed by the owner,
a former Broadway costume
designer, as well as a selection
of vintage clothes, are the
attractions at this cheery shop.
The Earnest Sewn Co.
821 Washington
Street/Gansevoort Street; tel:
212-242-3414; Sun–Fri
11am–7pm, Sat 11am–8pm;
map p. 154 A4
Walking into this store you
might think you have walked
into a general store of a
bygone era. Not quite that

long ago it functioned as a meat locker but now sells handcrafted denim 'sewn in earnest.'

Jussara Lee
11 Little West 12th Street/Ninth Avenue; tel: 212-242-4128; Mon–Sat 11am–7pm, Sun noon–6pm; map p.154 A4
Much of this Brazilian designer's work is straightforward – light wool pants, leather skirts, linen dresses – but can be embellished as the client wishes. It also offers a service that turns a customer's own design into a finished garment.

La Petite Coquette
51 University Place/East 9th Street; tel: 212-473-2478; Mon–Sat 11am–7pm, Thur to 8pm, Sun noon–6pm; map p.154 C3
This saucy shop – the name means 'little flirt' – does great lingerie, from everyday to seductive.

Marc Jacobs
403–405 Bleecker Street/West 11th Street; tel: 212-924-0026; daily noon–8pm; map p.154 B3
This shop carries Marc Jacobs's line of casual separates, shoes, and accessories. Lines are classic, fabrics luxurious, and prices

Below: retail therapy break in Greenwich Village.

Eighth Street between Sixth Avenue and Broadway in Greenwich Village is known as Shoe Row. The number of shoe stores has declined in recent years, but if you're looking for stylish kicks at reasonable prices, this is still a good place to shop.

as steep as you would expect. (Also at: 163 Mercer Street/Prince Street, tel: 212-343-1490; 301 West 4th Street, tel: 212-929-0304.)

Urban Outfitters
628 Broadway/West Houston Street; tel: 212-475-0009; Mon–Sat 10am–10pm, Sun noon–8pm; map p.154 C2
Packed with teenage girls searching for the season's urban fashions, make-up, accessories, and other must-have items. Five more branches in Manhattan, including another on Broadway. (Also at: 2081 Broadway/West 72nd Street, tel: 212-579-3912 and various other locations.)

JEWELRY AND ACCESSORIES
Catherine Angiel's Gallery Eclectic
43 Greenwich Avenue/Seventh Avenue; tel: 212-924-4314; Mon–Sat noon–7pm, Sun noon–6pm; map p.154 B4
With jewelry by local designers such as Nathan Levy and owner Catherine Angiel, this shop is popular with couples shopping for wedding rings.

East Village to Chinatown

CLOTHES AND SHOES
American Apparel
183 East Houston Street/First Avenue; tel: 212-598-4600; Mon–Wed 11am–11pm, Thur–Sat 11am–midnight, Sun 11am–10pm; map p.155 C1
Few clothes manufacturers can claim to be sweatshop

free – this is the rare exception. You'll find comfy T-shirts and cotton goods for men, women, and children, all made at their own factory. Sixteen more branches around Manhattan.

Bawa
70 East 1st Street/First and Second avenues; tel: 212-254-1249; Wed–Sat 1–8pm, Sun noon–7pm; map p.155 C1
Indian designer Alpana Bawa's clothes are fabulous if you're looking for something out of the ordinary. Designs include men's cotton shirts with embroidery, as well as women's silk tops and wool-and-silk dresses.

By Robert James
75 Orchard Street/Grand Street; tel: 212-253-2121; Mon 1–8pm, Tue–Sat noon–8pm, Sun noon–6pm; map p.157 D4
Lower Eastside designer Robert James uses local manufacturers and local materials to craft his contemporary menswear. His hand-printed graphic tees are popular. In addition to the menswear collection he also carries some vintage men's clothing and vintage women's jewelry.

Below: a street fit for fashionistas of all types and stripes.

F

Foley & Corinna
114 Stanton Street/Essex Street; tel: 212-529-2338; Sun–Mon noon–7pm, Tue–Sat noon–8pm; map p.157 D4

A stylish range of women's clothes combining fancy and funky designs by Dana Foley with top-notch vintage clothes by Anna Corinna.

MoMo FaLana
43 Avenue A/East 3rd Street; tel: 212-979-9595; Wed–Mon 12.30–8.30pm, Tue 12.30–7pm; map p.155 D1

Hand-painted silks make this shop an East Village staple. The designs are like tie-dye but on fine fabrics and have been profiled in numerous fashion magazines. Great option for weddings.

Tokio 7
64 East 7th Street/First and Second avenues; tel: 212-353-8443; Sun–Fri noon–8pm, Sat noon–8.30pm; map p.155 D2

To catch your attention, this resale/consignment shop usually has a Prada dress featured in the window. Once inside, you will find a wide range of men's and women's designer wear; most items look as good as new.

SoHo and TriBeCa

CLOTHES AND SHOES
Agent Provocateur
133 Mercer Street/Prince Street; tel: 212-965-0229; Mon–Sat 11am–7pm, Sun noon–6pm; map p.154 B1

Ultra-fancy lingerie for the adventurous at heart – now more tasteful than raunchy.

Anna Sui
113 Greene Street/Prince Street; tel: 212-941-8406; Mon–Sat 11.30am–7pm, Sun noon–6pm; map p.154 B2

Chinese-American designer Anna Sui finds inspiration in everything from sharp 1950s cuts to 1960s psychedelia and 1970s glam rock.

Intermix
98 Prince Street/Mercer Street; tel: 212-966-5303; Mon–Sat 11am–8pm, Sun noon–7pm; map p.154 B1

This 'Sex and the City' store is for hardened style slaves. It has a small men's collection. (Also at: 1003 Madison Avenue/East 77th Street, tel: 212-249-7858; 210 Columbus Avenue/West 69th Street, tel: 212-769-9116; 125 Fifth Avenue/East 19th Street, tel: 212-533-9720; 365 Bleecker Street/Charles Street, tel: 212-929-7180.)

Issey Miyake
119 Hudson Street/North Moore Street; tel: 212-226-0100; Mon–Sat 11am–7pm, Sun noon–6pm; map p.154 A1

The first designer to make an appearance in TriBeCa, Miyake appeals to fashionistas who want to turn all heads with a sleek and cutting-edge look.

John Varvatos
122 Spring Street/Greene Street; tel: 212-965-0700; Mon–Sat 11am–7pm, Sun noon–6pm; map p.154 B1

This men's clothier creates designs that are both practical and unique, from striped shirts and leather shoes to blue-velvet suits and sandals.

Morgane Le Fay
67 Wooster Street/Broome and Spring streets; tel: 212-219-7672; daily 11am–7pm; map p.154 B1

Layers of silk, chiffon, organza, and other fine fabrics are used to create the kind of wispy romantic dresses that little girls dream of.

Only Hearts
230 Mott Street/Prince Street; tel: 212-431-3694; Mon–Sat noon–8pm, Sun noon–7pm; map p.154 C1

Only Hearts has its own line of sexy lingerie but also carries other designers such as Capucine and Cosabella. They also stock bags, bath oils, jewelry, and other gift items. All have a heart motif.

Philosophy di Alberta Ferretti
452 West Broadway/Prince Street; tel: 212-460-5500; Mon–Sat 11am–7pm, Sun noon–6pm; map p.154 B2

The (supposedly) cheaper label from Italian women's clothes designer Alberta Ferretti. When everything else in

SoHo and Tribeca are cast-iron cool. Many stores are situated in former warehouses and loft spaces, with one – Prada *(see below)* – even occupying the site of the Guggenheim Museum's former downtown premises. It's worth a visit for the building alone.

SoHo starts to look alike, come here.

Prada
575 Broadway/Prince Street; tel: 212-334-8888; Mon–Wed 11am–7pm, Thur–Sat 11am–8pm, Sun noon–7pm; map p.154 B1

Formerly the Guggenheim Museum's Downtown branch, this wonderful space was acquired and converted by Prada to exhibit its high-end fashions. Even if prices are out of reach, this shop is a spectacle in itself.

R by 45rpm
169 Mercer Street/West Houston Street; tel: 917-237-0045; Mon–Sat 11am–7pm, Sun 11am–6pm; map p.154 B2

R is a clothing line from 45rpm, a Japanese firm that specializes in casual clothes inspired by American styles of the 1950s and 1960s. The fashions are displayed amid bamboo and waterfalls.

Scoop
473–475 Broadway/Grand Street; tel: 212-925-3539; Mon–Sat 11am–8pm, Sun 11am–7pm; map p.154 B1

Scoop offers up-to-the-minute urban chic displayed by color rather than designer label. For sale items, head for the 'Scoop It Up' section. (Also at: 430 West 14th Street/ Ninth and Tenth avenues, tel: 212-929-1244; 1273 Third Avenue/East 73rd Street, tel: 212-535-5577.)

Left: style in the Meatpacking District. **Right:** industrial design meets forward-looking fashion.

Right: the devil (and anyone who can afford it) wears Prada.

Steven Alan
103 Franklin Street/Church Street; tel: 212-343-0692; Mon–Sat 11.30am–7pm, Thur to 8pm, Sun noon–6pm; map p.156 B4

Steven Alan has perfected the art of the effortless preppy shirt; not too loose, never too tight. The flagship TriBeCa store has men and women's clothes under his own label alongside items by more avant garde designers, like Comme des Garçons. (Also at: 69 Eighth Avenue/West 13th Street, tel: 212-242-2677; 465 Amsterdam Avenue/West 82nd Street, tel: 212-595-8451; 229 Elizabeth Street/Prince Street, tel: 212-226-7482.)

Topshop
478 Broadway/Broome Street; tel: 212-966-9555; Mon–Sat 10am–9pm, Sun 11am–8pm; map p.154 B1

This British chain finally made its long-anticipated debut in New York with a multi-level flagship store on Broadway. You'll find cutting-edge styles at reasonable prices and lots of accessories.

JEWELRY AND ACCESSORIES
Anya Hindmarch
115 Greene Street/Prince Street;

tel: 212-343-8147; Mon–Sat 11am–7pm, Sun noon–6pm; map p.154 B2

London designer Hindmarch is famed for her unmistakable handbags, in particular her playful use of photos. Prices tend to be steep.

The Hat Shop
120 Thompson Street/Prince Street; tel: 212-219-1445; Mon–Sat noon–7pm, Sun 1–6pm; map p.154 B2

When Hollywood needs hats, they call The Hat Shop. Countless designs and colors provide hours of fun.

Jill Platner
113 Crosby Street/Prince Street; tel: 212-324-1298; Tue–Sat noon–7pm; map p.154 C1

This silver designer's studio is downstairs from the store, so you are guaranteed that the rings, belt buckles, and other body art are not mass-produced elsewhere.

Kate Spade
454 Broome Street/Mercer Street; tel: 212-274-1991; Mon–Sat 11am–7pm, Sun noon–6pm; map p.154 B1

Kate Spade's terminally hip handbags share her boutique with funky shoes, sunglasses, and other accessories.

57

Festivals and Events

Festivals seem almost redundant in a city as culturally rich as this one. Still, New Yorkers have a knack for throwing parties, and they do so quite often. Some events are celebrations of ethnic identity – the St Patrick's Day Parade, and the Puerto Rican Day Parade. Others focus on the arts or sporting events. The grandaddy of them all is the New Year's Eve bash in Times Square, when up to a million people brave frigid temperatures to watch the big ball drop at the stroke of midnight. For film festivals, *see also Movies, p.87–9.*

January

Martin Luther King, Jr. Day Parade
Fifth Avenue/East 61st to 86th streets.

Winter Antiques Show
Seventh Regiment Armory, East 67th Street/Park Avenue; tel: 718-292-7392

February

The Art Show
Seventh Regiment Armory, East 67th Street/Park Avenue; tel: 212-488-5550

Chinese New Year parades and celebrations
Chinatown, Mott, Mulberry and Bayard streets

Westminster Kennel Club Dog Show
Madison Square Garden; tel: 212-213-3165

March

St Patrick's Day Parade
Fifth Avenue/44th to 86th streets

Whitney Biennial (in even years, 2010, 2012)
Whitney Museum of American Art, 945 Madison Avenue/East 75th Street; tel: 212-570-3676

April

Cherry Blossom Festival (Sakura Matsuri)
Brooklyn Botanic Garden, 1000 Washington Avenue, Brooklyn; tel: 718-623-7200

Earth Day
Earth Day New York, 201 East 42nd Street; tel: 212-922-0048

Easter Parade
Fifth Avenue/East 49th to 57th streets

Tribeca Film Festival
Tribeca Cinemas (box office), 54 Varick Street; tel: 212-941-2400; www.tribecafilm festival.org

May

Five Borough Bike Tour and Festival
Bike New York, 891 Amsterdam Avenue; tel: 212-932-2453

One of the world's most unusual footraces is the **Empire State Building Run-Up**, a race up 1,576 steps to the 86th-floor Observatory. The event is held in February.

Ninth Avenue International Food Festival
Ninth Avenue Association; tel: 212-581-7029

Ukrainian Festival
East 7th Street/Second and Third Avenues

Washington Square Outdoor Art Exhibit
Washington Square Park; tel: 212-982-6255

June

River to River Festival
Lower Manhattan; www.rivertorivernyc.com

Feast of St Anthony
Little Italy: Mulberry Street, and Broome and Spring streets

Gay and Lesbian Pride Day Parade
Fifth Avenue; tel: 212-807-7433; www.hopinc.org

Mermaid Parade
Coney Island, 1208 Surf Avenue, Brooklyn; tel: 718-372-5159

Left: Little Italy's Feast of St Anthony is in June.

Left: Times Square's dropping of the ball is a New Year's Eve tradition.

September

West Indian American Day Carnival (Labor Day)
Eastern Parkway, Brooklyn; tel: 718-467-1797; www.wiadca.org

October

Columbus Day Parade
Fifth Avenue/44th and 79th streets; tel: 212-249-9923

Halloween Parade
Greenwich Village, Sixth Avenue/Spring and 23rd streets; www.halloween-nyc.com

New York Film Festival
Lincoln Center; tel: 212-875-5600; www.filmlinc.org

Next Wave Festival
Brooklyn Academy of Music, 30 Lafayette Avenue; tel: 718-636-4100; www.bam.org

November

Macy's Thanksgiving Day Parade
77th Street and Central Park to Broadway and 34th Street; tel: 212-494-4495

New York City Marathon
Staten Island to Central Park; www.nycmarathon.org

December

Christmas Tree Lighting
Rockefeller Center

New Year's Eve
Times Square; tel: 212-768-1560; www.timessquarenyc.org

Museum Mile Festival
Fifth Avenue/82nd to 105th streets; www.museummilefestival.org

Puerto Rican Day Parade
Fifth Avenue/44th to 86th Streets; tel: 718-401-0404

July

Macy's Fourth of July Fireworks
East River, spectators can watch from FDR Drive; tel: 212-494-4495

Mostly Mozart Festival
Lincoln Center for the Performing Arts, 70 Lincoln Center Plaza; tel: 212-875-5000; www.lincolncenter.org

Thunderbird American Indian Midsummer Powwow
Queens County Farm Museum, 73-50 Little Neck Pkwy, Floral Park; tel: 718-347-3276

Washington Square Music Festival
Washington Square; tel: 212-252-3621

August

Harlem Jazz and Music Festival
Venues throughout Harlem; tel: 212-862-7200; http://harlemjazz.harlemdiscover.com

Howl! Festival of East Village Arts
Venues around Tompkins Square Park; www.howlfestival.com

New York International Fringe Festival
More than 20 Downtown venues; tel: 212-279-4488; www.fringenyc.org

US Open Tennis Championship
USTA National Tennis Center, Queens; www.usopen.org

Right: Manhattan's Gay and Lesbian Pride Day Parade starts on Fifth Avenue and ends in Greenwich Village.

59

Food and Drink

When it comes to 'food glorious food,' New Yorkers are spoiled rotten. In addition to some of the food world's most celebrated restaurants, there are scores of gourmet shops, delis, bakeries, wine purveyors, and farmers' markets where residents and visitors alike stock up on the finest food and wine the city has to offer. Imported cheeses? Hundreds. Fine chocolate? Tons. Beluga caviar? Naturally. But there's more to the gourmet scene than exotic delicacies. Even homespun foods like bagels, apple pie, and peanut butter get gourmet treatment in this city. This chapter lists the best places to shop for New York's finest foods.

Midtown

Little Pie Company
424 West 43rd Street/Ninth and Tenth avenues; tel: 212-736-4780; Mon–Fri 9am–6pm, Sat 10am–6pm, Sun 11am–6pm; map p.152 B4
Sweet or savory, old-fashioned or new-fangled, the pies here will not disappoint. (Also at: Grand Central Terminal, tel: 212-983-3538.)

Whole Foods Market
10 Columbus Circle/Broadway; tel: 212-823-9600; daily 8am–11pm; map p.150 C2
Nirvana for health-conscious eaters, this natural foods market is filled with organic produce, meat, baked goods, vegan specialties, and much more. (Also at: 250 Seventh Avenue/West 24th Street, tel: 212-924-5969; 4 Union Square/Broadway, tel: 212-673-5388, and throughout the city.)

Uptown

Barney Greengrass
541 Amsterdam Avenue/West 86th Street; tel: 212-724-4707; Tue–Sun 8am–6pm
On weekends this store and restaurant is packed with

Above: fresh produce from the Greenmarket in Union Square.

brunch eaters with a craving for bagels with lox and cream cheese. The delicatessen section has a mouthwatering selection of smoked fish, caviar, and other jarred and canned specialty foods.

Citarella
2135 Broadway/West 75th Street; tel: 212-874-0383; Mon–Sat 7am–9pm, Sun 9am–7pm; map p.150 C4
Originally a seafood specialist, Citarella has expanded to supply every kind of gourmet foods. (Also at: 1313 Third Avenue/East 75th Street; 424 Sixth Avenue/West 9th Street; 461 West 125th Street/Amsterdam Avenue.)

H & H Bagels
2239 Broadway/West 78th Street; tel: 212-595-8003; daily 24 hours; map p.150 C4
More than 60,000 fresh bagels are baked on the premises every day. Pick up a dozen of these warm and doughy delights for an authentic taste of New York. (Also at: 1551 Second Avenue/East 80th and 81st streets, tel: 212-717-7312.)

La Maison Du Chocolat
1018 Madison Avenue/between East 78th and 79th streets; tel: 212-744-7117; Mon–Sat 10am–7pm, Sun noon–6pm; map p.151 E3
The confections at this Paris chocolatier's New York outpost look (almost) too good to eat. Browsers can purchase chocolates by the piece, addicts by the pound. (Also at: 30 Rockefeller Plaza, tel: 212-265-9404.)

Murray's Sturgeon Shop
2429 Broadway/West 89th and 90th streets; tel: 212-724-2650; times vary
Smoked fish, rare meats, homemade salads, a selection of caviars, and favorites like *knishes* and *kugel* can all

Left: Dean & DeLuca sell SoHo's most delectable edibles.

A converted 19th-century biscuit factory houses more than 20 gourmet stores, bakeries, cafés and eateries in the heart of Chelsea.

Greenmarket
Union Square, Broadway/East 17th Street; Mon, Wed, Fri–Sat 8am–6pm; map p.155 C4
Don't miss this farmers' market, which takes over the north end of Union Square several days a week. Regional farmers offer fresh produce, meats, eggs, flowers, baked goods, and cheese.

T. Salon
459 West 15th Street/Ninth Avenue (in Chelsea Market); tel: 212-243-0432; Mon–Sat 9am–8.30pm, Sun 10am–8pm; map p.154 B4
Breeze in for a wide variety of exotic teas, sample a cup or two in the salon, or sign up for a tea-tasting seminar.

WINE AND SPIRITS
Italian Wine Merchants
108 East 16th Street/Park Avenue South; tel: 212-473-2323; Mon–Fri 10am–7pm, Sat 11am–7pm; map p.155 C3
Take advantage of the owners' expertise and treat yourself to one of their specialty Italian wines. Tastings are offered on Saturday.

West Side restaurants, gourmet shops, and street vendors offer visitors their finest fare at the **Ninth Avenue Food Festival**, a feast held in May between West 37th and 57th streets.

be taken to go or ordered and shipped. A long-time favorite on the Upper West Side.

The Vinegar Factory
431 East 91st Street/York and First avenues; tel: 212-987-0885; daily 7am–9pm
A personal venture of Eli Zabar, of the same family as the legendary food store *(see below)*, this East Side temple of gourmet delights is filled to the rafters with fine cheeses, breads, smoked fish, meats, produce, coffees, and many other foods.

Zabar's Gourmet Foods
2245 Broadway/West 80th Street; tel: 212-787-2000; Mon–Fri 8am–7.30pm, Sat 8am–8pm, Sun 9am–6pm; map p.150 C4
For over 70 years, the Zabar family's world-famous gourmet shop has been providing high-quality fare to New Yorkers and others who travel here from far and

wide. Famous for its smoked fish and other Jewish delicacies, the store also offers a wonderful choice of coffee, bread, and cheese, and a selection of cookware and houseware.

WINE AND SPIRITS
Nancy's Wines for Food
313 Columbus Avenue/West 75th Street; tel: 212-877-4040; Mon–Sat 10am–9pm, Sun noon–7pm; map p. 151 C4
A two-room shop that has been a neighborhood favorite since 1992 with focus on small producers.

Sherry-Lehmann
505 Park Avenue/East 59th Street; tel: 212-838-7500; Mon–Sat 9am–8pm; map p.151 D1
Purveyors of fine wines and spirits since 1934. The sign offering delivery to the Hamptons is indicative of their upmarket clientele. The expert staff know their stuff.

Chelsea to Gramercy
Chelsea Market
75 Ninth Avenue/West 15th and 16th streets; Mon–Sat 7am–10pm, Sun 8am–8pm; map p.154 B4

Below: Chelsea Market.

Above: Jewish delights are part of the city's deli scene.

Greenwich Village

Chocolate Bar
19 Eighth Avenue/Jane and West 12th streets; tel: 212-367-7181; Mon–Fri 7.30am–10pm, Sat–Sun 10am–9pm; map p.154 B4
Nothing satisfies a chocolate fan like a visit to this inviting little shop, where you can pull up a chair and sample the mouthwatering selection of truffles, bon-bons, toffee, and steamy hot chocolate.

Magnolia Bakery
401 Bleecker Street/West 11th Street; tel: 212-462-2572; Sun–Thur 9am–11.30pm, Fri–Sat 9am–12.30am; map p.154 B3
This little shop smells just like grandma's kitchen, assuming your grandma is a world-class baker. Treats include peanut-butter pie, banana pudding with vanilla wafers, and irresistible cupcakes.

Murray's Cheese Shop
254 Bleecker Street/Sixth and Seventh avenues; tel: 212-243-3289; Mon–Sat 8am–8pm, Sun 10am–7pm; map p.154 B3
Sample hundreds of cheeses at this Greenwich Village institution, which has regular tastings and classes. (Also at: Grand Central Terminal, tel: 212-922-1540.)

O. Ottomanelli & Sons
285 Bleecker Street/Seventh Avenue South; tel: 212-675-4217; Mon–Sat 8.30am–6pm; map p.154 B3
This is the butcher shop of every carnivore's dreams, where the staff ply their trade with the skill of surgeons. The products range from the finest cuts of beef, poultry, and lamb to exotic game, and the butchers are happy to give cooking advice.

Peanut Butter & Co.
240 Sullivan Street/Bleecker and West 3rd streets; tel: 212-677-3995; Sun–Thur 11am–9pm, Fri–Sat 11am–10pm; map p.154 B2
Choose from more than 20 varieties of peanut butter or order a sandwich – perhaps a traditional P&J, or something more daring like spicy peanut butter, grilled chicken, and pineapple jam.

WINE AND SPIRITS

IS-WINE
24 West 8th Street/Fifth and Sixth avenues; tel: 212-254-7800; Mon–Sat noon–9pm, Sun noon–7pm; map p.154 B3
This self-described 'innovative wine merchants' offers free tastings every Saturday afternoon – a great way to wrap up a shopping spree or work up the inspiration to spend a few more bucks.

East Village to Chinatown

Clinton Street Bakery
4 Clinton Street/East Houston and Stanton streets; tel: 646-602-6263; Mon–Fri 8am–4pm and 6–11pm, Sat 10am–4pm and 6–11pm, Sun 10am–4pm; map p.157 E4
This company's freshly baked goods are sold in other locations throughout New York, but it's good to come to the source. It's also a great breakfast, lunch, and early dinner spot, and is popular with locals.

Doughnut Plant
379 Grand Street/Norfolk Street; tel: 212-505-3700; Tue–Sun 6.30am–until doughnuts sell out (between 6pm and 7pm); map p.157 D3
Can a doughnut be healthy? Well, let's just say that some are healthier than others, like the sweet, spongy ringlets made at this commercial bakery, which has a small retail operation in front. You have to get up early to enjoy them; the day's supply is baked early and sells quickly.

East Village Cheese
40 Third Avenue/East 10th Street; tel: 212-477-2601; daily 8.30am–6.30pm; map p.155 C2
You will find scores of quality imported and domestic cheeses at rock-bottom prices at this snug East Village shop.

Below: Guss' Pickles is one of the oldest in New York.

Guss' Pickles

85 Orchard Street/Broome Street; tel: 212-334-3616; Sun–Thur 10.30am–6pm, Fri to 4pm; map p.157 D4

Reach into the barrel at this old-time Lower East Side shop for a snappy, salty pickle.

Porto Rico Coffee Co.

40½ St Mark's Place/First and Second avenues; tel: 212-533-1982; Mon–Sat 9am–8pm, Sun noon–7pm; map p.155 D2

Sample some of the city's finest coffee, and have some ground up to take home. (Also at: 107 Thompson/Prince and Spring streets, 212-966-5758; and various other locations.)

Russ & Daughters

179 East Houston Street/Allen and Orchard streets; tel: 212-475-4880; Mon–Fri 8am–8pm, Sat 9am–7pm, Sun 8am–5.30pm; map p.155 D1

Lox, sable, herring, and other smoked fish are the stock in trade of this Lower East Side landmark, serving the neighbourhood since 1914. You'll also find a tasty selection of cheese, pastry, chocolate, and caviar.

Veniero's Pasticceria

342 East 11th Street/First and Second avenues; tel: 212-674-7070; Sun–Thur 8am–12am, Fri–Sat 8am–1am; map p.155 D2

A classic Italian pastry shop and café in the East Village, popular with tourists.

SoHo and TriBeCa

A.L. Bazzini

339 Greenwich Street/Harrison Street; tel: 212-334-1280; Mon–Fri 8am–7.30pm, Sat 8.30am–7pm, Sun 8.30am–6.30pm; map p.156 B4

This gourmet shop stocks more than 20 kinds of imported olive oil, dried fruits, and nuts as well as fresh produce, baked goods, and prepared dishes.

A cavernous hall in Grand Central Terminal (Park Avenue at East 42nd Street) houses the food stalls of Grand Central Market. Vendors here sell everything from pastries and produce to prosciutto and prawns; if you're staying in Midtown, this is a good place to stock up on snacks for your hotel room.

Dean & DeLuca

560 Broadway/Prince Street; tel: 212-226-6800; Mon–Fri 7am–8pm, Sat–Sun 8am–8pm; map p.154 B1

A New York institution that stocks everything for the gourmand – those hard-to-find herbs and spices, chocolates, charcuterie, cheese, seafood, foie gras, even kitchenware – but quality comes at a price. A coffee bar, too. (Also at: 75 University Place/West 11th Street, tel: 212-473-1908; 235 West 46th Street/Broadway, tel: 212-869-6890; Time Warner Center, 10 Columbus Circle, tel: 212-765-4400.)

Gourmet Garage

453 Broome Street/Mercer Street; tel: 212-941-5850; daily 7am–9pm; map p.154 B1

A gourmet grocery store with a bountiful selection of high-quality cheeses, seafood, meat, produce, baked goods, and prepared foods. (Also at: 2567 Broadway/West 96th Street, tel: 212-663-0656; 301 East 64th Street/First Avenue, tel: 212-535-6271; 1245 Park Avenue/East 96th Street, tel: 212-348-5850.)

Lower Manhattan

Godiva Chocolatier

South Street Seaport, 21 Fulton Street; tel: 212-571-6965; Mon–Sat 10am–7pm, Sun 11am–6pm; map p.156 B2

This maker and purveyor of quality Belgian chocolates has locations around the city; this one has the advantage of being situated in one of New York's oldest buildings. (Also at: Times Square, 1460 Broadway/West 41st Street, tel: 212-840-6758; Time Warner Center, 10 Columbus Circle, tel: 212-823-9462.)

Brooklyn

Bedford Cheese Shop

229 Bedford Avenue/North 4th Street; tel: 718-599-7588; Mon–Sat 11am–9pm, Sun 10am–8pm

Knowledgeable cheesemongers dole out samples and advice at this pungent neighborhood shop, stocked with domestic and imported cheeses. They also run classes on matters cheesy.

Below: Veniero's Pasticceria in the East Village has been owned and operated by the same family since 1894.

Galleries

Painters, sculptors, and dealers rub elbows with prospective buyers, as well as those who are merely curious, at the city's art venues. There are more than 500 galleries in New York, from hushed Uptown venues full of Old Masters to impromptu spaces with experimental art. In some cases, gallery collections rival those of established museums. In others, they provide a fascinating glimpse into the ever-changing currents of contemporary art and the fickle tastes of the art-buying public. In general, however, even commerical galleries will be happy for you to have a walk around. For museums of art, *see Museums, p.90–105.*

The Gallery Scene

You could say that the city's contemporary gallery scene was born in the Abstract Expressionist movement of the 1940s. That's when Peggy Guggenheim – niece of Solomon, for whom the world-famous funnel-shaped museum on Fifth Avenue is named – opened a gallery at 30 West 57th Street. Called 'Art of This Century,' it became the city's most stimulating

Below: contemporary art against a classic facade.

venue for contemporary art, showcasing her favorite French surrealists as well as edgy new work by a Wyoming-born painter named Jackson Pollock.

As practiced by Pollock, Willem de Kooning, Mark Rothko, and others, Abstract Expressionism was a purely American phenomenon. Reaching its peak in the 1950s, the movement's geographic center was New York, where the majority of artists lived and worked, often within a block or two of each other's Greenwich Village studios. Manhattan suddenly became the mecca of the international art scene, although its galleries remained firmly Uptown.

In the 1960s, driven out by rising rents in the Village, artists began exploring the neighborhood south of Houston Street, where industrial spaces were available. They were perfect for conversion into artists' lofts and cheap, too. The area's fate was more or less sealed in 1971, when the late Leo

Castelli moved his highly successful gallery from the Upper East Side to West Broadway.

By the late 1970s, the gallery scene was in full swing, reaching its zenith in the 1980s, when exhibits by artists like Keith Haring and Jean-Michel Basquiat attracted hordes of black-clad hipsters and well-heeled collectors. By then the neighborhood was overflowing with boutiques and restaurants, a trend that accelerated in the 1990s. As Uptown designers opened glossy ateliers in SoHo, galleries closed or moved.

By the mid-1990s, a mass exodus was under way, with a number of galleries moving to the industrial Chelsea neighborhood of the West 20s in a uniquely New York-style art-and-real-estate circle. (The artists themselves had long gone in search of greener pastures, including Brooklyn's Williamsburg and DUMBO quarters.) By 2000, Chelsea had become the center of the gallery scene.

Left: spend an afternoon in Chelsea touring the galleries.

Uptown

David Findlay
984 Madison Avenue; tel: 212-249-2909; Tue–Sat 10am–5pm; map p.151 E3
Contemporary Impressionist and Expressionist painting.

Hirschl & Adler Galleries
21 East 70th Street; tel: 212-535-8810; Tue–Fri 9.30am–5.15pm, Sat until 4.45pm; map p.151 D2
American and European painting, sculpture and decorative arts from the 18th to the early 20th centuries.

Knoedler & Co.
19 East 70th Street; tel: 212-794-0550; Tue–Fri 9.30–5pm, Sat 10am–5.30pm; map p.151 D2
Works by the major artists of the late 20th century and the contemporary period.

Kouros
23 East 73rd Street; tel: 212-288-5888; Tue–Sat 10am–6pm; map p.151 D2
Twentieth-century and contemporary painters and sculptors.

Praxis International Art
25 East 73rd Street, 4th Floor; tel: 212-772-9478; Tue–Fri

Below: there are over 500 galleries in New York City.

Midtown

Alexandre Gallery
41 East 57th Street, 13th Floor; tel: 212-755-2828; Tue–Sat 10am–5.30pm; map p.153 E4
American art from the early 20th century to the present.

AXA Gallery
787 Seventh Avenue/West 51st Street; tel: 212-554-4818; Mon–Fri 11am–6pm, Sat noon–5pm; map p.153 D4
A gallery in the atrium lobby of the Equitable Tower showing a wide range of work.

Babcock
724 Fifth Avenue, 11th Floor; tel: 212-767-1852; Mon–Fri 10am–5pm; map p.153 D4
Significant works by American masters of all periods.

Bernarducci Meisel
37 West 57th Street, 6th Floor; tel: 212-593-3757; Tue–Sat 10am–5.30pm; map p.151 C1
Realist art of the 20th and 21st centuries.

Bonni Benrubi
41 East 57th Street, 13th floor; tel: 212-888-6007; Tue–Sat 10am–6pm; map p.153 E4
Twentieth-century and contemporary American photography.

DC Moore
724 Fifth Avenue, 8th Floor; tel: 212-247-2111; Tue–Sat 10am–5.30pm; map p.153 D4
American 20th-century and contemporary art.

Laurence Miller
20 West 57th Street; tel: 212-397-3930; Tue–Fri 10am–5.30pm, Sat 11am–5.30pm; map p.151 C1
Modern and contemporary fine art photography.

Marlborough Gallery
40 West 57th Street; tel: 212-541-4900; Mon–Sat 10am–5.30pm; map p.151 C1
Prominent 20th-century American and European artists.

Mary Boone Gallery
745 Fifth Avenue/57th and 58th Streets; tel: 212-752-2929; Tue–Sat 10am–6pm; map p.151 D1
Boone opened a SoHo gallery in 1977 and became a major force with shows of 1980s art-world stars like Jean-Michel Basquiat and David Salle. She continues a policy of cutting-edge exhibits at her Fifth Avenue gallery. (Also at: 541 West 24th Street.)

10am–6pm; map p.151 D2
Contemporary Latin American artists.

Chelsea to Gramercy

303 Gallery
525 West 22nd Street; tel: 212-255-1121; Tue–Sat 10am–6pm; map p.152 A2
Emerging and mid-career artists.

Agora
530 West 25th Street; tel: 212-226-4151; Tue–Sat noon–6pm; map p.152 A2
New and promising work from America and abroad.

Atlantic
135 West 29th Street; tel: 212-219-3183; Tue–Sat noon–6pm; map p.152 A3
Emerging artists in a variety of media and styles.

Exit Art
475 Tenth Avenue at West 36th Street; tel: 212-966-7745; Tue–Thur 10am–6pm, Fri 10am–8pm, Sat noon–8pm; map p.152 B3
Home of innovative works by emerging artists.

Galerie Lelong
528 West 26th Street; tel: 212-315-0470; Tue–Sat 10am–6pm; map p.152 A2
Contemporary artists of Europe and the Americas.

George Adams Gallery
525 West 26th Street; tel: 212-

The trees on 22nd Street from 10th to 11th avenues are part of a worldwide installation by the late conceptual artist Joseph Beuys. Entitled *7000 Oaks* (actually there are only about 23 trees here; the others are in Kassel, Germany), the work was partly underwritten by the Dia Center for the Arts, a Chelsea pioneer that opened an exhibition space in 1987. There are a variety of species of trees including Pin Oak, Red Oak, Elm Honey, Gingko and Linden.

Be aware that many galleries, especially those in Chelsea and SoHo, are closed on Sundays and Mondays. During summer months galleries often have reduced hours and closures.

564-8480; Tue–Sat 10am–6pm; map p.152 A2
Works of well-known North and South American artists.

I-20 Gallery
557 West 23rd Street; tel: 212-645-1100; Tue–Sat 11am–6pm; map p.152 A2
Contemporary art, with an emphasis on new media and emerging artists.

Kent Gallery
541 West 25th Street; tel: 212-627-3680; Tue–Sat 10am–6pm; map p.152 A2
Mid-career artists from the US and abroad.

Marlborough Chelsea
545 West 25th Street; tel: 212-463-8634; Tue–Sat 10am–5.30pm; map p.152 A2
Works by major contemporary artists.

Mary Ryan
527 West 26th Street; tel: 212-397-0669; Tue–Fri 10am–6pm; map p.152 C1
Twentieth-century and current American and British work.

Matthew Marks
522 West 22nd Street; tel: 212-243-0200; Tue–Sat 10am–6pm; map p.152 A2
One of the first major galleries to make the move to Chelsea, this influential dealer often presents drawings, photographs, prints, and other works on paper, as well as prominent contemporary painters such as Lucian Freud and Ellsworth Kelly.

Max Protetch
511 West 22nd Street; tel: 212-

633-6999; Tue–Sat 11am–6pm; map p.152 A2
A varied selection of contemporary works, ranging from architectural design and photographs to conceptual art.

PaceWildenstein
534 West 25th Street; tel: 212-929-7000; Tue–Sat 10am–6pm; map p.152 A2
Influential gallery showing prominent 20th-century and contemporary artists.

Paula Cooper
534 West 21st Street; tel: 212-255-1105; Tue–Sat 10am–6pm; map p.152 A2
This former SoHo pioneer offers an intriguing mix of conceptual and minimalist artwork.

P.P.O.W.
555 West 25th Street; tel: 212-647-1044; Tue–Sat 10am–6pm; map p.152 A2
A former East Village gallery that specializes in works by artists 'outside the norm.'

Robert Miller
524 West 26th Street; tel: 212-366-4774; Tue–Sat 10am–6pm; map p.152 A2
Contemporary international work, with a special interest in photography.

White Columns
320 West 13th Street; tel: 212-924-4212; Tue–Sat noon–6pm; map p.154 B4
An artist-owned gallery dedicated to showing the work of developing artists and challenging ideas.

SoHo and TriBeCa

Arcadia Gallery
51 Greene Street; tel: 212-965-1387; Mon–Fri 10am–6pm, Sat–Sun 11am–6pm; map p.154 B1
Classic and contemporary realist work.

Artists Space
38 Greene Street, 3rd floor; tel: 212-226-3970; Tue–Sat noon–6pm; map p.154 B1
Was a showcase for emerging artists like Robert Mapplethorpe and Cindy Sherman.

Deitch Projects
76 Grand Street; tel: 212-343-7300; Tue–Sat noon–6pm; map p.154 B1
Emerging and contemporary artists often with focus on multimedia and performance projects.

The Drawing Center
35 Wooster Street; tel: 212-219-2166; Tue–Fri 10am–6pm, Sat 11am–6pm; map p.154 B1
A nonprofit gallery with drawings of all periods by masters and little known artists.

Franklin Bowles Gallery
431 West Broadway; tel: 212-226-1616; Mon–Sun 11am–7pm; map p.154 B2
American and European masters in both modern and traditional styles.

Louis K. Meisel
141 Prince Street; tel: 212-677-1340; Tue–Sat 10am–6pm; map p.154 B2
Contemporary artists, with an emphasis on photorealists.

The Painting Center
52 Greene Street, 2nd Floor; tel: 212-343-1060; Tue–Sat 11am–6pm; map p.154 B1
Run by artists and dedicated to contemporary painting.

Peter Blum
99 Wooster Street; tel: 212-343-0441; Tue–Fri 10am–6pm, Sat 11am–6pm; map p.154 B1
Well-known contemporary painters, sculptors, and makers of installation art.

Staley-Wise Gallery
560 Broadway; tel: 212-966-6223; Tue–Sat 11am–5pm; map p. 154 B1
Photography including fashion, Hollywood portraiture, landscape, still life, and nudes.

Westwood Gallery
568 Broadway; tel: 212-925-5700; Tue–Sat 11am–6pm; map p.154 B1
Contemporary, 20th- and 19th-century artists in a wide variety of media and styles.

Sonnabend Gallery
536 West 22nd Street; tel: 212-627-1018; Tue–Sat 10am–6pm; map p.152 A2
Big-name contemporary American and European artists are shown at a multi-roomed gallery.

Greenwich Village

Grey Art Gallery
100 Washington Square East; tel: 212-998-6780; Tue–Thur 11am–6pm, Wed 11am–8pm, Fri 11am–6pm, Sat 11am–5pm; map p.154 C2
New York University's Grey Gallery has a mission, which is to 'collect, preserve, study, document, interpret, and exhibit the evidence of human culture.' This means you're likely to see shows of post-Revolution Cuban photography to police photography to the Czech avant-garde. Exhibits occasionally draw from NYU's collection of American paintings, which includes several by New York's seminal cadre of Abstract Expressionists.

Right: Brooklyn's DUMBO is an area popular with artists.

Gay and Lesbian

The traditional epicenter of New York's gay community is Greenwich Village – the West Village in particular, on and around Christopher Street. This is where the Stonewall Riots occurred in 1969, an event widely regarded as the opening salvo in the gay rights movement. Trendier are the adjacent Meatpacking District, Chelsea, and Hell's Kitchen areas, which claim some of the city's hottest new nightclubs and restaurants. Beyond these, gay and lesbian travelers will find Manhattan a mostly tolerant and friendly place and are likely to encounter few if any problems.

Accommodations

Chelsea Inn
46 West 17th Street; tel: 212-645-8989, 800-640-6469; http://chelseainn.com; map p.154 C4
This B&B is in a four-story walk-up in the Flatiron District.

Chelsea Mews Guest House
344 West 15th Street/Eighth Avenue; tel: 212-255-9174; www.chelseamewsguest house.com; map p.154 B4
A male-only B&B in a Victorian building.

Chelsea Pines Inn
317 West 14th Street/Eighth Avenue; tel: 212-929-1023; www.chelseapinesinn.com; map p.154 B4
Each room at this stylish B&B is named after a classic movie star and decorated with Hollywood memorabilia. All rooms have a private shower, but some share a hall toilet.

Contact **Big Onion Walking Tours** (tel: 212-439-1090; http://bigonion.com) for a view of gay and lesbian history in Greenwich Village.

Above: comic book from a New York store.

Colonial House Inn
318 West 22nd Street/Eighth Avenue; tel: 212-243-9669; www.colonialhouseinn.com; map p.152 B1
This Chelsea townhouse has homey guest rooms and an art gallery in the lobby.

Bars and Cafés

The Cubby Hole
281 West 12th Street/West 4th Street; tel: 212-243-9041; Mon–Fri 4pm–4am, Sat–Sun 2pm–2am; map p.154 B4
A laid-back lesbian bar in the West Village that attracts a diverse clientele – gay and straight, male and female.

G Lounge
225 West 19th Street/Seventh and Eighth avenues; tel: 212-929-1085; daily 4pm–4am; map p.152 B1
This Chelsea *boîte* describes itself as New York's premier gay bar. Popular with the buff and beautiful, it exudes a cool, modern vibe in tune with the area's studied hipness.

Henrietta Hudson
438 Hudson Street/Morton Street; tel: 212-924-3347; Mon–Fri 4pm–4am, Sat–Sun 2pm–4am; map p.154 A3
A lesbian bar with the vibe of a neighborhood tavern, this long-running West Village hangout has a pool table and a relaxed attitude.

Splash Bar
50 West 17th Street/Fifth Avenue; tel: 212-691-0073; Mon–Sat 4pm–4am, Sun 3pm–4am; map p.155 C4
Booze and cruise at this Chelsea dance club, known for its shirtless bartenders, friendly go-go boys, and basement sex shop.

Therapy
348 West 52nd Street/Eighth

Left: the Henrietta Hudson.

4pm–8pm, Sat noon–5pm
Provides information about all aspects of gay life in New York, including recommendations for bars, restaurants, legal counseling, etc.

Gay Men's Health Crisis
119 West 24th Street; tel: 212-367-1000, 800-243-7692; www.gmhc.org; map p.152 B1
This nonprofit group assists people with HIV/Aids and is dedicated to the prevention and treatment of the disease.

Lesbian, Gay, Bisexual, and Transgender Community Center
208 West 13th Street/Seventh Avenue; tel: 212-620-7310; www.gaycenter.org; daily 9am–11pm; map p.154 B4
This large and helpful organization offers a wide range of services and events, ranging from health education, counseling, and political action to dances and parties.

NYC Gay & Lesbian Anti-Violence Project
240 West 35th Street; tel: 212-714-1184; www.avp.org; map p.152 B3
The organization provides legal advocacy for victims of anti-gay violence.

Below: taking a walk through the West Village.

and Ninth Avenues; tel: 212-397-1700; daily 5pm–5am; map p.150 B1
A contemporary setting and congenial crowd make for a pleasant night of socializing. Cocktails are named after your favorite psychosis – oral fixation, delerium, psychotic episode, and more.

Vlada Lounge
331 West 51st Street/Eighth and Ninth Avenues; tel: 212-974-8030; daily 4pm–4am; map p.150 B1
Russian-themed bar with, of course, an extensive vodka-based drink menu. Part of growing Hell's Kitchen bar scene. With its proximity to theater district, Broadway performers often stop by.

Festivals

Halloween Parade
Greenwich Village, Sixth Avenue/Spring and 23rd streets; tel: 845-758-5519; www.halloween-nyc.com
A spectacle of wild costumes and flamboyant characters.

NewFest
Tel: 718-923-1450; www.newfest.org
A year-round gay and lesbian

film series, which features a 'best of' weekend at the Brooklyn Academy of Music in September.

Pride Week
Heritage of Pride; tel: 212-807-7433; www.nycpride.org
A weeklong series of events and tours culminating in the Gay and Lesbian Pride Day Parade on Fifth Avenue.

Publications

Gay City News
http://gaycitynews.com
A newspaper covering local, national, and international news and events.

HX: Homo Xtra
www.hx.com
Gay lifestyle magazine with good events listings.

New York Blade
http://theblade.net
News for the gay and lesbian community.

Next
www.nextmagazine.net
A slick magazine dedicated to entertainment and nightlife in gay New York.

Useful Resources

Gay and Lesbian Hotline
Tel: 212-989-0999; Mon–Fri

History

1626

Peter Minuit, director general of New Amsterdam, purchases Manhattan from Algonquin Indians for 60 guilders' worth of trinkets – the equivalent of $24 in today's currency.

1647

Peter Stuyvesant becomes director general of New Amsterdam. He later directs the colonists to build a fence along what is now Wall Street to protect New Amsterdam from British incursion.

1664

Stuyvesant surrenders the town to the British without a fight. New Amsterdam is renamed New York, after King Charles II's brother, James, Duke of York.

1673

The Dutch recapture New York, only to return it the next year as a result of the Treaty of Westminster.

1776

The American Revolution begins. George Washington, in command of the colonial troops, loses the Battle of Long Island. British troops occupy New York until 1783.

1789

George Washington is inaugurated president at the site of Federal Hall on Wall Street. New York briefly serves as the US capital.

1820

A formal Stock Exchange replaces the outdoor money market on Wall Street.

1825

The Erie Canal connects the Hudson River to the Great Lakes and Midwest markets, enhancing New York's status as a center of commerce. Irish and German immigrants begin arriving in great numbers. The city's population soon tops 200,000.

1835

Manhattan between South Broad and Wall Street is ravaged by the 'Great Fire.'

1858

Calvert Vaux and Frederick Law Olmsted submit plans for Central Park.

1861

The American Civil War begins. New York is the largest metropolis in the US.

1863

Draft protestors attack African-Americans and police. About 100 people are killed during the Draft Riots.

1877

The Museum of Natural History opens, followed in 1880 by the Metropolitan Museum of Art.

1883

The Brooklyn Bridge opens, followed in 1886 by the Statue of Liberty.

1929

Wall Street crashes; the Great Depression begins.

1930

Construction of the Chrysler Building, the world's tallest, is completed, only to be surpassed in 1931 by the Empire State Building.

1933
Fiorello LaGuardia is elected mayor and uses federal money to mitigate the effects of Depression.

1939
Ten years after its foundation by Abby Aldrich Rockefeller, the Museum of Modern Art moves into a new home on West 53rd Street.

1941
The US enters World War II.

1946
The United Nations begins meeting in New York. Permanent buildings are completed six years later.

1959
The Guggenheim Museum opens; construction begins on Lincoln Center.

1973
The World Trade Center opens. The 110-story Twin Towers are the world's tallest buildings.

1975
A loan from the federal government prevents the city from sliding into bankruptcy.

1977
A 27-hour blackout prompts widespread looting.

1978
Ed Koch is elected mayor and remains in office until 1989.

1990
David Dinkins becomes the city's first African-American mayor.

1993
A bomb explodes below the World Trade Center. Six people are killed and more than 1,000 injured.

1997
Mayor Rudolph Giuliani's anti-crime campaign is effective; NY becomes one of the safest large cities in the US.

2001
Terrorists crash two planes into the World Trade Center; nearly 3,000 people are killed. Michael Bloomberg is elected mayor.

2004
The Museum of Modern Art reopens in Manhattan after extensive expansion.

2006
President George Bush visits the new World Trade Center Tribute Visitors Center.

2007
The New Museum of Contemporary Art opens on the Lower East Side.

2008
New Yorkers celebrate election of President Barack Obama.

71

Hotels

Small and expensive. That, in a phrase, is what you can expect of a hotel room in New York. There are exceptions, of course. Some properties give their guests extra elbow room; others offer weekend discounts or package deals, though they don't often volunteer this information unless you ask. But with occupancy rates regularly between 80 and 85 percent, topping 90 percent during holidays and special events, there's little incentive for hotels to drop their rates. The best strategy is to prowl the online discounters, check out the current promotional deals, or travel during the off-seasons – February, March, and August.

Midtown

The Algonquin
59 West 44th Street/Fifth and Sixth avenues; tel: 212-840-6800, 888-304-2047; www.algonquinhotel.com; $$$–$$$$; map p.153 D3
Once a haven for New York's literary Round Table, and still an all-time favorite, The Algonquin retains a low-key, oak-paneled charm. Clubby and Victorian in demeanor, civilized in its treatment of guests, it's near theaters and not as expensive as its competitors. A recent renovation managed to upgrade everything but change very little.

Casablanca Hotel
147 West 43rd Street/Broadway and Sixth Avenue; tel: 212-869-1212; www.casablanca hotel.com; $$$; map p.153 C3
Just off Times Square, this romantic boutique hotel has a Moroccan-via-Hollywood

Price categories are for a double room without breakfast:
$$$$	over $400
$$$	$250–$400
$$	$200–$250
$	under $200

Above: outside the New York Palace Hotel, *see p.75.*

theme. Rick's Café serves a complimentary breakfast, free tea in the afternoon, and wine and cheese in the evening. Ask about special summer and corporate rates.

Comfort Inn Manhattan
42 West 35th Street/Fifth and Sixth avenues; tel: 212-947-0200, 877-424-6423; www.comfortinnmanhattan.com, www.comfortinn.com; $–$$; map p.153 C2
The Comfort Inns don't offer special luxuries, and rooms are generally quite small, but they provide reliable, good-value comfort and intelligent service, in several well-placed Manhattan locations, putting them among the best mid-price options. (Also in Midtown at: Comfort Inn Midtown, 129 West 46th Street/Sixth and Seventh avenues, tel: 212-221-2600, 877-424-6423; Comfort Inn Javits Center, 442 West 36th Street, tel: 212-714-6699.)

Hotel 57
130 East 57th Street/Lexington and Park avenues; tel: 212-753-8841, 866-240-8604; www.hotel 57.com; $$$; map p.153 E4
Until recently a budget hotel, this building has become another spot in New York's style-hotel line-up. Rooms are still small, but they're now very sharply designed, with luxury touches like Egyptian cotton sheets and sophisticated electronics throughout, and some have great views.

The Hotel at Times Square
59 West 46th Street/Fifth Avenue; tel: 212-719 2300, 800-848-0020; www.applecorehotels.com; $–$$$; map p.153 C4
Another reasonably priced hotel from Apple Core Hotels, mainly geared to business travelers, with a business

Left: the lavish lobby of the Waldorf-Astoria, *see p.76*.

style maestro Philippe Starck, is even more striking than at other Schrager hotels. If you don't mind the mini-scale rooms, rates can be quite reasonable for upscale New York. It's a favorite due to its location near the Time Warner Center, and a restaurant, Hudson Cafeteria, that's a magnet for high-fashion nightlife.

InterContinental The Barclay New York
111 East 48th Street/Park Avenue; tel: 212-755-5900, 800-782 8021; http://new-york-barclay.intercontinental.com; $$$–$$$$; map p.153 D3
Opened in the 1920s just as the Barclay, this hotel blends executive-class efficiency with majestic spaces and a range of pampering services. Public rooms include two fine restaurants, a clothier, and a luxury gift shop.

The Iroquois
49 West 44th Street/Fifth and Sixth avenues; tel: 212-840-3080, 800-332-7220; www.iroquoisny.com;

There are ways of softening the blow (at least a little) of New York hotel prices. One is to book a flight and hotel together when you arrange your trip: several websites offer combination bookings with hotels at discounted rates, such as expedia.com, travelocity.com, lastminute.com, which operate around the world. Within the US and Canada only there are also hotwire.com, orbitz.com, and kayak.com, among others. Some websites offer discount rates on hotels only, without flights, such as hotels.com or quikbook.com. And when booking directly with a hotel, online or by phone, be sure to check out whatever promotional or weekend rates they are currently offering – dependent on when you are visiting, these deals and packages can be quite abundant.

center and conference rooms. Breakfast is included, and there's free WiFi throughout.

Hotel Pennsylvania
401 Seventh Avenue/West 33rd Street; tel: 212-736-5000, 800-223-8585; www.hotelpenn.com;

$–$$$; map p.152 C2
With 1,700 rooms, this huge hotel is centrally located across from Madison Square Garden and Penn Station. Built in 1919 by the Pennsylvania Railroad, it was designed by the renowned firm of McKim, Mead, & White, and the hotel's Café Rouge Ballroom played host to the greats of the big-band era, including Count Basie, Duke Ellington and the Glenn Miller Orchestra – who immortalized the hotel's phone number in the 1938 hit *Pennsylvania 6-5000*. It has kept the same number ever since. The hotel's range of packages are good value.

Hudson Hotel
356 West 58th Street/Eighth and Ninth avenues; tel: 212-247-0769; www.hudsonhotel.com; $$$; map p.150 B2
Part of the Ian Schrager design-hotel stable like Morgans *(see p.74)*, the Hudson has around 1,000 rooms – so they're often very small, although the overall design, by

Right: a classy setting at the Iroquois.

$$$–$$$$; map p.153 D3
Built in the 1920s, this once-shabby hotel has been comprehensively facelifted and now offers upscale rooms and suites and a calm, opulent atmosphere. The James Dean Suite commemorates the time when the actor lived here in the 1950s, when the hotel offered none of the luxuries it does today.

La Quinta Manhattan
17 West 32nd Street/Broadway; tel: 212-736-1600, 800-551-2303; www.applecorehotels. com; $$–$$$; map p.152 C2
Apple Core Hotels run several good-value mid-to-budget-range hotels in New York. The 182-room La Quinta, a short walk from Macy's and Madison Square Garden, is typical of their style: rates are extremely reasonable, especially considering that the comfortable rooms come with such conveniences as data ports and voice mail. There's also complimentary breakfast, a lobby café with entertainment, room service, and –

rare at this price – an open-air rooftop bar where music and snacks can be enjoyed in summer, along with views of the Empire State Building.

Marriott ExecuStay Aurora
556 Third Avenue/East 36th and 37th streets; tel: 212-953-5707, 800-877-2800; www.execustay. com; $$–$$$; map p.153 D2
Fully equipped apartments for long- and short-term stays (usually with a minimum stay of at least three nights; very often a 30-night stay is required.). The surrounding area is hectic, but it's a great bargain. The ExecuStay branch of the Marriott group also has many other similar apartments around Manhattan.

Milford Plaza Hotel
700 Eighth Avenue/West 45th Street; tel: 212-869-3600, 800-221-2690; www.milfordplaza. com; $–$$; map p.152 C4
In the hectic heart of the theater district not far from Times Square, this hotel is big, with reasonable rates, and popular with tour groups. If you're taking in a Broadway show, a room at the Milford is a smart way to save.

Millennium UN Plaza
United Nations Plaza, East 44th Street/First Avenue; tel: 212-758-1234, 866-866-8086; www.millennium-hotels.com;

$$$; map p.153 E2
The location is a bit far from the heart of town, but guests appreciate the busy atmosphere as United Nations representatives bustle through the heroically proportioned lobby. Other benefits include views of the East River, a fitness center, a tennis court and a pool, and decent rates.

Morgans
237 Madison Avenue/East 37th Street; tel: 212-686-0300, 800-697-1791; www.morganshotel. com; $$$–$$$$; map p.153 D2
The original boutique hotel, created by Ian Schrager and the late Steve Rubell – once the driving forces behind 1970s disco Studio 54 – and designer Andrée Putnam in 1954, and the inspiration for every chic modern design hotel that has sprung up since then around the world. Schrager himself went on to create the Royalton, the Hudson, and many other ventures. Surprisingly for ultra-trendy New York, Morgans itself is still one of the most fashionable hotels in Manhattan, with a clientele of movie stars and millionaires. The decor's original stark grays have been replaced by warmer tones, but there's still a minimalist ambience. Service is famously extraordinary.

Left: the Royal Suite of the Waldorf-Astoria, *see p.76.*

Murray Hill East Suites
149 East 39th Street/Lexington and Third avenues; tel: 212-661-2100, 800-248-9999; $$$; map p.153 D2

Set in the heart of Murray Hill, this all-suites hotel is a bit shabby in parts, and service can be erratic, but the spaciousness of its rooms makes it reasonable value. Each suite has a kitchenette.

New York Palace
455 Madison Avenue/East 50th Street; tel: 212-888-7000, 800-804-7035; www.newyorkpalace.com; $$$$; map p.153 D4

A grand monument to American pomp and excess. Appointed in a style that can only be called postmodern Rococo, the Palace has a regime of flawlessly detailed service that can make the average guest feel like an imperial pasha. A brash New York experience.

Omni Berkshire Place
21 East 52nd Street/Madison Avenue; tel: 212-753-5800, 888-444-6664; www.omnihotels.com; $$$–$$$$; map p.153 D4

Although it's been acquired by the Omni chain, the Berkshire retains its old-fashioned grace and attention to personal service. Known by some guests as a junior Plaza, it's comfortable and comforting, a tastefully appointed oasis of calm in the heart of Midtown.

The Paramount
235 West 46th Street/Broadway and Eighth Avenue; tel: 212-764-5500, 866-760-3174; www.nycparamount.com; $$–$$$; map p.153 C4

Right on Times Square, this hotel was originally launched as the biggest venture in Ian Schrager's design-hotel sta-

Students and budget travelers might consider staying at one of several hostels. Most offer dorm-style accommodations, shared bathrooms, and a common kichen for a fraction of the cost of a standard hotel. Manhattan locations include Big Apple Hostel (119 West 45th Street/Sixth Avenue; tel: 212-302-2603; www.bigapple hostel.com); Chelsea International Hostel (251 West 20th Street/Seventh and Eighth avenues; tel: 212-647-0010; www.chelseahostel.com); and HI-New York (891 Amsterdam Avenue/West 103rd Street; tel: 212-932-2300; www.hinewyork.org).

ble, like the Hudson and the Royalton pre-redesign, with out-to-dazzle Philippe Starck design, but has been sold to the Spanish Solmelia group. It's not really as spectacular as it first appears – rooms are New York cramped – but amenities include beds with headboards reproducing famous paintings, a fitness club, a kids' playroom, and suitably trendsetting bars and restaurants.

Le Parker Meridien
118 West 57th Street/Sixth and Seventh avenues; tel: 212-245-5000, 800-543-4300; www.parkermeridien.com; $$$–$$$$; map p.150 C1

This hotel, now part of the

Starwoods Hotels and Resorts Group, has been transformed with a very New York style into a chic modern boutique hotel – fresh, airy, and with excellent restaurants and ample health facilities that include a top-floor swimming pool with a fabulous view.

Peninsula New York
700 Fifth Avenue/East 55th Street; tel: 212-956-2888, 866-382-8388; www.peninsula.com; $$$$; map p.153 D4

One of the city's most lavish hotels, with richly appointed rooms, a truly luxurious health club, spa and pool with superb views, and a prime Fifth Avenue location.

The Pod Hotel
230 East 51st Street/Third Avenue; tel: 212-355-0300, 800-742-5945; www.thepod hotel.com; $–$$$; map p.153 E3

One more New York budget hotel that has suddenly got style: long known as the Pickwick Arms, this place has been made over and relaunched as The Pod, with bright hipster decor and right-now electronics (WiFi, iPod docks, etc) in all its still-tiny rooms. Very handily located, it's perfect for budget-conscious travellers looking for a modern hotel experience, and as well as full en suite rooms for around $300 there are others with shared bathrooms or 'bunk rooms' for around $170.

Right: upmarket snacks at the Peninsula New York.

Renaissance New York Times Square
714 Seventh Avenue/West 43rd Street; tel: 212-765-7676; www.marriott.com/renaissance-hotel; $$$$; map p.153 C4

A star of the improved and cleaned up Times Square, with 300-plus rooms, most of them featuring wide-screen TVs, oversized baths, and other comforts. It's very convenient for theaters, restaurants, and Midtown shopping, and prices are often lower than those of other hotels with similar facilities.

The Royalton
44 West 44th Street/Fifth and Sixth avenues; tel: 212-869-4400, 800-697-1791; www.royaltonhotel.com; $$$$; map p.153 D3

Ian Schrager is credited by many with having invented the modern 'boutique hotel' concept with Morgans (see p.74) in 1984, and The Royalton followed four years later. Every fitting and detail – from lobby lighting to lavatories – was designed as an integral part of the high-style image, as boldly futuristic as the set of a sci-fi film. After 19 years, The Royalton was comprehensively renovated in 2007, with a new design that has divided critics. Old or new, clients are consistently pampered (for a hefty price).

W New York
541 Lexington Avenue/East 49th Street; tel: 212-755-1200; www.starwoodhotels.com/who-tels; $$–$$$$; map p.153 E3

The W hotels are the luxury boutique-hotel brand of the Starwood Hotel group, also

Above: views to die for at The Carlyle.

in charge of Sheraton and many other hotel fleets, and this is the chain's flagship. The very deliberately stylish interior was designed by entertainment architect David Rockwell, with Zen-inspired rooms where (a little) grass grows on the windowsills and quilts are inscribed with New Age aphorisms. There's a juice bar, a spa with good fitness facilities and a trend-setting restaurant, Heartbeat.

The Waldorf-Astoria
301 Park Avenue/East 50th Street; tel: 212-355-3000, 800-925-3673; www.waldorf.com; $$$–$$$$; map p.153 E3

The most famous hotel in the city in its heyday in the 1930s and 1940s, with an Art Deco panache that's been restored to something like its early glory. The public spaces combine H.G. Wells's heroic concept of the future with Cecil B. DeMille's view of ancient Egypt: a style mix that never fails to lift the spirits. Rooms have an old-world charm, and the location is equally convenient for Midtown shopping, the theater, and business districts.

Wellington Hotel
871 Seventh Avenue/West 55th Street; tel: 212-247-3900, 800-652-1212; www.wellington hotel.com; $–$$; map p.150 C1

The side-street entrance in a congested neighborhood is useful, and the location is great for Central Park, Lincoln Center, and Carnegie Hall. A reliable standby, with reasonable rates for NY.

Westin New York
270 West 43rd Street/Seventh and Eighth avenues; tel: 212-201-2700, 888-837-4183; www.westinny.com; $$$; map p.152 C4

Architecturally dazzling, with a multicolored, mirrored exterior, this 45-story hotel has become a visual attraction in the Times Square area and is one of the newer luxury hotels in the neighborhood.

Uptown

Beacon Hotel
2130 Broadway/West 75th Street; tel: 212-787-1100, 800-572-4969; www.beaconhotel.com; $$–$$$; map p.150 C4

This busy, friendly Upper West Side favorite is adjacent to the Beacon Theater, a busy music venue. Deals are to be had for families who book rooms with fold-away couches. The location is a great launch pad, with good subway connections nearby.

The Carlyle
35 East 76th Street/Madison Avenue; tel: 212-744-1600;

Price categories are for a double room without breakfast:
$$$$	over $400
$$$	$250–$400
$$	$200–$250
$	under $200

Added to your hotel bill will be city and state taxes of 14.25 percent plus a room charge of $3.50 per night.

www.thecarlyle.com; $$$$; map p.151 E3

Posh, serene, and very expensive, the Carlyle remains one of the city's most acclaimed luxury hotels. The appointments are exquisite, the furnishings antique, the service formal. Home of Café Carlyle and Bemelmans Bar, two of the city's most enduring upscale evening spots.

Comfort Inn Central Park West

31 West 71st Street/Central Park West; tel: 212-721-4770, 877-424-6423; www.comfort inn.com; $$–$$$; map p.151 C3

Uptown branch of the Comfort Inn chain *(see p.72)*, with the usual reliably good value. It also has an excellent Upper West Side location, less than a block from Central Park.

The Franklin

164 East 87th Street/Lexington and Third avenues; tel: 212-369-1000, 877-607-4009; www. franklinhotel.com; $$$–$$$$

This snug East Side boutique hotel has recently upgraded, but rates are still lower than average for this kind of plush comfort. The atmosphere is charming, the breakfast delicious, the beds heavenly. Guests enjoy plasma TV, WiFi, and in-room movies from a library of classic films.

Gracie Inn

502 East 81st Street/York Avenue; tel: 212-628-1700, 800-404-2252; www.thegracie inn.com; $–$$

On a quiet side street near the East River and Gracie Mansion (the mayor's residence), this is a cross between a townhouse and a country inn. It's an apartment-hotel, since all the very comfortable studios and rooms of different sizes have kitchenettes. Rates may be reduced depending on the length of your stay, and it's one of NY's best bargains.

Hotel Bentley

500 East 62nd Street/York Avenue; tel: 212-644-6000, 800-555-7555; www.hotelbentley newyork.com; $$–$$$

This sleek, contemporary high-rise hotel is in a quiet part of the Upper East Side, near the East River, and has spectacular views. Rooms are spacious, breakfast is included, and rates are reasonable. Free cappuccino too, in a library by the lobby.

Hotel Excelsior

45 West 81st Street/Columbus Avenue and Central Park West; tel: 212-362-9200; www.excelsiorhotelny.com; $$$; map p.151 D4

This 1920s hotel has been renovated in the last few years, and is set on a pleasant block near Columbus Avenue shopping, several museums, and Central Park.

Hotel Wales

1295 Madison Avenue/East 92nd Street; tel: 212-876-6000, 866-925-3746; www.wales hotel.com; $$$–$$$$

The Wales was once known for both low rates and splendid views of Central Park. Today it costs a good deal more, but still offers a great location in the Carnegie Hill neighborhood near Museum Mile and the Park. You can feast on the city's best breakfast next door at **Sarabeth's** *(see p.122)*, or enjoy the light breakfast offered in the hotel's tea salon, also the setting for afternoon tea and chamber music.

Loews Regency Hotel

540 Park Avenue/East 61st Street; tel: 212-759-4100, 866-563-9792; www.loewshotels. com; $$$$; map p.151 D1

A bastion of tranquility with a cozy bar and fine restaurant. The Regency has rooms sumptuously decorated in soothing tones and high-quality fabrics, and equipped with flat-screen TVs, CD players, and high-speed WiFi. It's a favorite of showbiz folks and high-profile corporate types.

The Lowell

28 East 63rd Street/Madison Avenue; tel: 212-838-1400, 800-221-4444; www.lowell hotel.com; $$$$; map p.151 D1

Understated elegance and

Below: the Trump International Hotel & Tower, *see p.79*.

Price categories are for a
double room without breakfast:

$$$$	over $400
$$$	$250–$400
$$	$200–$250
$	under $200

sumptuous traditional decor
are bywords at this polished
property off high-powered
Madison Avenue. With only
72 rooms and suites, it's
more intimate than some of
the giant luxury hotels, and is
known for its plush tea salon.

Mandarin Oriental
80 Columbus Circle/West 60th
Street; tel: 212-805-8800, 866-
801-8800; www.mandarinorien-
tal.com; $$$$; map p.150 C2
One of the newest luxury
hotels, in the upper floors of
the Time Warner Center – so
guests enjoy spectacular
views over the city and Central Park. In addition, hushed
surroundings and the latest
of everything make this a
sought-after spot for (very)
high-end visitors.

Marrakech Hotel
2688 Broadway/West 103rd
Street; tel: 212-222-2954;
www.marrakechhotelnyc.com;
$$–$$$
This long-running hotel on
the Upper West Side (once
the Malibu) has been given a
very groovy makeover, with
Moroccan-themed fantasy
decor. Aimed at hip younger
travelers, its rooms are a
great bargain, even though it
lacks a few frills (such as an
elevator). It's a quick subway
ride from every part of town.

The Milburn
242 West 76th Street/Broadway;
tel: 212-362-1006, 800-833-
9622; www.milburnhotel.com;
$–$$$; map p.150 C4
The decor is straightforward,
but this hotel is a very good

deal, with studio rooms and
suites all with TVs, Internet
connection and kitchenettes.
They come in different sizes,
so rates vary as well. It also
has a recently added fitness
facility. It is situated on a
quiet street, an easy walk
from Lincoln Center and Cen-
tral Park. A minimum stay of
2–3 nights is often required.

On The Ave Hotel
222 West 77th Street/Broadway;
tel: 212-362-1100, 800-509-
7598; www.ontheave-nyc.com;
$$$; map p.150 C4
Out of the same boutique-
hotel stable as Hotel 57 (see
p.72), this recent addition to
the Upper West Side has
similarly chic modern rooms
with queen- or king-size beds
and designer fittings. There's
a great balcony with views of
the Hudson River or Central
Park, and several rooms have
their own balconies. It's an
easy walk from Lincoln Center, and though rates are not
budget, they're good value
for this style and location.

The Pierre
2 East 61st Street/Fifth Avenue;
tel: 212-838-8000, 800-743-
7734; www.the-pierre.com;
$$$$; map p.151 D1
Justly renowned as one of
New York's finest hotels, with
a fabulous pedigree of guests
that goes back to its opening
in 1930. The location is per-

fect for those intent on business or Midtown shopping,
and there is a lovely view of
Central Park. Rooms are
large and elegant, service is
top flight, and dining in Café
Pierre or tea in the beautiful
Rotunda are among the city's
most civilized experiences.
The Pierre is undergoing
extensive renovation to
update all 200 rooms.

The Plaza
Fifth Avenue/East 59th Street; tel:
212-759-3000; www.fairmont.
com; $$$$; map p.151 D1
One of the grandest grand
hotels, the 1909 Plaza has
emerged from a three-year
renovation that has turned
most of its 19 floors into ultra-
luxurious condo apartments.
The lower floors are still hotel
rooms, though, and they and
the public areas, like the
famous Palm Court, retain the
hotel's Edwardian splendor.

Sherry-Netherland
781 Fifth Avenue/East 59th
Street; tel: 212-355-2800;
www.sherrynetherland.com;
$$$$; map p.151 D1
An old-fashioned luxury hotel
redolent of the 1920s, with
such a faithful club of visitors
that reservations must be
made well ahead. Guests
enjoy grand spaces, both in
the public areas and the 40
rooms and suites, royal treatment to match, and, from the

Right: be a part of New
York's edgy history.

Left: the Jade Bar at the now-fashionable Gramercy Park Hotel.

vary from a few inexpensive student rooms to suites; as is renowned, there are discounts for long stays.

Hotel Roger Williams

131 Madison Avenue/East 31st Street; tel: 212-448-7000, 888-448-7788; www.hotelroger williams.com; $$$$; map p.153 C2

The chic Roger Williams has exchanged its sleek, stark style for a warmer approach, using bold colors and natural wood. The lobby has a soaring atrium, and the bedrooms are cozy, with lots of space, thick bathrobes, down comforters to curl up under, CD and DVD players and free WiFi. Penthouses have lovely little balconies with great views of the Empire State.

Inn at Irving Place

56 Irving Place/East 18th Street; tel: 212-533-4600, 800-685-1447; www.innatirving.com; $$$–$$$$; map p.155 D3

A pair of graceful townhouses have been transformed into a near-facsimile of a 19th-century inn, with a fireplace-lit tea salon and 12 elegant rooms and suites featuring four-poster beds (plus all modern comforts and high-grade electronics). This Henry James-ian little world is two blocks from Gramercy Park, and a short distance from Union Square. There's a nice little restaurant, with room service.

Ramada Inn Eastside

161 Lexington Avenue/East 30th

best rooms, glorious views over Central Park.

Trump International Hotel & Tower

1 Central Park West/West 60th Street; tel: 212-299-1000, 800-448 7467; www.trumpintl.com; $$$$; map p.150 C2

As well as floor-to-ceiling windows overlooking Central Park, the hotel has a full spa and indoor pool. As flashy as its owner, it houses a celebrated restaurant, Jean Georges, and has an enormous globe sculpture marking its spot at Columbus Circle.

Chelsea to Gramercy

Gershwin Hotel

7 East 27th Street/Fifth and Madison avenues; tel: 212-545-8000; www.gershwinhotel.com; $–$$; map p.153 C1

A very artsy, intimate hotel just north of Madison Square Park with a Warhol-inspired look and aimed at the young, fashionable, and cash-strapped (there are chic little bunk-bed rooms reserved as housing for tyro models, new to the big city). It's also amazing value: there are bunk beds for around $50, full-size rooms for around $200 and attractive package rates for families and weekend stays, and the whole hotel is nicely kept.

Gramercy Park Hotel

2 Lexington Avenue/East 20th Street; tel: 212-920-3300, 866-

784-1300; www.gramercypark hotel.com; $$$$; map p.155 D4

Once a faded relic from the Jazz Age, this Ian Schrager property has been reborn as a lavish, idiosyncratic hotel, designed by artist Julian Schnabel, adorned with a mix of modern art and rich velvets and neo-Baroque chandeliers. The Rose and Jade bars are favorite celebrity hangouts, which means the Gramercy is not for those seeking discreet tranquility.

Hampton Inn Manhattan-Chelsea

108 West 24th Street/Sixth Avenue; tel: 212-414-1000; www.hamptoninn.com; $$–$$$; map p.152 B1

Hi-tech facilities and ample comforts set the tone at this Chelsea spot at the doorstep of the gallery scene. Shopping abounds on Sixth Avenue.

Hotel Chelsea

222 West 23rd Street/Seventh Avenue; tel: 212-243-3700; www.hotelchelsea.com; $$–$$$; map p.152 B1

A Victorian red-brick landmark of bohemian decadence, home to Dylan Thomas, Beatnik poets, then Warhol drag queens, then Sid Vicious, and now... a few of all of the above plus ordinary guests. For some, a stay at the Chelsea is part of a ritual pilgrimage to all that is hip and edgy. Accommodations

Few people are more useful to first-time visitors than a knowledgeable concierge. Searching for a romantic bistro, a hip nightclub, hard-to-get theater tickets? A good concierge will be able to help you out.

Street; tel: 212-545-1800; www.applecorehotels.com; $$$; map p.153 D1

This cozy hotel was built in the early 1900s, but has been comprehensively refurbished with modern fittings and extras, and has friendly staff. Some of its 100 reasonably priced rooms have views of the Empire State Building.

W New York Union Square
201 Park Avenue South/East 17th Street; tel: 212-253-9119; www.starwoodhotels.com/who-tels; $$$–$$$$; map p.155 D3

A Downtown outlet for W Hotels' take on the boutique concept (see also p.76). Bordering the fashionable Flatiron District, this stylish hotel has one foot in Gramercy Park and the other in Downtown attitude. Everything here is top-of-the-line, including a trendy bar and restaurant, Olives.

Greenwich Village

Abingdon Guest House
21 Eighth Avenue/West 12th and Jane streets; tel: 212-243-5384; www.abingdonguesthouse.com; $$–$$$; map p.154 B4

It's romance on a shoestring at this exceptional-value nine-room hostelry between the West Village and the Meatpacking District. Tiny, individually decorated rooms are

spread over two townhouses: some have four-poster beds, some fireplaces. Rooms facing Eighth Avenue can be a little noisy, so ask for a room at the back. A two-night minimum stay may be required.

Hotel Gansevoort
18 Ninth Avenue/West 13th Street; tel: 212-206-6700, 877-426-7386; www.hotelgansevoort. com; $$$$; map p.154 B4

The Meatpacking District's first luxury boutique hotel has as its pièce de résistance a roof garden, bar, and swimming pool, with breathtaking skyline views. Bedrooms are naturally the last word in chic (think neutral colors and a single orchid), and the lobby, with subtly changing colors, is spectacular. If your room faces west, the Hudson River will be on the horizon, and the Meatpacking action will be directly below, nonstop.

The Jane
113 Jane Street/West 12th and 14th streets; tel: 212-929-0060; www.thejanenyc.com; $; map p.154 A4

A restored 1907 waterfront hotel geared to young travelers with more dash than cash. Luxury train cabins inspired design of cabin rooms with bathrooms down the hall. A single cabin with

Bed and breakfast accommodations in New York range from a room in someone's apartment to a full apartment or small guest house. For information, contact City Lights (tel: 212-737-7049; www.citylights newyork.com) or Bed and Breakfast Network of New York (tel: 212-645-8134, 800-900-8134; www.bedandbreakfast netny.com).

shared bathroom is $99. Many of the over 200 rooms have riverfront views. Only single-bed rooms currently available while hotel is undergoing renovation. Queen and king beds will all have communal bathrooms.

Maritime Hotel
363 West 16th Street/Ninth Avenue; tel: 212-242-4300; www.themaritimehotel.com; $$$$; map p.152 A1

Porthole windows recall the days when this 1966 building was the headquarters of the National Maritime Union. The nautical theme is evident in the rooms, which have a resemblance to shipboard cabins, but naturally offer lots of modern extras. The lobby bar is a hip gathering place for the Meatpacking crowd.

Washington Square Hotel
103 Waverly Place/Macdougal Street; tel: 212-777-9515, 800-222-0418; www.washington squarehotel.com; $$–$$$; map p.154 B3

A century-old hotel with an ideal Village location on Washington Square. Rooms are small but nicely appointed. Back in the 1960s, this was the seedy hotel where The Mamas & the Papas are said to have written California Dreaming. Though done up, the hotel still has a boho air, and is still very good value.

Left: a view from Soho Grand.

Left: outside the Mercer Hotel in SoHo.

East Village to Chinatown

Blue Moon Hotel
100 Orchard Street/Delancey and Broome streets; tel: 212-533-9080; www.bluemoon-nyc.com; $$$–$$$$; map p.157 D4
In the heart of the old immigrant Lower East Side, this formerly run-down tenement has been converted into a distinctly cozy small modern hotel that seeks to maintain a feel of the past. Rooms are named after stars of the Vaudeville and Swing eras (Al Jolson, Tommy Dorsey…), and are twice the size of an average NY hotel room.

The Hotel on Rivington
107 Rivington Street/Ludlow Street; tel: 212-475-2600; www.hotelonrivington.com; $$$$; map p.155 D1
The Lower East Side had never been associated with hotels, so gentrification moved on apace when this glass-walled tower appeared among the old tenement blocks. Its floor-to-ceiling windows and high-end design are much appreciated by a young, fashionable clientele.

SoHo and TriBeCa

Holiday Inn Downtown
138 Lafayette Street/Howard Street; tel: 212-966-8898; www.hidowntown-nyc.com; $$–$$$; map p.156 C4
This hotel on the edge of Chinatown has more individuality than most chain hotels in this price range.

Mercer Hotel
147 Mercer Street/Prince Street; tel: 212-966-6060, 888-918-6060; www.mercerhotel.com; $$$$; map p.154 B1
This 1890s landmark in the heart of SoHo has been converted into an opulent boutique hotel with 75 rooms with high ceilings, arched windows, and (unusually for New York) large, sumptuous bathrooms. Owner André Balazs also owns Chateau Marmont in Los Angeles, and the clientele is equally stylish. Facilities include a roof garden, a library bar open 24 hours, and the **Mercer Kitchen** restaurant.
SEE ALSO RESTAURANTS, P.129

Soho Grand Hotel
310 West Broadway/Grand and Canal streets; tel: 212-965-3000; www.sohogrand.com; $$$–$$$$; map p.154 B1
Expect excellent service at this 15-story hotel, with industrial-chic decor and magnificent top-floor views. The lobby and bar are a rendezvous of choice for cool New York. As befits a place owned by the heir to a pet-food empire, pets are welcome (in rooms far from guests with allergies). Those who arrive without an animal companion but still feel the need are provided with a bowl of goldfish.

Tribeca Grand
2 Sixth Avenue/Walker and White streets; tel: 212-519-6600; www.tribecagrand.com; $$$–$$$$; map p.154 B1
Sister-hotel to the Soho Grand, and maybe even more dazzling as a style showpiece. Rooms are mellow and ultra-comfortable, while the Church Lounge is one of *the* spots in the city to meet up for cocktails or brunch.

Lower Manhattan

Best Western Seaport Inn
33 Peck Slip/Front Street; tel: 212-766-6600, 800-468-3569; www.seaportinn.com; $$–$$$; map p.156 C2
A block from South Street Seaport, this converted warehouse has Federal-era antiques and modern amenities. Some upper-floor rooms have Jacuzzis and/or terraces with great views of the Brooklyn Bridge.

Millennium Hilton
55 Church Street/Fulton Street; tel: 212-693-2001, 800-445-8667; www1.hilton.com; $$$–$$$$; map p.156 B3
Adjacent to the glass canyons of Wall Street, this hotel gives guests the opportunity to be near cooling Hudson River breezes.

Price categories are for a double room without breakfast:
$$$$ over $400
$$$ $250–$400
$$ $200–$250
$ under $200

81

Literature

The year 1888, when writer William Dean Howells abandoned Boston for the Big Apple, is often seen as the moment when New York moved into the lead of America's literary enterprise. And so it remains. The industry nurtured such major talents as Henry James and Edith Wharton, who forged an old New York mystique later augmented by waves of writers coming from other cultures – Jewish, Irish, African-American, Italian, and, nowadays, a diverse range of creative potential representing other worlds, other people, other sensibilities. For bookstores, *see Shopping, p.134–6.*

History

Downtown: My Manhattan by Pete Hamill. Little, Brown, and Company, 2004. An inveterate New York journalist and novelist rambles through the history of downtown Manhattan.

Fifth Avenue: The Best Address by Jerry E. Patterson. Rizzoli International Publications, 1998. Describes the gradual development of the city's most famous boulevard, from rocky dirt path to shanty row to elegant thoroughfare.

Flatbush Odyssey: A Journey Through the Heart of Brooklyn by Alan Abel. McClelland & Stewart, 1997. A fond reminiscence by an expat writer (now a Canadian) who grew up in one of Brooklyn's most colorful neighborhoods.

The Gangs of New York: An Informal History of the Underworld by Herbert Asbury. Thunder's Mouth Press, 2001. The book on which the Martin Scorsese film is based takes readers on a journey to a bygone New York, when violent gangs ruled the Five Points near present-day City Hall.

Gotham: A History of New York to 1898 by Mike Wallace and Edwin G. Burrows. Oxford University Press, 1998. Pulitzer Prize-winning narrative about the city's early years; in-depth, with an emphasis on some of its characters.

How the Other Half Lives by Jacob Riis. Dover, 1971. Groundbreaking account of the squalid tenements and sweatshops of the 19th century.

Low Life by Luc Sante. Vintage Books, 1992. The gangs, gangsters, and riff-raff of 19th-century New York.

Manhattan '45 by Jan Morris. Johns Hopkins University Press, 1998. An engaging portrait of the city on the brink of the postwar era.

Mannahatta: A Natural History of New York by Eric W. Sanderson. Abrams Books, 2009. Imagines and reconstructs, using modern ecological principles and computer modeling, what Manhattan looked like 400 years ago, when Henry Hudson first laid eyes on it, in its complete wild and natural state.

Stork Club by Ralph Blumenthal. Little, Brown, and Company, 2000. Historical account of New York's café society from the speakeasy era to the 1960s.

Publishers show off their latest titles during the fall **New York Is Book Country** festival. Author readings, panel discussions, and a variety of parties and receptions are held in venues around the city. The *New Yorker* Festival, also in the fall, is a popular festival featuring New Yorker writers in panel discussions and conducting interviews with high-profile writers, movers, and shakers.

Left: the magnificent New York Public Library *(see p.33).*

weaves a story of love and loss in the wake of the World Trade Center attack.

Netherland by Joseph O'Neill. Pantheon, 2009. O'Neill tells the story of a Dutchman living in the Hotel Chelsea in the wake of September 11th. Hans van den Broek befriends a Trinidadian who introduces him to cricket and the 'other' New York of immigrants.

The Nanny Diaries by Emma Mclaughlin and Nicola Kraus. St Martin's Griffin, 2003. A satirical take on the parenting habits of Uptown families by two former nannies.

Wonderful Town: New York Stories from *The New Yorker* edited by David Remnick. Random House, 2000. Work by Philip Roth, John Cheever, Susan Sontag, and others is collected in this anthology of short stories from the venerable literary magazine.

Writing New York: A Literary Anthology edited by Philip Lopate. The Library of America, 1998. Observations about life in New York by such literary folk as Henry David Thoreau, Walt Whitman, Maxim Gorky, and F. Scott Fitzgerald.

Contemporary Nonfiction

New York Eats: The Food Shopper's Guide to the Freshest Ingredients, the Best Takeout and Baked Goods and the Most Unusual Marketplaces in All of New York by Ed Levine. St Martin's, 1997. A guide to and celebration of the city's delectable variety of ethnic foods and eateries.

New York Stories: The Best of the City Section of the *New York Times* edited by Constance Rosenblum. An anthology of essays about city life from the *Times*.

Rats: Observations on the History and Habitat of the City's Most Unwanted Inhabitants by Robert Sullivan. Bloomsbury, 2004. A fascinating investigation of the city's rat population by an author who specializes in exploring marginal habitats.

Sex and the City by Candace Bushnell. Warner Books, 1997. These sex columns from the *New York Observer* served as the inspiration for the popular TV series.

Still Life in Harlem by Eddy L. Harris. Henry Holt and Company, Inc., 1996. An autobiographical take on this storied African-American neighborhood.

Fiction

The Age of Innocence by Edith Wharton. Modern Library Classics, 1999. A portrait of upper-crust New York in the 19th century.

The Bonfire of the Vanities by Tom Wolfe. Bantam, 1990. Satirical novel set in the New York of the 1980s.

Bright Lights, Big City by Jay McInerney. Vintage, 1984. Novel set in yuppie New York during the cocaine-saturated 1980s by one of the period's rising literary stars.

The Good Life by Jay McInerney. Vintage, 2007. Over two decades after *Bright Lights, Big City*, McInerney

---

Readers of mystery novels can choose from a long list of authors who set their tales in New York. Lawrence Block is among the most prolific. His world-weary PI Matthew Scudder appears in more than a dozen novels chronicling the city's dark side. Donald E. Westlake's books are lighter in tone; his protagonist, John Dortmunder, is a master thief whose capers go hilariously wrong. Annette Meyers conjures a vivid picture of Jazz Age Greenwich Village in her books featuring bohemian poet and amateur sleuth Olivia Brown. And Robert K. Tanenbaum explores political intrigue inside the Manhattan DA's office in novels such as *Hoax, Counterplay,* and *Fury.* Two anthologies – *Manhattan Noir* and *Brooklyn Noir* – collect short mysteries.

Media

Visitors should have no trouble getting the message in New York, the so-called 'Communications Capital of the World.' Facts and figures are thrust at you by everything from neon newsflashes crawling around buildings to a range of free publications pushed by street hawkers. Manhattan is the headquarters of major players like the prestigious *New York Times*, *Wall Street Journal*, and the Associated Press, by powerful TV and radio broadcasters, by the marketing pitchmen of Madison Avenue, and by the new-media industry termed 'Silicon Alley.' MTV has headquarters in Times Square.

Print

The internationally known *New York Times* is the paper of choice for most well-informed readers, with its bulky Sunday edition listing virtually everything of consequence. Two papers compete for the tabloid market: the *New York Post* and the *Daily News*. There are two commuter dailies distributed free in the mornings: *AM New York* and *Metro*. The free alternative weekly *Village Voice* has comprehensive listings and classified ads, as does the *New York Observer* and *New York Press*. Local magazines with extensive event listings include *New York*, *Time Out New York*, and the biweekly *L Magazine*.

Television

The three major networks – all with New York headquarters – are ABC (77 W. 66th Street; tel: 212-456-7777); CBS (51 W. 52nd Street; tel: 212-975-4321); NBC (30 Rockefeller Plaza; tel: 212-664-4444) and Fox News national offices (1211 Sixth Avenue; tel: 212-301-3000). CNN has offices at the Time Warner Center at

Above: New York City is the publishing capital of the US.

Columbus Circle. The Public Broadcasting Service (PBS) can be found on channels 13 and 21 on the VHF band (for those without cable). The other three local stations are affiliated with the Fox (5), UPN (9), and CW (11) networks. These channels broadcast nationally aired shows as well as local programing. In addition, half a dozen UHF stations broadcast in Spanish and other languages. Various cable companies offer 50 or more basic cable and movie channels, although the exact number varies depending on the cable service provider.

How to Attend a Television Broadcast

With advance planning, it's possible to join the audience of a New York-based TV show, many of them shown overseas. For more details, go to nycgo.com. Here's a selection:

Late Show with David Letterman
Late Night Tickets, Ed Sullivan Theater, 1697 Broadway; tel: 212-975-1003 or 975-2476; www.lateshowaudience.com; subway: 7th Ave; map p.150 B1
Tapings of this popular, comedic talk show are Mon–Fri at 5.30pm. Audience members must be 18 or older; ID is required. Apply for tickets online or by visiting the show's theater and making an in-person request. Standby tickets may be available by calling 212-247-6497 from 11am on the day of the broadcast or taping.

Live With Regis and Kelly
ABC Studios, W. 66th Street (between Columbus Avenue and Central Park West); tel: 212-456-3054; subway: 72nd St; map p.150 C3
To get tickets, mail a post-

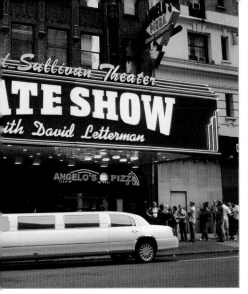

Left: attending a TV broadcast is popular with out-of-towners.

Who Wants to Be a Millionaire

ABC Studios, 30 W. 67th Street (between Columbus Avenue and Central Park West); tel: 212-479-7755. www. millionairetv.com; subway: 72nd St map p.150 C3

This popular game show is taped Tue–Fri. Tickets for the studio audience and contestant auditions are available by phone and on the Web. You must be 18 or older to attend.

Websites

Websites that provide helpful information include: www.newyork.citysearch.com for listings and reviews of current arts and entertainment events, as well as restaurants and shopping, www.nyc.gov, the official site of the City of New York, contains news items, mayoral updates, city agency information, and parking regulations; nycgo.com is the official New York City visitor website; www.nypl.org is for everything there is to know about the New York Public Library. There's also an online information service.

Radio

There are more than 70 radio stations in New York City. Some of the better stations with local news include:

WNYC 93.9fm/820am
WABC 770am
WCBS 880am
WINS 1010am
WBBR 1130am

---

card at least a year in advance. Otherwise, a limited number of standby tickets are available at the corner of 67th Street and Columbus Avenue. Arrive by 7am for your best chance. Standbys are seated on a first-come, first-served basis after regular ticketholders are seated.

Saturday Night Live

NBC Studios, GE Building, 30 Rockefeller Plaza; tel: 212-664-3056; email: snltickets@nbc uni.com; subway: 50th St/Rockefeller Center; map p.153 D4

This sketch comedy show is taped on Saturday, 11.30pm–1am. Audience members must be 16 or older. A ticket lottery is held each August. Only one e-mail per person sent in August will be

accepted, for two tickets each. Standby tickets are given out for the dress rehearsal and the live show at 7am at the 49th Street entrance, but do not guarantee admission.

The Today Show

NBC Studios, GE Building, 30 Rockefeller Plaza; tel: 212-664-4602; subway: 50th St/Rockefeller Center; map p.153 D4

Tapings of this early-morning show are Mon–Fri from 7–9am. An audience is encouraged to watch from the street outside – and perhaps be televised – but get there by dawn. The best spot to stand is at the corner of 49th Street and Rockefeller Center. Go to the kiosks at 30 Rockefeller Plaza for information.

The View

ABC Studios, 320 W. 66th Street (near West End Avenue); www.abc.abcnews.go.com/the view; subway: 72nd St; map p.150 C3

Request free tickets by mail (send a postcard only) or on the Web. The show airs live Mon–Thur 11am–noon with Friday show taping earlier in the week.

Below: CNN has offices at the Time Warner Center.

Movies

There's something about New York that loves the camera. From all those wide-angle sweeps up, down, and across the city's imposing skyscrapers to the down-and-dirty peeks at what lies beneath, moviemakers have found Gotham an irresistible backdrop. Indeed, the first movie projectors to operate in the United States date from 1896 in New York, and the first studios were based in the metropolis. It's a time-honored connection that includes everything from *The Broadway Melody* (1929) and *The Asphalt Jungle* (1950) to *New York, New York* (1977), and *Gangs of New York* (2002).

Hollywood on the Hudson

Ever since *The Lights of New York* was released in 1927, the city and its landmarks have been illuminating the big screens of the world's celluloid consciousness. King Kong atop the Empire State Building is an enduring image – although the 1976 remake was so bad it's remarkable that actress Jessica Lange's fledgling career survived the premiere. The Empire struck back when New York writer-turned-director Nora Ephron made *Sleepless in Seattle*, itself a pastiche of the 1957 three-hankie tear-jerker *An Affair to Remember*.

Greenwich Village has featured in everything from Fonda and Redford going *Barefoot in the Park* to Scorsese's *Raging Bull* (the swimming pool by St Luke's Place). The 1953 Marilyn Monroe comedy *How to Marry a Millionaire* revolved around an East Side penthouse, where three tyro models set themselves up in order to ensnare the money-bags of the title, while the

Above: Audrey Hepburn ready for *Breakfast at Tiffany's*.

classy apartment occupied by *Rosemary's Baby* is in the famed Dakota on Central Park West. The realities of contemporary life in Brooklyn have been vividly conveyed by director Spike Lee in movie such as *Do the Right Thing* and *Jungle Fever*.

Despite high costs, over 250 films are made in New York each year, many at the Kaufman Astoria Studios in Queens, and the number rises annually; so there's no *Escape from New York* to Hollywood just yet.

Shot in New York

Here's just a short selection of iconic New York movies.

Miracle on 34th Street, 1947
A classic Christmas story. The 1994 remake is even more sugary than the original, but Richard Attenborough makes a good Santa Claus.

The Seven-Year Itch, 1955
Billy Wilder's comedy is best known for the shot of Marilyn Monroe with her dress billowing over a subway grate.

An Affair to Remember, 1957
Cary Grant and Deborah Kerr find love atop the Empire State Building.

Breakfast at Tiffany's, 1961
Audrey Hepburn and George Peppard search for love, diamonds, and breakfast in a bittersweet tale based (with some huge liberties taken) on the Truman Capote novel.

West Side Story, 1961
Romeo and Juliet are transported to Hell's Kitchen with irresistible energy in this near-definitive New York musical by Leonard Bernstein and Stephen Sondheim.

Left: Woody Allen and Diane Keaton in *Manhattan*.

Big, 1988
A romantic comedy with Tom Hanks, who dances memorably (with Robert Loggia) on a giant electronic keyboard in FAO Schwarz.

Do the Right Thing, 1989
Spike Lee riffs on racial tensions in Brooklyn's Bedford-Stuyvesant neighborhood.

When Harry Met Sally, 1989
The city looks fantastic in this romantic comedy about friendship and love, with Meg Ryan and Billy Crystal.

Basquiat, 1996
A film by Julian Schnabel about Brooklyn-born graffiti artist Jean-Michel Basquiat, who made a big splash in the Downtown art scene of the 1980s. Jeffrey Wright plays Basquiat; David Bowie plays his mentor, Andy Warhol.

World Trade Center, 2006
The first Hollywood film about the 2001 World Trade Center attack focuses on two Port Authority cops trapped beneath the rubble.

Nick and Norah's Infinite Playlist, 2008
A coming-of-age romantic comedy in the world of indie rock which takes place in one evening mostly in the Lower East Side and East Village.

Sex and the City: The Movie, 2008
The much-loved TV series back for a film treatment with New York as the real star.

Film Festivals

Havana Film Festival New York
Tel: 212-687-2146; www.hffny.com; dates: Apr
Feature films, documentaries, shorts, and animation by Latin American filmmakers, shown at various venues.

The **Museum of the Moving Image** in Astoria, Queens, presents numerous film series throughout the year, as well as events with filmmakers, actors, and authors, and screenings of classic movie serials. *See Museums, p.105.*

Midnight Cowboy, 1969
Dustin Hoffman and Jon Voight are down-on-their-luck hustlers in this vivid evocation of 1960s street life.

The French Connection, 1971
A riveting performance by Gene Hackman as cop Popeye Doyle, and the daddy of all New York car chases.

The Godfather I and II, 1972 and 1974
Francis Ford Coppola's Mafia epics chronicle the fortunes of the Corleone family, and create a whole mythology of immigrant/underworld life.

Dog Day Afternoon, 1975
Al Pacino is a crazed bank robber who needs money for his boy/girlfriend's sex change operation in Sidney Lumet's film about a Brooklyn bank job gone bad.

Taxi Driver, 1976
Martin Scorsese directs Robert De Niro as a psychotic cabbie who tries to save a child prostitute played by Jodie Foster.

Saturday Night Fever, 1977
John Travolta is a dancing fool in this portrait of the 1970s suburban disco scene, with music by the Bee Gees that just stays in your head.

Manhattan, 1978
Woody Allen's ode to his hometown and his own neuroses is shot in black and white and stars Allen, Diane Keaton, Meryl Streep, and a young Mariel Hemingway.

Escape from New York, 1981
Imagine the whole of Manhattan is a high-security prison. Now imagine the US president has been taken hostage by the inmates. That's the premise of this over-the-top sci-fi action flick starring Kurt Russell.

Wall Street, 1987
'Greed is good,' declares Michael Douglas in this Oliver Stone film, neatly summing up the excesses of the go-go 1980s.

Human Rights Watch International Film Festival

Tel: 212-216-1264; http://hrw.org/iff; dates: June
The Walter Reade Theater at Lincoln Center is the host for this program of feature films, documentaries, and shorts, related to human rights issues.

New Directors/New Films

Tel: 212-875-5600; www.filmlinc.com; dates: Mar/Apr
For over years this festival, a collaboration between the Film Society of Lincoln Center and the Museum of Modern Art, has featured the work of emerging filmmakers.

NewFest

Tel: 718-923-1950; www.newfest.org; dates: June
New York's lesbian, gay, bisexual, and transgender film-fest, which presents a worldwide mix of LGBT-related films and other events in the first half of June. Most screenings are at AMC Loews 34th Street *(see right)*.

New York African Film Festival

Tel: 212-352-1720; www.african filmny.org; dates: usually Apr
Films from across Africa, and discussions on related themes, at Lincoln Center and the Brooklyn Academy of Music. Each summer it organizes free outdoor screenings in parks in Harlem, Queens, and Brooklyn.

New York Film Festival

Lincoln Center; tel: 212-875-5610; www.filmlinc.com; dates: late Sept–Oct
The Film Society of Lincoln Center presents this prestigious festival, showcasing

> To find out what's on at the movies in New York at any time, check the listings in daily papers (especially Friday and Sunday's *New York Times*), and the weekly *New York* magazine.

Above: shooting outside the Tribeca Film Center: New York plays a role in over 250 movie productions every year.

new films by American and international directors. The event runs for 17 days.

New York International Children's Film Festival

Tel: 212-349-0330; www.gkids. com; dates: usually Mar
Largest festival for children and teens in North America. Features animated, live action and experimental shorts for ages 3–18.

New York International Latino Film Festival

Tel: 646-723-1428; www.ny latinofilm.com; dates: late July
Emerging and established Latino filmmakers screen their work at this July event, which includes Cinema under the Stars screenings at Thomas Jefferson Park (First Avenue and East 112th Street).

TriBeCa Film Festival

Tel: 212-941-2400; www.tribecafilm.com; dates: late Apr–early May
Robert De Niro and his team launched this festival in 2002 to help reinvigorate the neighborhood after 9/11. Now it's one of the industry's biggest events, with premieres of Hollywood, indie, and international films. Discussions, live music, outdoor screenings, a sports film section and a family festival round out the program.

Movie Theaters

MIDTOWN

AMC Empire 25

234 West 42nd Street/Seventh and Eighth avenues; tel: 212-398-3939; map p.152 C3
A mammoth multiplex with stadium-style seating and the latest sound technology.

AMC Loews 34th Street 14

312 West 34th Street/Eighth Avenue; tel: 212-244-4556; map p.152 B3
State-of-the-art multiplex near Times Square, which is also a venue for NewFest *(see left)*.

Clearview Ziegfeld

141 West 54th Street/Sixth and Seventh avenues; tel: 212-307-1862; map p.150 C1
A grand theater on the site of the old Ziegfeld Follies.

Paris Theatre

4 West 58th Street/Fifth Avenue; tel: 212-688-3800; map p.151 D1
Film aficionados enjoy a dash of style at this older theater, a favorite for catching international and independent cinema, new films, and revivals.

UPTOWN

AMC Loews Lincoln Square 13 with IMAX

1998 Broadway/West 68th Street; tel: 212-336-5020; map p.150 C3
This modern theater has design touches reminiscent

of old-style movie palaces, plus a giant IMAX screen.

Clearview First & 62nd
400 East 62nd Street/First Avenue; tel: 212-752-0694; map p.151 E1
Mainstream fare, plus a few foreign or indie pictures.

IMAX Theatre – American Museum of Natural History
Central Park West/West 79th Street; tel: 212-769-5200; map p.151 C4
Spectacular large-format films: *Dinosaurs Alive!* is the main picture.

Lincoln Plaza Cinemas
1886 Broadway/West 62nd and 63rd streets; tel: 212-757-2280; map p.150 C2
A tasteful, varied mix of high-quality indie and international films. In intermissions you can enjoy carefully chosen music and superior snacks.

Walter Reade Theater, Lincoln Center
70 Lincoln Center Plaza, at West 65th Street/Amsterdam Avenue; tel: 212-875-5600; map p.150 B3
This is the way films ought to be viewed, in a spacious theater with big screen and state-of-the-art sound. Programs run the gamut of world cinema, and it hosts the New York Film Festival *(see p.88)*.

CHELSEA TO GRAMERCY
Clearview Chelsea
260 West 23rd Street/Eighth Avenue; tel: 212-691-5519; map p.152 B1
Eclectic mix of mainstream and more challenging fare.

GREENWICH VILLAGE
Angelika Film Center
18 West Houston Street/Mercer Street; tel: 212-995-2000; map p.154 B2
Popular arthouse with six snug underground theaters.

Cinema Village
22 East 12th Street/University Place and Fifth Avenue; tel: 212-924-3363; map p.154 C3

Foreign and American indie films are the specialties at this renovated movie house.

Film Forum
209 West Houston Street/Sixth and Seventh avenues; tel: 212-727-8110; map p.154 B2
Short on comfort but long on taste, this arthouse features an intriguing selection of foreign, indie, and cult classics.

IFC Center
323 Sixth Avenue/West 3rd Street; tel: 212-924-7771; map p.154 B3
A modern arthouse within a venerable theater, with varied programs and a great café.

EAST VILLAGE TO CHINATOWN
Anthology Film Archives
32 Second Avenue/East 2nd Street; tel: 212-505-5181; map p.155 C2
Film buffs will find plenty of alternative fare at this theater, run by serious cinephiles.

Landmark's Sunshine Cinema
143 East Houston Street/Forsyth and Eldridge streets; tel: 212-330-8182; map p.155 C1
In a gracious building that once housed a Yiddish theater, this new-style arthouse has all the bells, whistles, and comforts of a multiplex.

Village East Cinema
181–189 Second Avenue/East

12th Street; tel: 212-529-6799; map p.155 D2
A former Yiddish theater built in 1926. Now restored, it is has seven screens, including the main auditorium with stadium and balcony seating, and remains one of best places in city to watch a movie.

SOHO AND TRIBECA
Tribeca Cinemas
54 Varick Street/Laight Street; tel: 212-941-2001; map p.154 A1
Part of Robert De Niro's Tribeca Film Center, this venue doesn't have regular programming but hosts the TriBeCa Film Festival *(see p.88)* and a range of other film series through the year, as well as (usually invitation-only) movie-biz events.

BROOKLYN
BAM Rose Cinemas
30 Lafayette Avenue/Ashland Place and St Felix Street, Brooklyn; tel: 718-636-4100
A classy four-screen complex showing arthouse fare as well as new independent and foreign films.

Brooklyn Heights Cinemas I & II
70 Henry Street/Orange Street; tel: 718-596-7070
A small but comfortable independent movie house with a loyal neighborhood following.

Below: no more broken-down seats: Landmark's Sunshine offers East Village movie buffs an all-new level of comfort.

Museums

So you want to do New York's museums? You'll have no lack of choices. The tendency among most travelers is to make a beeline to one of the Big Five – the Met, the MoMA, the Guggenheim, the Whitney, and the American Museum of Natural History – but even this leaves you with more options than you could possibly manage in a single visit. And what of the dozens of lesser-known museums, most of which, if located in a smaller city, would be star attractions in their own right? Some are world-class institutions; others no more than a snug gallery or two. *See also Galleries, p.64–7.*

Midtown

American Folk Art Museum

45 West 53rd Street; tel: 212-265-1040; www.folkart museum.org; Tue–Sun 10.30am–5.30pm, Fri to 7.30pm; entrance charge; subway: 49th St; map p.153 D4

Traditional work and that of contemporary self-taught artists are the mainstays of this museum, which features so-called primitive work by vernacular artists. The collection includes a great variety of objects, ranging from rare Shaker needlework to paintings and visionary sculpture by untrained artists. The museum holds a year-round series of special exhibitions, lectures, symposia and performances by folk musicians and storytellers.

International Center of Photography

1133 Sixth Avenue/West 43rd Street; tel: 212-857-0000; www.icp.org; Tue–Thur 10am–6pm, Fri 10am–8pm, Sat–Sun 10am–6pm; entrance charge; subway: 42nd St; map p.153 C3

ICP had its genesis more than a quarter of a century ago,

Above: the Morgan features some notable Old Masters.

when *Life* magazine photographer Cornell Capa created a repository for images captured by his brother, celebrated photojournalist Robert Capa, killed by a landmine in Indochina in 1954. Since then, the center has amassed some of the finest work of scores of photojournalists and art photographers. It is the city's only museum dedicated to photography and is the largest photo museum and photography school in the world.

Intrepid Sea, Air, & Space Museum

Pier 86/West 46th Street and Twelfth Avenue; tel: 212-245-0072; www.intrepidmuseum.org; Tue–Sun 10am–5pm, Apr–Sept 30: Mon–Fri 10am–5pm, Sat–Sun 10am–6pm; entrance charge; subway: 42nd St/Port Authority; map p.150 A1

The USS *Intrepid* was rescued from the junkyard in 1976. Having served the nation in war and peace for nearly three decades, the aircraft carrier was born again as a floating museum anchored on the Hudson River. It was launched on its new mission in 1982, when patriotic visitors came to stand atop her 900ft (270m) long flight deck and try to imagine what it was like when bomb-laden Navy planes took off for the skies of Tokyo. Another attraction was the bridge, where officers once steered a course and looked for trouble. On the hangar deck is a range of exhibits showcasing aircraft, military, and scientific equipment.

Morgan Library

225 Madison Avenue/East 36th Street; tel: 212-685-0008; www.themorgan.org; Tue–Thur 10.30am–5pm, Fri 10.30am–9pm, Sat 10am–6pm, Sun 11am–6pm; entrance charge;

Left: MoMA's renovation set the New York art world alight.

in clay, glass, wood, metal, and fiber. Open Studios: Artists at Work on the 6th floor allows visitors a behind-the-scenes view of the artistic practice.

Museum of Modern Art

11 West 53rd Street/Fifth and Sixth avenues; tel: 212-708-9400; www.moma.org; Wed–Sun 10.30am–5.30pm, Fri 10.30am–8pm; entrance charge; subway: 53rd St/Fifth Ave; map p.153 D4

You know what you are getting by virtue of the name, but what you are not prepared for is the size, with 150,000 or so objects in the collection, now displayed in a fully renovated and expanded facility. The breadth of the museum's collection is impressive, with offerings of Cubism, Surrealism, Abstract Expressionism, and all the labeled and unlabeled movements of Modernist design. And besides all the paintings and sculpture are hundreds of drawings, photos, and films, and a wide range of distinctive objects ranging from sewing machines to cups and saucers.

Entrance Charges

Visitors will find that pretty much everywhere and every attraction in New York charges an entrance fee. Some of these are surprisingly expensive, especially the major galleries: MoMA and the Met are $20 each; the Guggenheim is $18; and the Whitney and the American Museum of Natural History are $15 apiece.

---

comprehensively renovated and given a new 'campus' by brilliant Italian architect Renzo Piano.

Museum of Arts and Design

2 Columbus Circle; tel: 212-299-7777; www.madmuseum.org; Wed–Sun 11am–6pm, Thur to 9pm; entrance charge; subway: 50th St/Rockefeller Center; map p.150 C1

Recently relocated to a new, larger home at Columbus Circle, the museum features arts, craft, and design work

subway: 33rd St; map p.153 D2

John Pierpont Morgan, the banker known for his railroad and steel empires, was a master collector whose tastes and vast wealth underlie the considerable resources of the Morgan Library. Morgan bought Chinese ceramics, medieval tapestries, and Near Eastern antiquities as well as paintings by the Old Masters. Turning to manuscripts and printed works, he acquired illuminated books of hours, a Gutenberg Bible, and letters by luminaries such as Jefferson, Washington, and Napoleon, and manuscripts by Dickens, Keats, and others. The Morgan has been

Below: Vincent van Gogh's *The Starry Night*, painted in 1889, is just one of the fabulous artworks in the Museum of Modern Art.

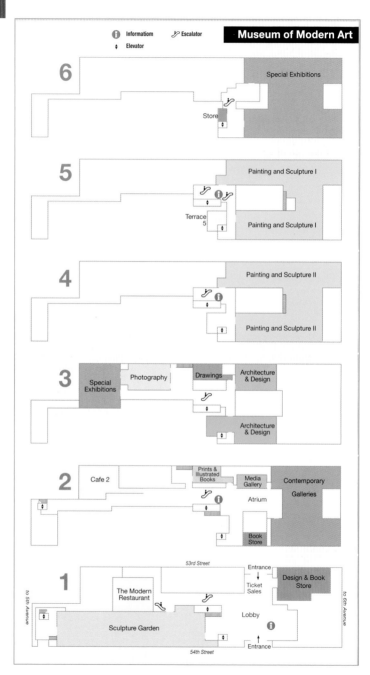

At the heart of the collection are some 3,500 paintings and sculptures dating to the 1880s, when rebellious artists began a process that favored abstraction over objective representation, setting new aesthetic standards even as their work was criticized as somehow dehumanizing, perverse, or plain ugly. The twists and turns in modern art's development are evident in the chronological arrangement of the works. The roster of modern masters is astounding – Van Gogh, Seurat, Cézanne, Gauguin, Monet, Picasso, Matisse, Dalí, Pollock, Wyeth, and countless others.

Museum of Sex
233 Fifth Avenue/27th Street; tel: 212-689-6337; www.museumofsex.com; Sun–Fri 11am–6.30pm, last tickets at 5.45pm, Sat 11am–8pm, last tickets at 7.15pm; entrance charge; subway: 28th St; map p.153 C1

This is a slightly surprising addition to Fifth Avenue; though perhaps not, given the country's uneasy mix of prudishness and a multi-billion-dollar porn industry.

The museum's aim is to 'present the history, evolution, and cultural significance of human sexuality,' in word and song, film and video, pictures and naughty postcards. Famous *femmes fatales* such as Blaze Starr, Gypsy Rose Lee, Linda Lovelace, and Xavier Hollander get a mention.

Men are included, too, like the straying preacher-man Henry Ward Beecher, the anti-vice crusader Anthony Comstock, and the master 'cheesecake' illustrator Alberto Vargas. The permanent collection displays whips, stag films, and other things devoted to explicating

America's fondness for porn. Included in the focus are such social developments as the porn industry, the Playboy 'mystique,' the Stonewall uprising of 1969 that gave rise to the gay-pride movement, and the emergence of Aids.

Paley Center for Media
25 West 52nd Street/Fifth and Sixth avenues; tel: 212-621-6800; www.paleycenter.org; Tue–Sun noon–6pm, Thur noon–8pm; entrance charge; subway: 50th St/Rockefeller Center; map p.153 D4

The museum was established by the legendary William S. Paley, longtime CBS chairman, who began collecting tapes of radio and television programs in 1975. The archive has grown enormously since Paley's death in 1990 (it now encompasses more than 140,000 programs), and the mission has been broadened to include more talks and workshops related to media. Visitors entering the museum can reserve a viewing or listening

One of MoMA's unexpected pleasures is the industrial design collection. Exhibits range from vacuum cleaners, tea kettles and ball bearings to a Cistalia 202 GT sports car and a Bell & Howell helicopter. You'll never look at an ordinary object the same way again.

console, then search the computer database for the TV or radio show of their choice. Programs are also presented several days of the week in screening rooms and theaters.

Uptown

American Museum of Natural History
Central Park West/79th Street; tel: 212-769-5100; www.amnh.org; daily 10am–5.45pm; entrance charge; subway: 81st St; map p.151 D4

The facade of this 23-building complex may look forbidding, but the enormous exhibition space inside is devoted to an impressive series of exhibits on natural

Below: the Museum of Modern Art's newest gallery was designed by Japanese architect Yoshio Taniguchi.

history, anthropology, and paleontology. It's ideal for children: there are dinosaur and whale skeletons; the gem collection contains the largest cut sapphire in the world (the Star of India); the Hall of South American Peoples contains shrunken heads and blowpipes; and the IMAX Theater has a screen four stories high.

If you have time to see only one thing, head directly to the fourth floor, where you'll find the world's largest exhibition of dinosaur fossils. A major overhaul in the late 1990s led to the repositioning of several skeletons, reflecting the view that the great beasts were agile, possibly warm-blooded creatures instead of the ponderous, tail-dragging behemoths envisioned by early paleontologists.

Next door, the dazzling Rose Center for Earth and Space includes the Hayden Planetarium, which features a four-story sphere housing a high-tech star projector.

SEE ALSO CHILDREN, P.43

> The Food Court at the American Museum of Natural History is several cuts above typical museum cafeterias, with fresh salads, grilled specialties, stone-oven pizza and an appealing choice of cakes and pastries.

Asia Society

725 Park Avenue/70th Street; tel: 212-288-6400; www.asiasociety.com; Tue–Sun 11am–6pm, Fri to 9pm; entrance charge; subway: 68th St at Hunter College; map p.151 E2

The Society came into being in 1956 thanks to John D. Rockefeller III. Enamored with life in East Asia after traveling there, he wanted a center to facilitate cultural exchange between the US and Asia. Art exhibitions have been held here ever since, many showcasing Rockefeller's own collection. Gallery space features a glass-enclosed garden court that floods the lobby with natural light. Digital signage and touch screens allow visitors to explore Asian art and culture interactively.

Children's Museum of Manhattan

The Tisch Building, 212 West 83rd Street/Broadway and Amsterdam Avenue; tel: 212-721-1234; www.cmom.org; Tue–Sun 10am–5pm; entrance charge; subway: 79th St

The museum is a wonderama tailored for youngsters, but adults can learn a thing or two as well.

Cooper-Hewitt National Design Museum

2 East 91st Street/Fifth Avenue; tel: 212-849-8400; www.cooperhewitt.org; Mon–Fri 10am–5pm, Sat 10am–6pm, Sun noon–6pm; entrance charge; subway: 86th St

Housed in Andrew Carnegie's East Side mansion, this branch of the Smithsonian Institution showcases centuries of achievement in the art of design. The museum has collections of decorative and applied arts and industrial design, fulfilling its original mission as a 'visual library' of the history of style.

El Museo del Barrio

1230 Fifth Avenue/East 104th Street; tel: 212-831-7272; www.elmuseo.org; temporarily

Below: the stately facade of the AMNH.

Below: kids of all ages love the dinosaurs at the American Museum of Natural History.

closed for final stage of renovation; entrance charge; subway: 103rd St

The art and culture of Puerto Rico, Latin America, and the Caribbean are brought to life with a series of exhibitions and special events. Exploring the fusion of cultures that took place following the Spanish conquest, selections from the permanent collection focus on folkloric and religious artifacts. Secular artwork traces the movement of Latinos to the urban centers of North America. Paintings, prints, sculptures, and photographs round out the museum's holdings. El Museo mounts at least four special exhibitions each year, highlighting artists and artistic movements in the Latino communities of the metropolitan area. Festivals are held throughout the year.

The Frick Collection
1 East 70th Street; tel: 212-288-0700; www.frick.org; Tue–Sat 10am–6pm, Sun 11am–5pm; entrance charge; subway: 68th St Hunter College; map p.151 D2
Steel magnate Henry Clay Frick built his mansion around a spectacular collection of art dating from the Renaissance through to the late 19th century. Intended from the beginning as a legacy to future generations, it remains one of the world's finest testaments to a connoisseur's vision. The collection focuses on European paintings (including three Vermeers) and furnishings, and represents one of the city's most successful combinations of art and environment. The ambience is one of quiet gentility. Leave plenty of time for the central courtyard, a soothing respite from the city streets.

Jewish Museum
1109 Fifth Avenue/East 92nd Street; tel: 212-423-3200;

Above: the Rose Center for Earth and Space in the American Museum of Natural History.

www.jewishmuseum.org; Sat–Wed 11am–5.45pm, Thur 11am–8pm; entrance charge; subway: 86th St
This fine old French Renaissance mansion was built around 1908 for banker-philanthropist Felix Warburg. The designer of this New York landmark was Charles Gilbert, son of the even more renowned architect Cass Gilbert, and inside is one of the world's greatest collections of Judaica – art, artifacts, and antiques that tell the story of Jewish persistence in an age-old struggle for survival. The centerpiece of the collection is an exhibition entitled 'Culture and Continuity: The Jewish Journey' that illuminates cultural history extending back more than 4,000 years and points up a people's resilience in the face of oppression.

Metropolitan Museum of Art
1000 Fifth Avenue/East 82nd Street; tel: 212-535-7710; www.metmuseum.org; Fri–Sat 9.30am–9pm, Sun, Tue–Thur 9.30am–5.30pm; entrance charge; subway: 86th St; map p.151 E4

This wonderful museum is a labyrinth of corridors and galleries crammed with paintings and sculpture, furniture and textiles, knights' armor and rare violins, and all manner of precious objects.

The Met, as New Yorkers call the museum, accommodates under one roof an encyclopedic collection of cultural history. An errant step in this warehouse of art can take the unsuspecting visitor from a 5,000-year-old relic of Iranian pottery to a modern manifesto of in-your-face Abstract Expressionism – say, perhaps, Jackson Pollock's paint-splattered *Autumn Rhythm* of 1950.

There are 3 million objects, more or less, only a fraction of which can be shown at any one time. Visitors should consult floor plans, decide on their list of most-favored art, and be prepared to devote a full day for appreciation. Some genres are especially popular, like the relics of ancient Egypt, the famous European paintings, medieval arms and armor, and 60,000 articles of

95

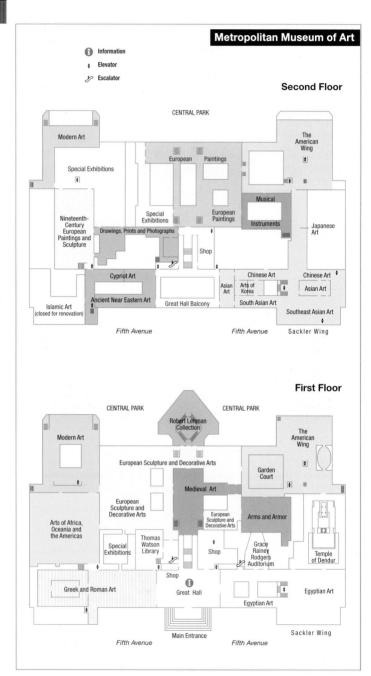

Metropolitan Museum of Art

- Information
- Elevator
- Escalator

Second Floor

CENTRAL PARK

Modern Art

Special Exhibitions

Nineteenth-Century European Paintings and Sculpture

European Paintings

Special Exhibitions

Drawings, Prints and Photographs

European Paintings

Musical Instruments

The American Wing

Japanese Art

Shop

Cypriot Art

Islamic Art (closed for renovation)

Ancient Near Eastern Art

Great Hall Balcony

Asian Art

Arts of Korea

Chinese Art

South Asian Art

Chinese Art

Asian Art

Southeast Asian Art

Fifth Avenue

Fifth Avenue

Sackler Wing

First Floor

CENTRAL PARK

CENTRAL PARK

Robert Lehman Collection

Modern Art

European Sculpture and Decorative Arts

Medieval Art

European Sculpture and Decorative Arts

European Sculpture and Decorative Arts

Garden Court

The American Wing

Arts of Africa, Oceania and the Americas

Special Exhibitions

Thomas Watson Library

European Sculpture and Decorative Arts

Arms and Armor

Shop

Grace Rainey Rodgers Auditorium

Temple of Dendur

Greek and Roman Art

Shop

Great Hall

Egyptian Art

Egyptian Art

Fifth Avenue

Main Entrance

Fifth Avenue

Sackler Wing

garb and costumes that include everything from tribal headgear to haute couture. Be sure to visit the newly renovated Greek and Roman galleries.

Mount Vernon Hotel Museum
421 East 61st Street/First and York avenues; tel: 212-838-6878; www.mvhm.org; Tue–Sun 11am–4pm; entrance charge; subway: 59th St

This stone hotel was originally constructed in 1799 as a carriage house on the estate of Colonel William Stephen Smith and his wife Abigail Adams Smith, daughter of President John Adams. Later converted into a 'day hotel,' it is now furnished with more than 1,000 works of art and decorative objects from the early 19th century.

Museum of the City of New York
1220 Fifth Avenue/East 103rd Street; tel: 212-534-1672; www.mcny.org; Tue–Sun 10am–5pm; entrance charge; subway: 103rd St

The museum chronicles the story of New York from Dutch colonial times to the present. The collection encompasses more than 1½ million artifacts and artworks related to the city's ever-changing character and phenomenal growth, including historic paintings, vintage firefighting equipment, antique toys, and much more.

> The Met's holdings of ancient Egyptian artifacts are as comprehensive as any museum outside Cairo. The collection encompasses some 36,000 objects from Dynastic and Pre-Dynastic times, including the famous Temple of Dendur, housed in a glass-sided wing overlooking Central Park.

Above: inside the Metropolitan Museum's elegant walls are close to 3 million exhibits and objects.

National Academy Museum
1083 Fifth Avenue/East 89th Street; tel: 212-369-4880; www.nationalacademy.org; Wed–Thur noon–5pm, Fri–Sun 11am–6pm; entrance charge; subway: Lexington Ave; map p.151 E4

The National Academy has a golden history, a majestic setting, and a quiet devotion to resurrecting the work of important artists. The Academy was established in 1825 and has been described by art critic Robert Hughes as 'the most powerful taste-forming body of the American Renaissance.' The country's oldest artist-run organization upholds a quaint custom: members – including, over the decades, such notable figures as Frederic East Church, Winslow Homer, John Singer Sargent, Robert Henri, and Jasper Johns – are required to submit a self-portrait and a representative example of their work, a tradition that fortifies the Academy's collection of 2,200 paintings, 240 sculptures, and 5,000 works on paper.

Neue Galerie
1048 Fifth Avenue/East 86th Street; tel: 212-628-6200; www.neuegalerie.org; Thur–Mon 11am–6pm; entrance charge; subway: 86th St; map p.151 E4

There was a Neue Galerie in Vienna in the 1920s devoted to German and Austrian art, and now there's one in New York. The credit goes to Ron Lauder, the son of Estée Lauder and heir to her cosmetics fortune. He's also a former ambassador to Austria and a collector long interested in German-Austrian art, and he has deep pockets to indulge his desire for art and decorative objects. The fine things in this collection are quite at home at its swanky address; the mansion, erected 1912–14, is the work of Carrère & Hastings, the same firm that gave us the grandly elegant New York Public Library.
SEE ALSO CAFÉS, P.38

New York Historical Society
170 Central Park West/West 76th and 77th streets; tel: 212-873-3400; www.nyhistory.org; Tue–Sat 10am–6pm, Fri to 8pm, Sun 11am–5.45pm; entrance charge; subway: 81st St; map p.151 C4

This stately building contains a treasure trove of Americana, much of it very odd – an illustrious wooden leg, a mesmerizing death mask, a ceramic cockroach

97

Since 1932, the Whitney has mounted a major series of exhibitions held every other year and called, appropriately, the Biennial. An invitational show, the Biennial is dedicated to the most provocative American work of the previous two years – 'a mirror of our culture and of who we are now,' as its curators attest.

trap. Visitors explore history through a collection of 40,000 objects, including galleries of rare 18th- and 19th-century paintings.

Solomon R. Guggenheim Museum

1071 Fifth Avenue/East 89th Street; tel: 212-423-3500; www.guggenheim.org; Sat–Wed 10am–5.45pm, Fri 10am–7.45pm; entrance charge; subway: 86th St; map p.151 E4

The Guggenheim's prominence is due in no small measure to Frank Lloyd Wright, America's most renowned architect. He was asked in 1943 by mining magnate Solomon R. Guggenheim to design a place where Guggenheim could show off his collection of paintings. It was Wright's only New York commission. His final blueprint called for a concrete structure that reminded people of everything from a corkscrew to a marshmallow.

At the core of the collection are the works of some of the leading artists since Modernism reared its head in the latter part of the 19th century. Many were associated with movements such as Expressionism, Cubism, and the trend toward abstraction – such painters as Klee, Kandinsky, Mon-

drian, Modigliani, Léger, Picasso, Pollock, and others.

Whitney Museum of American Art

945 Madison Avenue/75th Street; tel: 212-570-3600; www.whitney.org; Wed–Thur 11am–6pm, Fri 1–9pm, Sat–Sun 11am–6pm; entrance charge; subway: 77th St; map p.151 E3

Strong in both historical and contemporary trends, the Whitney is regarded as holding the world's finest collection of 20th-century American art. The museum building is a work of art in its own right. Cloaked in gray granite, its sleek bulk arranged in progressively overhanging masses, the building showcases the fact that in his youth, architect Marcel Breuer was apprenticed to the Bauhaus school.

The collection was founded in 1931 by Gertrude Vanderbilt Whitney, whose taste tended toward American realists like Edward Hopper (whose widow,

Josephine, donated 2,500 paintings, watercolors, drawings, and prints in 1970) and George Bellows. Since then, the museum's policy has been to acquire pieces that represent the range of 20th- and 21st-century American art, including important works by Georgia O'Keeffe, Willem de Kooning, Jackson Pollock, and Jasper Johns.

Harlem and Beyond

The Cloisters

Fort Tryon Park; tel: 212-923-3700; www.metmuseum.org; Mar–Oct: Tue–Sun 9.30am–5.15pm, Nov–Feb: Tue–Sun 9.30am–4.45pm; entrance charge; subway: 190th St

If the city's frenetic pace is getting on your nerves, take a trip to this branch of the Metropolitan Museum of Art, devoted to medieval art and architecture. The exhibits are integrated into the building, much of it reconstructed from fragments of 12th-century monasteries. The result is an enchanting

Right: the spiral ramp inside the Guggenheim Museum.

composite of old and new that recreates the atmosphere of a medieval cloister. Serene and fascinating, it's about as far away from Manhattan as you can get without leaving the island. Built by John D. Rockefeller, Jr, the structure rises like a castle from a hilltop overlooking the Hudson River.

The exhibits are laid out in roughly chronological order, including outdoor cloisters and two chapels with 12th-century frescoes. The museum's most famous possessions are the 15th-century Unicorn Tapestries, which were woven in Brussels. The brilliant colors in the seven tapestries are derived from only three dye plants, and depict the hunt of the mythological unicorn, whose capture, death, and restoration many think represents the incarnation, death, and resurrection of Jesus Christ.

The Cloisters is situated in Fort Tryon Park, a green and

Above: The Cloisters is partly assembled from older structures.

Above: this branch of the Met Museum is serene and secluded.

tranquil area that once played an important role in the American Revolution. It was from near here that George Washington and his troops made a retreat that placed the city of New York in British hands for the rest of the Revolutionary War.

Hispanic Society of America

Audubon Terrace, 613 West 155th Street/Broadway; tel: 212-926-2234; www.hispanic society.org; Sept–July: Tue–Sat 10am–4.30pm, Sun 1–4pm; free; subway: 157th S

The museum is dedicated to the classic art and literature of Spain and Portugal. The collection features works by some of the immortal names of Spanish painting – most notably El Greco, Velázquez, and Goya.

Studio Museum in Harlem

144 West 125th Street/Lenox and Seventh avenues; tel: 212-864-4500; www.studio museum.org; Wed–Fri noon–6pm, Sat 10am–6pm, Sun noon–6pm; suggested donation; subway: 125th St

The museum presents a wide range of African-American and African art, but its strongest exhibitions are devoted to contemporary work. Topics cover broad

themes, ranging from explorations of cultural identity, racism, and gender roles to the re-evaluation of black artists whose work has been overlooked by critics.

Chelsea to Gramercy

Chelsea Art Museum

556 West 22nd Street/11th Avenue; tel: 212-255-0719; chelseaartmuseum.org; Tue–Sat 11am–6pm, Thur to 8pm; entrance charge; subway: 23rd St; map p.152 A2

An international roster of emerging and established artists show their work at this landmark building near the Hudson waterfront.

Rubin Museum of Art

150 West 17th Street/Sixth and Seventh avenues; tel: 212-620-5000; www.rmanyc.org; Mon 11am–5pm, Wed 11am–7pm, Thur 11am–5pm, Fri 11am–10pm, Sat–Sun 11am–6pm; entrance charge; subway: 14th St; map: p.154 B4

Himalayan art is the focus of this museum, which has a collection of paintings, sculptures, and textiles dating back some 2,000 years.

Greenwich Village

Forbes Magazine Galleries

62 Fifth Avenue/West 12th

Street; tel: 212-206-5548; www.forbesgalleries.com; Tue–Wed, Fri–Sat 10am–4pm; free; subway: 14th St; map p.154 C3

This collection reflects the broad range of interests of the late publisher Malcolm S. Forbes. Although known as an avid balloonist, biker, and party-giver, Forbes was also an inveterate collector. His most celebrated acquisitions are the bejeweled eggs created by Peter Carl Fabergé for the last three Romanov czars. Two galleries are devoted to over 4,000 items written by US presidents. Toy soldiers were another Forbes passion; some 10,000 are arrayed in historical battle scenes. The eclectic borders on the eccentric in a pair of galleries devoted to the history of the board game Monopoly and to a collection of trophies honoring such peculiar achievements as victory in egg-laying and pie-eating contests. There is also a room devoted to the firm's treasury of 19th-century paintings.

East Village to Chinatown

Lower East Side Tenement Museum
108 Orchard Street/Delancey Street; tel: 212-982-8420; www.tenement.org; daily 11am–5pm; entrance charge; subway: Delancey St; map p.157 D4

Around the turn of the 20th century, the Lower East Side was the most densely populated place in the world, with nearly 1/2 million people per sq mile (181,000 per sq km). The Orchard Street block where this former apartment building stands had more than 2,300 inhabitants. Over a span of seven decades, this one building housed more than 7,000 people from some 20 countries. Closed in 1935, the apartments stood empty for more than 50 years, their interiors left as an inadvertent time capsule. Then, in 1989, a group of New Yorkers intent on creating an immigrant memorial selected 97 Orchard Street as the focus for a museum. Guides recount stories culled from the lives of for-

In the Lower East Side Tenement Museum's 'ruin apartment,' time stands still, frozen at the moment when the last tenants moved out and the apartment was sealed. Plaster lies where it fell from the cracked ceiling, and smudged walls still bear the inventory notations left by garment workers when the space was used for storage.

mer residents and escort visitors through the apartments, some of which are furnished.

Merchant's House Museum
29 East 4th Street/Lafayette Street; tel: 212-777-1089; www.merchantshouse.com; Thur–Mon noon–5pm; entrance charge; subway: 8th St; map p.155 C2

In 1835, wealthy merchant Seabury Tredwell moved with his family into a row house in an upscale 'suburb' to the north of Lower Manhattan. The house remained in the Tredwell family until the 1930s, when it opened as a museum. Seven rooms and the Tredwell's 'secret' garden serve as a time capsule of upper-class life in the 19th and early 20th centuries.

Museum of the Chinese in America
211–215 Center Street/Canal Street; tel: 212-619-4785; www.moca-nyc.org; Mon 11am–5pm, Thur 11am–9pm, Fri 11am–5pm, Sat–Sun 10am–5pm; entrance charge; subway: Canal St; map p.156 C4

Major expansion brings a new home by architect Maya Lin. The museum explores and preserves the experience of people of Chinese descent in the United States.

New Museum
235 Bowery; tel: 212-219-1222; www.newmuseum.org; Wed

Below: moccasins from dozens of tribes form an exhibit at the National Museum of the American Indian (*see p.102*).

Above: the Ellis Island Immigration Museum *(see p.103).*

Drawing on an archive of some 10,000 artifacts and documents, the museum focuses on the rise of capital markets in New York and the nation since the days when securities were traded under a buttonwood tree by the founders of the New York Stock Exchange.

Museum of Jewish Heritage

36 Battery Place; tel: 646-437-4200; www.mjhnyc.org; Sun–Thur 10am–5.45pm, Wed to 8pm, Fri 10am–3pm, summer 10am–5pm; entrance charge; subway: Bowling Green; map p.156 A2

The museum opened its doors in 1997, close to the spot where Jews first set foot in North America in 1654. The three-level building has six sides to evoke the Star of David and honor the 6 million Jews who died in the Holocaust. Exhibits present the story of the Jewish people in the 20th century, weaving together themes of joy, tradition, and tragedy, and putting the

noon–6pm, Thur–Fri noon–9pm, Sat–Sun noon–6pm; entrance charge; subway: Bowery; map p.157 D4

A major force in contemporary art, with an emphasis on social commentary, technology, and global perspectives, the museum has opened this new facility on the Bowery. The building itself is a significant architectural contribution to the Downtown urban landscape.

SoHo and TriBeCa

Children's Museum of the Arts

182 Lafayette Street; tel: 212-274-0986; www.cmany.org; Wed–Sun noon–5pm, Thur noon–6pm; entrance charge; subway: Canal St; map p.156 C4

Brightly painted windows mark the entrance to a space that is part museum and part artist's studio. Here, children learn about the arts by becoming artists. Everything is built half-size. Parents may feel a bit cramped, but kids are instantly at home, scampering from one work space to another, plunging into fingerpaints, sculpting clay, collages, and costumes.

New York City Fire Museum

278 Spring Street; tel: 212-691-1303; www.nycfiremuseum.org;

Tue–Sat 10am–5pm, Sun 10am–4pm; suggested donation; subway: Spring St; map p.154 A2

An old firehouse contains a comprehensive collection of firefighting artifacts from the 18th century to the present, including a moving tribute to more than 300 New York City firefighters who died in the line of duty during the World Trade Center attack on September 11, 2001.

Lower Manhattan

Fraunces Tavern Museum

54 Pearl Street/Broad Street; tel: 212-425-1778; www.frauncestavernmuseum.org; Mon–Sat noon–5pm; entrance charge; subway: Whitehall St; map p.156 B1

George Washington ate here several times, but never more memorably than on December 4, 1783. Late on that morning he and his officers met in an upstairs room before the General headed south into retirement. Today the site is both a working tavern and a museum, with a collection of period furnishings.

Museum of American Finance

48 Wall Street; tel: 212-908-4110; www.moaf.org; Tue–Sat 10am–4pm; entrance charge; subway: Wall St; map p.156 B2

Below: the Merchant's House Museum in the East Village.

Holocaust into the context of Jewish history.

National Museum of the American Indian

One Bowling Green/Battery Park; tel: 212-514-3700; www.nmai.si.edu; daily 10am–5pm, Thur to 8pm; entrance free; subway: Bowling Green; map p.156 A1

Housed in a Beaux Arts temple designed by Cass Gilbert, this branch of the Smithsonian's Museum of the American Indian showcases highlights from a vast collection of Native art and artifacts, assembled by collector George Gustav Heye in the late 19th and early 20th centuries.

New York City Police Museum

100 Old Slip/FDR Drive; tel: 212-480-3100; www.nycpolicemuseum.org; Mon–Sat 10am–5pm; suggested donation; subway: Wall St; map p.156 B1

In a former precinct house, the collection draws from both sides of the law. Here are the tools of every variety of criminal trade, from switchblades and brass knuckles to an armory of illegal firepower. The 'good guys' portion of the collection includes examples of every style of NYPD badge as well

Right: the Statue of Liberty was a gift to America from France.

as uniforms worn by officers since the 1870s. A Hall of Heroes honors those killed in the line of duty.

Skyscraper Museum

39 Battery Place; tel: 212-968-1961; www.skyscraper.org; Wed–Sun noon–6pm; entrance charge; subway: Bowling Green; map p.156 A2

Housed in an intriguing new gallery, the museum explores the history and technology behind the construction of high-rise buildings.

South Street Seaport Museum

12–14 Fulton Street; tel: 212-748-8600; www.southstreet seaportmuseum.org; daily 10am–6pm, Jan–Mar 10am–5pm; entrance charge; subway: Nassau St; map p.156 C2

Not a museum in the conventional sense, the Seaport is an 11-block historic district on the East River that was the country's busiest port in the mid-1800s. The advent of large steamships shifted sea traffic to the deeper waters of the Hudson River, and by the early 20th century South Street was in decline. A restoration campaign in the late 1960s saved it from high-rise development.

The old ships tied up at Piers 15 and 16 are the main attraction. Nearby is the Pier 17 Pavilion, with stores, cafés, and a food court offering vistas of the Brooklyn Bridge. Also nearby is Schermerhorn Row, built in 1810–12 to house offices and warehouses.

Staten and Ellis Islands and the Statue of Liberty

Alice Austen House

2 Hylan Boulevard; tel: 718-816-4506; www.aliceausten.org; Thur–Sun, noon–5pm; suggested donation

'Clear Comfort' is the restored Victorian Gothic home and garden of Alice Austen, one of America's first female documentary photographers. Austen chose

Below: the South Street Seaport Museum in Lower Manhattan calls itself 'a museum without walls.'

Statue of Liberty

Liberty Island; tel: 212-363-3200; www.nps.gov/stli; ferry tickets: Castle Clinton, Battery Park; daily 9am–5pm, extended summer hours; free, but charge for ferry; subway; South Ferry; map p.156 A1

The Statue of Liberty was a gift to the United States from the people of France. It was conceived by a French admirer of American democracy named Edouard-René Lefèvre de Laboulaye, who conveyed his enthusiasm to the sculptor Frédéric-Auguste Bartholdi, who not only designed the monument, but raised 1 million francs – worth about $400,000 at the time – to fund the project.

Bartholdi began with a clay model of his statue, enlarging it in three stages until the copper segments of its outer surface were ready to be assembled. The iron frame was designed by Alexandre-Gustave Eiffel, the engineer who later created the Eiffel Tower. On July 4, 1884, the finished work was presented to the United States at a ceremony in Paris. It remained for the statue to be dismantled, shipped to New York, and reassembled. The US government had already

great age of American immigration in the late 19th and early 20th centuries. Today, it is a national monument and one of the city's most popular tourist destinations. The original immigration station, which was transformed into a 'museum of the melting pot' in 1990, tells the stories of the millions who passed through here on their way to new lives in the US. An estimated 40 percent of Americans have at least one ancestor who entered the country via Ellis Island.

Garibaldi-Meucci Museum

420 Tompkins Avenue; tel: 718-442-1608; www.garibaldi meuccimuseum.org; Tue–Fri 1–5pm, Sat–Sun noon–4pm; entrance charge

This historic home on Staten Island commemorates Antonio Meucci, who reputedly invented a telephone years before Alexander Graham Bell. Exhibits focus on his many inventions, as well as his friendship with Italian political crusader Giuseppe Garibaldi.

Jacques Marchais Museum of Tibetan Art

338 Lighthouse Avenue; tel: 718-987-3500; www.tibetan museum.org; Wed–Sun 1–5pm; entrance charge

Situated amid gardens on a Staten Island hillside is the country's only museum to display Tibetan art in an authentic setting. The museum is built in the style of a Tibetan *gompa*, or temple, and reflects its founder's lifelong enthusiasm for the art and culture of Tibet. Most of the collection is made up of devotional art, including sculptures of Buddhist deities, ritual masks, and figurines in metal and clay.

among her many subjects the immigrant community and other less genteel aspects of metropolitan life. Her house overlooking the Narrows at the entrance to New York Harbor recalls her roots in an older, more comfortable New York. Visitors can tour most rooms, including the formal parlor, Alice's bedroom, and the 18th-century dining room. Fifty of her photographs are on permanent display.

Ellis Island Immigration Museum

Ellis Island; tel: 212-363-3200; www.nps.gov/elis; ferry tickets: Castle Clinton, Battery Park; daily 9am–5.15pm, extended summer hours; free, but charge for ferry; subway: South Ferry

Ellis Island served as a gateway to the US during the

Below: the National Museum of the American Indian.

donated the island, which had outlived its military usefulness, but little had been done beyond laying the cornerstone for the massive pedestal, designed by Richard Morris Hunt. In what might be taken as indifference to France's monumental gift, fund-raising for the pedestal had slowed to a trickle.

To the rescue came a prominent New Yorker who was himself an immigrant. He was the owner and publisher of the *New York World*, Joseph Pulitzer, who raised more than $100,000 to put Liberty on her pedestal. The dedication was celebrated on October 28, 1886, and the monument soon became a major tourist attraction.

Now that exhibits pertaining to immigration history are concentrated at Ellis Island, the small museum here is devoted to the history of the monument itself. Located in the base, it displays photographs, plans, tools, and models that trace the construction of Bartholdi's project, and of the 1980s restoration.

Although the staircase to the crown is closed, visitors can instead take in the view from the 10th-story pedestal observatory. Free ranger-led tours of the statue and the island are offered several times a day. Check the schedule at the information center.

Brooklyn

Brooklyn Museum of Art
200 Eastern Parkway; tel: 718-638-5000; www.brooklyn museum.org; Wed–Fri 10am–5pm, Sat–Sun 11am–6pm; entrance charge; subway: Eastern Parkway/Brooklyn Museum
Second in size only to the Metropolitan, New York's 'other' great art museum

Above: the P.S. 1 Art Center in Queens is inside an old school house and is an affiliate of MoMA.

contains more than a million objects, representing cultures reaching back to ancient Egypt, Rome, and Greece. The Egyptian collection is one of the best in the world, and the collection of modern masters, including works by Degas, Toulouse-Lautrec, Gauguin, Matisse, Rodin, O'Keeffe, and others, is no slouch either. The ethnographic collection is impressive, as are period rooms tracing the development of American decorative arts.

New York Transit Museum
Corner of Boerum Place/Schermerhorn Street;
tel: 718-694-1600;
www.mta.info/mta/museum;
Tue–Fri 10am–4pm, Sat–Sun noon–5pm; entrance charge; subway: Borough Hall
In a 1930s subway station, the museum has exhibits

One expression of Isamu Noguchi's genius is his Akari lights, paper sculptures illuminated from within. Their abstract geometric designs recall traditional Japanese paper lanterns. Scaled-down versions of the lights are sold in the museum shop.

---

about the city's public transportation systems, with vintage subway cars and buses on display.

Queens

Isamu Noguchi Garden Museum
32–37 Vernon Boulevard, Long Island City; tel: 718-204-7088; www.noguchi.org; Wed–Fri 10am–5pm, Sat–Sun 11am–6pm; entrance charge; subway: Broadway (in Queens)
When Japanese-American sculptor Isamu Noguchi purchased an old photoengraving plant to use as a studio, he engineered one of his boldest studies in contrast. In this gritty neighborhood, Noguchi created both a practical work space and a superb environment.

Museum for African Art
www.africandart.org
The museum organizes off-site exhibitions throughout the city from its temporary office space in Queens. The museum plans to move into a new building on Fifth Avenue's Museum Mile in 2010.

Right: performance at Bronx Museum of Art.

Museum of the Moving Image

37th Street (near thirty-fifth Avenue), Astoria; tel: 718-784-4520; www.movingimage.us; Tue–Fri 10am–3pm; entrance charge; subway: Steinway

Occupying an old movie studio built in 1920, the museum houses 95,000 objects related to American film and television. It is a treasury of the material culture of the moving image – photos, cameras, projectors, and special-effects paraphernalia. The museum is undergoing major expansion and set to reopen in fall 2010 with two new theaters, where film and video screenings will be offered daily. During construction film screenings are being presented off-site.

P.S. 1 Contemporary Art Center

22–25 Jackson Avenue/Forty-Sixth Avenue, Long Island City; tel: 718-784-2084; www.ps1.org; Thur–Mon noon–6pm; suggested donation; subway: 23rd St/Ely Ave

Now an affiliate of the Museum of Modern Art, this building started out as Public School 1, a handsome Romanesque Revival struc-

ture for 2,000 students. P.S. 1 fell into disuse, and the school closed in 1963, only to be transformed into a contemporary art center with a reputation for cutting-edge art. Each summer, P.S. 1 hosts Warm Up, a critically-acclaimed and much anticipated music series.

Queens Museum of Art

New York City Building, Flushing Meadows-Corona Park; tel: 718-592-9700; www.queensmuseum.org; Tue–Fri 10am–5pm, Sat–Sun noon–5pm; suggested donation; subway: Mets-Willets Point

The Queens Museum of Art comes off as a bit of a hodgepodge. The largest galleries are devoted to changing exhibitions of contemporary art, but the museum is also dedicated to preserving the legacy of New York's two 20th-century World's Fairs. Housed in the only major structure remaining from the 1939 and 1964 World's Fairs (look for the enormous steel globe Unisphere in the front plaza) are artifacts and photographs that speak volumes about American culture at those times. Particularly instructive are notions about the future –

some remarkably prescient, others comically off-key.

As a special attraction for the 1964 World's Fair, Robert Moses – the 'master builder' and political dynamo whose public works transformed the city in the 1930s, '40s, and '50s – commissioned a scale model of New York City. The result is the Panorama of the City of New York, the world's largest architectural model, containing 895,000 individual structures. Another QMA highlight is a collection of glass by Louis Comfort Tiffany, manufactured at the Tiffany studio in Corona, Queens.

The Bronx

Bronx Museum of the Arts

1040 Grand Concourse; tel: 718-681-6000; www.bronxmuseum.org; Thur–Sun noon–6pm, Fri to 8pm; suggested entrance charge; subway: 167 St/Grand Concourse

Originally a synagogue, this museum is encased in a glass facade that perfectly suits its latter-day function as a showplace for contemporary and 20th-century work. A 2006 expansion has been well received by the public.

Music

How do you get to Carnegie Hall? You got it: practice, practice. A bit overdone? Actually, there's a hidden message here that often gets overlooked – New York is crawling with musical talent. You see them around town, polished pros and wannabe virtuosos, lugging drum sets down subway stairs or cramming bass fiddles into taxicabs en route to that next gig in the Big Apple. The sounds come in all flavors. Bach and blues. Jazz and symphony. Opera, grand and otherwise. Folk and heavy metal. Country and cajun and karaoke and you name it. For music stores, *see also Shopping, p.134–5.*

Classical and Opera Companies

Amato Opera Company
319 Bowery/East 2nd Street; tel: 212-228-8200; www.amato.org; main season Sept–June; subway: Bleecker St; map p.155 C2
A small Downtown theater is the venue for grand opera on a modest scale, featuring up-and-coming talent and often overlooked works.

Chamber Music Society
Lincoln Center, Broadway/West 62nd and 65th streets; tel: 212-875-5788; www.chambermusicsociety.org; main season Sept–May; subway: 59th St-Columbus Circle; map p.150 B3
The company resides at Lincoln Center and performs a repertory of both traditional and new works. The Chamber Music Society presents concerts in a number of Lincoln Center venues including the newly transformed Alice Tully Hall.

DiCapo Opera Theater
184 East 76th Street/Lexington Avenue; tel: 212-288-9438; www.dicapo.com; main season Oct–May; subway: 77th St; map p.151 E3
An alternative to Lincoln Cen-

ter, often performing works outside that have slipped out of the traditional repertory.

Metropolitan Opera
Lincoln Center, Broadway/West 62nd and 65th streets; tel: 212-362-6000; www.metopera.org; main season Sept–May; subway: 59th St-Columbus Circle; map p.150 B2
One of the world's foremost opera companies stages the classics and new works in grand fashion, with the opera world's biggest stars.

New York City Opera
David H. Koch Theater, Lincoln Center, Broadway/West 62nd and 65th streets; tel: 212-870-5570; www.nycopera.com; main season Sept–Apr; subway: 59th St-Columbus Circle; map p.150 B2
A Lincoln Center company – less grand than the Met – that's renowned for performing lesser-known works and contemporary compositions, with an emphasis on cultivating rising American talent.

New York Philharmonic
Avery Fisher Hall, Lincoln Center, Broadway/West 62nd and 65th streets; tel: 212-875-5656; www.nyphil.org; main season

Sept–June; subway: 59th St-Columbus Circle; map p.150 B2
The oldest symphony orchestra in the US performs the classical canon and specially commissioned new works.

Performance Venues

Apollo Theater
253 West 125th Street/Eighth Avenue; tel: 212-531-5300; www.apollotheater.org; amateur night Wed 7.30pm; subway: 125th St
The famous Harlem theater has a history of showcasing African-American performers, including such past luminaries as Billie Holiday, James Brown and Stevie Wonder.

Beacon Theater
2124 Broadway/West 74th Street; tel: 212-307-1000; www.beacontheater.com; subway: 72nd St; map p.150 C4
This 80-year-old hall, recently emerged from a comprehensive renovation, has 2,800 seats and features pop, rock, jazz, and R&B acts.

Brooklyn Academy of Music (BAM)
30 Lafayette Avenue, Brooklyn, tel: 718-636-4100; www.bam.org; subway: Atlantic Ave

Left: Lincoln Center for the Performing Arts.

A landmark Art Deco theater that showcases pop performers of various genres – often veteran rock giants – and the high-kicking Rockettes.

Symphony Space
2537 Broadway/West 95th Street; tel: 212-864-5400; www.symphonyspace.org; subway: 96th St
A fine concert hall with a variety of inventive programming, including jazz and contemporary classical music.

Terminal 5
610 West 56th Street/11th and 12th avenues; www.terminal5nyc.com; subway: Columbus Circle; map p. 150 A2
A large multi-level venue on the far West Side with great views of the stage from the balconies.

Town Hall
123 West 43rd Street/Sixth Avenue; tel: 212-840-2824; www.the-townhall-nyc.org; subway: 42nd St; map p.153 C3
A midsized venue with excellent acoustics for an ultra-varied menu of music, dance, theater, and film – from Tony Bennett to orchestral classics and Chinese music.

Below: hear some of the best sounds in America here.

Students, professors, and visiting musicians associated with the world-famous **Juilliard School** stage performances nearly every week, many are free. For information, call 212-769-7406 or go to www.juilliard.edu.

A vibrant arts center with eclectic musical programming from classical and jazz to hip-hop, world, and pop.
SEE ALSO DANCE, P.47

Brooklyn Center for the Performing Arts
Brooklyn College, 2900 Campus Road, Brooklyn; tel: 718-951-4600; www.brooklyncenter.com; subway: Brooklyn College-Flatbush Ave
A complex with four theaters presenting classical, jazz, and pop music as well as drama, lectures, and films.

Carnegie Hall
57th Street/Seventh Avenue; tel: 212-247-7800; www.carnegiehall.org; subway: 57th St; map p.150 C1
This grand 19th-century concert hall is acclaimed for its excellent acoustics and splendid Gilded Age design.

The Fillmore NY at Irving Plaza
17 Irving Plaza/East 18th Street; tel: 212-777-6800; www.irving plaza.com; call or check website for schedule; subway: Union Square; map p.155 D3
A big, once-ramshackle hall that's gone through more than one incarnation, recently renovated yet again as a major music venue.

Madison Square Garden
Seventh Avenue/31st and 33rd streets; tel: 212-465-6741; www.thegarden.com; subway: 34th St; map p.152 B2
Legendary sports arena that's also the number-one venue for big-name pop and rock acts.

Merkin Concert Hall
129 West 67th Street/Broadway; tel: 212-501-3303; http://kaufman-center.org; subway: 72nd St; map p.150 C3
A 450-seat venue for intriguing jazz, classical, and world music performances.

Radio City Music Hall
1260 Sixth Avenue/West 50th and 51st streets; tel: 212-307-1000; www.radiocity.com; subway: 50th St-Rockefeller Center; map p.153 D4

Above: Wynton Marsalis playing at the Village Vanguard.

Jazz and Blues Clubs

B.B. King Blues Club and Grill

237 West 42nd Street/Seventh and Eighth avenues; tel: 212-997-4144; www.bbking blues.com; subway: 42nd St; map p.152 C3

The legendary bluesman's Times Square venture packs them in for the biggest names in R&B, and the King himself still drops by with his trusty guitar, Lucille.

Birdland

315 West 44th Street/Eighth Avenue; tel: 212-581-3080; www.birdlandjazz.com; Mon–Sat 5pm–3am, Sun noon–3am; subway: 42nd St; map p.152 C4

A big range of jazz styles features at this elegant club named for legendary bebopper Charlie 'Bird' Parker. Big bands and jazz greats often head the bill, though up-and-coming musicians also sometimes play. The music usually starts around 8.30pm, with a second set at 11pm. Expect a hefty cover charge.

Blue Note

131 West 3rd Street/Sixth Avenue; tel: 212-475-8592; www.bluenote.net; Mon–Thur 8pm and 10.30pm, Fri–Sat 8pm, 10.30pm and 12.30am, Sun 11.30am–4pm; subway: West 4th St; map p.154 B2

The West Village is home to the most famous jazz clubs in the world – first among them the Blue Note. It presents the best mainstream jazz, from time-honored greats to new acts. Weekend jam sessions often run to 4am.

Café Carlyle

35 East 76th Street/Madison Avenue; tel: 212-744-1600; www.thecarlyle.com; Mon–Sat 7.30pm–midnight; subway: 77th St; map p.151 E3

In the plush Carlyle Hotel, this upper-crust institution features top-notch cabaret and singers. Woody Allen sometimes sits in with Eddy Davis's New Orleans Jazz Band.

Feinstein's at the Regency

540 Park Avenue/East 61st Street; tel: 212-339-4095; www.feinsteinsattheregency.com; shows Sun–Thur 8.30pm, Fri–Sat 8.30pm and 11.30pm; subway: East 61st St-Lexington Ave; map p.151 D1

Singer Michael Feinstein is so devoted to cabaret he opened his own high-end club in the luxurious Regency Hotel.

Iridium

1650 Broadway/West 51st Street; tel: 212-582-2121; www.iridiumjazzclub.com; shows Sun–Thur 8pm and 10pm, Fri–Sat 8pm, 10pm, and midnight; subway: 50th St; map p.153 C4

Jazz greats old and new play this slick club and restaurant. Guitar legend Les Paul appears most Mondays.

Jazz at Lincoln Center/ Dizzy's Club Coca-Cola

Frederick P. Rose Hall, Broadway/West 60th Street; tel: 212-258-9800/9595; www.jalc.org; Dizzy's Club performances Sun–Thur 7.30pm and 9.30pm, Fri–Sat 7.30pm, 9.30pm, and 11.30pm; subway: 59th St-Columbus Circle; map p.150 C2

New York's most prestigious center for all things jazz, directed by Wynton Marsalis, has a concert hall and the intimate Dizzy's Club, which showcases the finest jazz musicians, including students and up-and-comers (the first Monday of each month). As well as Marsalis's stellar 15-piece Jazz at Lincoln Center orchestra, the center is also home to the Arturo O'Farrill's Afro-Latin Jazz Orchestra.

The Jazz Standard

116 East 27th Street/Park Avenue; tel: 212-576-2232; www.jazzstandard.net; daily 6.30pm–3am; subway: 28th St; map p.153 C1

This basement club features mainstream jazz, blues, and R&B, and has a great restaurant, the Blue Smoke.

Next Door at La Lanterna di Vittorio

129 MacDougal Street/West 3rd Street; tel: 212-529-5945; http://lalanternacaffe.com; Sun–Thur 6pm–2am, Fri–Sat 6pm–3am; subway: West 4th St; map p.154 B2

This cellar nightclub and restaurant offers an intimate setting for jazz and fine wine.

The Oak Room

Algonquin Hotel, 59 West 44th Street/Sixth Avenue; tel: 212-419-9331; www.algonquin hotel.com; Mon 6.30–10pm, Tue–Thur 7–10.30pm, Fri–Sat

Each September Brooklyn hosts the **Brooklyn Country Music Festival** (for details, see www.brooklyncountrymusic. com) and the **Park Slope Bluegrass Jamboree**, held at the Brooklyn Society for Ethical Culture (53 Prospect Park West, Brooklyn; tel: 718-768-2972).

7pm–12.30am, Sun noon–3pm; subway: 42nd St; map p.153 D3
This dark, intimate cabaret and jazz venue features great performers in a sophisticated setting. Go in your cocktail finery, not jeans or sneakers.

Smoke
2751 Broadway/West 105th Street; tel: 212-864-6662; www.smokejazz.com; daily 5pm–2am; subway: 103rd St
Latin jazz, bebop, blues, and soul play at this cozy Upper West Side haunt. There's no cover charge most nights; a bargain, especially if big names are playing.

Village Vanguard
178 Seventh Avenue South/Perry Street; tel: 212-255-4037; www. villagevanguard.com; shows Sun–Fri 9pm and 11pm, Sat 9pm, 11pm, and occasionally 12.30am (call club to confirm if late show); subway: 14th St; map p.154 B3
Born in 1935, this Greenwich Village boîte turned into a jazz landmark spotlighting major innovators like John Coltrane and Sonny Rollins. It hardly keeps up with the 'vanguard' anymore, but presents jazz's greats and near-greats.

Rock Clubs

Ace of Clubs
9 Great Jones Street/Broadway and Lafayette Street; tel: 212-677-6963; www.aceofclubs nyc.com; check website for schedule; subway: Broadway/ Lafayette; map p.154 C2

Right: the fun Cafe Wha? is a good bet for live music.

This tiny no-frills joint features two or more bands a night. You'll hear mostly indie rock, punk, and metal but you might also catch blues, reggae, country, and the occasional acoustic set.

Arlene's Grocery
95 Stanton Street/Ludlow and Orchard streets; tel: 212-995-1652; www.arlenesgrocery.net; daily 6pm–4am; subway: Delancey St; map p.155 D1
Basic Lower East Side venue with several bands a night – and rock 'n' roll karaoke every Monday.

Bowery Ballroom
6 Delancey Street/Bowery; tel: 212-533-2111; www.bowery ballroom.com; call or check website for schedule; subway: Grand St; map p.157 C4
This former vaudeville theater on the Lower East Side is now host to a variety of acts, ranging from graying rockers on a comeback tour to the latest alternative bands.

Cafe Wha?
115 MacDougal Street/West 3rd Street; tel: 212-254-3706; www.cafewha.com; daily 8.30pm–3am; subway: West 4th St; map p.154 B2
Ultra-popular club with a fresh approach to live music: Wed–Sun a house band plays rock and R&B, Mondays are Brazilian, Tuesdays are for funk: celebrities and new talents often drop in to jam.

Crash Mansion
199 Bowery/Spring Street; tel: 212-982-0740; www.crash mansion.com; subway: Spring St; map p.157 C4
An unusually polished venue for the Lower East Side, with two or more bands nightly.

Highline Ballroom
431 West 16th Street/Ninth and Tenth Avenues; tel: 212-414-5994; www.highline ballroom.com; subway: 14th Street; map p.152 A1
A popular venue catering to a broad range of music fans, presenting the best in cutting edge and eclectic music.

Mercury Lounge
217 East Houston Street/Ludlow and Essex streets; tel: 212-260-4700; www.mercurylounge nyc.com; check website or call for door times; subway: 2nd Ave; map p.157 D4
Stripped-down rock club on the Houston Street strip, with an impressive line-up of up-and-coming bands. See them here before they make it big.

The Village Underground
130 West 3rd Street/Sixth Avenue; tel: 212-777-7745. www.thevillageunderground. com; call or check website for schedule; map p.154 B3
For those who miss Tramps in Chelsea, its former booker picks the groups here – from world music to big rock names, and with an open mic night on Sundays at 9.30pm.

109

Nightlife

Manhattan clubs come and go quicker than a New York minute. This is especially true of the ultra-chic dance clubs, which seem to rise and fall overnight. Many of the nightclubs listed here present various types of live and recorded music, stand-up comedy, cabaret, karaoke, and even poetry readings, as well as DJs and club nights. Reservation policies, show times, and cover charges vary enormously, so call ahead or consult current listings in *Time Out New York*, *New York* magazine or the *Village Voice*. Dress up, dress down, but definitely go out on the town. This is, after all, the city that never sleeps. *See also Bars, p.34–7.*

Clubs

MIDTOWN

China Club
268 West 47th Street/Broadway and Eighth Avenue; tel: 212-398-3800; www.chinaclub nyc.com; Mon, Thur–Sat 10pm–4am; map p.153 C4
A sea of dancers undulate en masse at this high-profile club near Times Square. Though not quite as hot as it used to be in the 1980s and '90s, it still attracts Tony patrons and the occasional celebrity.

Pacha
618 West 46th Street/Eleventh and Twelfth avenues; tel: 212-209-7500; www.pachanyc.com; Thur 5pm–4am, Fri–Sat 10pm–6am; map p.152 B4
Part of the global nightclub franchise that started in Ibiza; you can expect crowd-pleasing music and big-name DJs in flasy surroundings – but check the schedule for details, as the quality can vary.

Roseland Ballroom
239 West 52nd Street/Broadway and Eighth avenues; tel: 212-247-0200; www.roselandball-room.com; call or check website for schedule; map p.150 B1
This old-time ballroom presents a wide variety of events, including performances by alternative rock bands, cabaret, DJ-driven dancing and private functions.

Swing 46
349 West 46th Street/Eighth and Ninth avenues; tel: 212-262-9554; www.swing46.com; daily, call or check website for schedule; map p.152 C4
In the theater district, this stylish supper club has swing dancing, live bands, and dance lessons to recre-

Below: stars of the screen, stage, and dance floor.

New York has one of the most dynamic nightlife and music scenes in the world, in which crossing boundaries – between genres, and between club nights and live acts – is a vital part of the menu. For music venues, many of which also host DJ nights, comedy and less classifiable acts, *see also Music, p.106–9.*

Left: decked out and addicted to nightlife.

Porky's NYC

55 West 21st Street/Fifth and Sixth avenues; tel: 212-675-8007; www.porkysnyc.com; daily noon–4am; map p.152 B1
There's a maybe off-putting frat house atmosphere at this party bar, where you are encouraged to 'eat like a pig, drink like a slob,' dance on the bar, 'dress like an idiot,' and guzzle drinks from fishbowls. Expect a young, male, raucous, and mostly inebriated crowd.

GREENWICH VILLAGE
Le Royale

21 Seventh Avenue South/Leroy Street; tel: 212-463-0700; www.leroyaleclub.com; daily 7pm–4am; map p.154 B2
The brainchild of a global DJ and a longtime club owner, Le Royale is an intimate spot for music lovers. Dance to cutting-edge music in a club that still flies a bit under the radar.

Sullivan Room

218 Sullivan Street/Bleecker and West 3rd Street; tel: 212-252-2151; www.suliivan

Below: cocktails and chat in a Manhattan club.

Getting past the velvet ropes at the hottest nightclubs may require a little strategy. For starters, dress sharply. Most clubs don't look kindly on T-shirts and sneakers. Be persistent but polite; obnoxious behavior is a surefire way to alienate the bouncers. Guys, don't try to get in all at once. Break up into two or three, or, better yet, enter with women. If all else fails, try palming the bouncer $20.

ate classic 1940s style every night. A rotating roster of house bands gets the joint jumping whenever they play.

CHELSEA, UNION SQUARE, FLATIRON, AND GRAMERCY
Cielo

18 Little West 12th Street/Washington Street; tel: 212-645-5700; www.cieloclub.com; usually daily 10pm–4am but call or check website; map p.154 A4
A gathering place for the beautiful and excruciatingly thin, this super-hip club in the Meatpacking District has a sexy, laid-back vibe suitable for sipping champagne and grooving on the sunken dance floor. Getting in can be a trial: expect to be interrogated at the velvet rope.

Home

532 West 27th Street/Tenth Avenue; tel: 212-273-3700; www.nyc.homeguesthouse.com; daily 10pm–4am; map p.152 A2
A fixture of the Chelsea nightlife scene, Home draws the crowds and its share of celebrities, although they have their own space on the 2nd floor. International DJs spin hip-hop, rock, and top 40 to keep everyone moving.

Marquee

289 Tenth Avenue/West 26th and 27th streets; tel: 646-473-0202; Tue–Sat 10pm–4am; map p.152 A2
A sleek and sexy club playing a mix of house and hip hop most nights. The mezzanine level overlooking the main dance floor is an interesting touch and a great spot for eyeing up the clientele, but it's up to you whether it's worth braving the notoriously picky door staff for. A favorite with celebrities.

room.com; Wed–Sun 10pm–5am; map p.154 B2

Still going strong after five years and a recent renovation, the Sullivan Room remains devoted to the underground music scene and boasts a relaxed, unpretentious vibe that really only gets going after midnight. Young local and international DJs keep electronic dance music lovers going all night.

EAST VILLAGE TO CHINATOWN
Element
225 East Houston Street/Essex Street; tel: 212-254-2200; www.elementny.com; call or check website; map p.155 D1

Once the studio of Jasper Johns, Element has had many incarnations, but its current status as people-friendly dance club is proving pretty successful. Check out **Vault**, situated in the basement, for a less mainstream club experience.

Stay
244 East Houston Street/Avenue A; tel: 212-982-3532; www.stay-nyc.com; Tue–Wed 9pm–3am, Thur 6pm–2am, Fri–Sat 9pm–4am; map p.155 D1

There's a laid-back vibe at this East Village club, which offers DJs, dancing, and specialty cocktails with minimal too-hip-for-the-room attitude.

Webster Hall
125 East 11th Street/Third and Fourth avenues; tel: 212-353-1600; www.websterhall.com; Thur–Sat 10pm–6am; map p.155 C3

This big, crowded East Village club draws a young, hip crowd for all-night dancing to rock, hip-hop, reggae, R&B, techno, and more. Theme nights include Circus Saturdays with fire breathers, a fly-

---

Cabaret Law: due to a 78-year-old law requiring bars to apply for a special licence for dancing, it's pretty hard to find a small venue for a casual boogie away from the masses. Although the law is currently being reviewed, it has been used as an excuse not only to close any bars whose patrons indulge in a little impromptu dancing, but also to shut down any clubs deemed 'unsuitable' by the police.

---

ing trapeze and snake charmers.

SOHO AND TRIBECA
M1–5
52 Walker Street/Broadway and Church Street; tel: 212-965-1701; www.m1-5.com; daily 4pm–4am; map p.156 B4

A deceptively small doorway leads down to this huge bar and club all painted out in deep deep red, a hotspot on the local singles scene. As well as regular DJs there are frequent theme events, and speed-dating sessions.

S.O.B.'s
204 Varick Street/West Houston Street; tel: 212-243-4940; www.sobs.com; call or check website for schedule; map p.154 B2

The Sounds of Brazil – aka S.O.B.'s – is a red-hot dance and dinner club with live Latin and Caribbean music ranging from salsa, reggae, and calypso to traditional Brazilian acts. Bring your dancing shoes.

Comedy and Cabaret
The Bitter End
147 Bleecker Street/Thompson Street and LaGuardia Place; tel: 212-673-7030; www.bitterend.com; call or check website for schedule; map p.154 B2

A Village landmark, The Bitter End books an eclectic mix of folk, rock, blues, and some comedy and cabaret. Eternally bohemian, it's popular with young tourists and is often mobbed on weekends.

Caroline's on Broadway
1626 Broadway/West 49th and 50th streets; tel: 212-757-4100; www.carolines.com; daily, call or check website for schedule; map p.153 C4

A plush restaurant and com-

Right: hot sounds at S.O.B.'s (Sounds of Brazil).

edy club that has helped launch some of the biggest names in the biz – Jerry Seinfeld, Chris Rock – and showcases a raft of new talent. Some shows are taped for broadcast on cable TV.

The Comedy Cellar
117 MacDougal Street/Minetta Lane; tel: 212-254-3480; www.comedycellar.com; bar daily 11am–2.30am; shows Sun–Thur 9pm and 11pm, Fri 8pm, 9.45pm, and 11.30pm, Sat 7.30pm, 9.15pm, 11pm, and 12.45am; map p.154 B2

A cramped basement room where the tables are packed so close together that, even if you don't get the jokes, you may make some new friends.

Comic Strip
1568 Second Avenue/East 82nd Street; tel: 212-861-9386; www.comicstriplive.com; Mon–Thur 8.30pm–midnight, Fri 8.30pm–2am, Sat 6pm–2am, Sun 8pm–midnight

A casual, popular proving ground for stand-up comics, both known and unknown. Open seven days a week, with three shows on Friday and Saturday nights.

Above: M1-5 on Walker Street is open weekdays 4pm to 4am and 8pm to 4am on Saturdays, with free pool on Mondays.

Don't Tell Mama
343 West 46th Street/Eighth and Ninth avenues; tel: 212-757-0788; www.donttellmama nyc.com; daily 4pm–4am; map p.152 C4

Camp rules at this jolly spot, a longtime favorite of the theater crowd. There are sing-alongs at the piano bar in front; the back room is a non-stop cabaret featuring comedians and torch singers. Leave inhibitions behind, and bring cash; credit cards are not accepted.

The Duplex
61 Christopher Street/Seventh Avenue; tel: 212-255-5438; www.theduplex.com; daily 4pm–4am; map p.155 B3

Expect camp fun at this landmark piano bar and cabaret in the heart of the West Village gay scene. Entertainment includes drag shows, sing-alongs, stand-up, and abbreviated musicals.

Gotham Comedy Club
208 West 23rd Street/Seventh and Eighth avenues; tel: 212-967-7555/212-539-8778; www.gothamcomedyclub.com; shows Sun–Thur 8.30pm, Fri 8.30pm and 10.30pm, Sat 8pm, 10pm, and 11.45pm; map p.152 B1

This Chelsea club runs the gamut from unknown comics trying to break into the business to old pros taping shows

for broadcast. Think you're funny? Take the stage at the 'new talent showcase.'

Joe's Pub
425 Lafayette Street/West 4th Street and Astor Place; tel: 212-239-6200; www.joespub.com; daily 6pm–4am; map p.155 C2

An eclectic mix of performance artists, musicians, comics, dance companies, acting troupes, and others appear at this small venue adjacent to Joseph Papp's legendary Public Theater.

Nuyorican Poets Café
236 East 3rd Street/Avenues B and C; tel: 212-505-8183; www.nuyorican.org; call or check website for schedule; map p.155 D1

Experience everything from poetry slams, hip-hop acts, stand-up comedy, Latin jazz, film, and theater at this cutting-edge East Village outpost for the arts of the New York-Latino cultural milieu.

Stand-Up NY
236 West 78th Street/Broadway; tel: 212-595-0850; www.standupny.com; shows Sun–Thur 9pm, Fri 8pm and 10pm, Sat 8pm, 10pm and midnight; map p.150 C4

This small Upper West Side club often takes the inventive approach of searching for the 'funniest doctor,' 'funniest banker' with hilarious results.

113

Pampering

It can be tough to slow down in a 'city that never sleeps.' If you need help relaxing, consider indulging yourself at a day spa, where the list of services will include facials, manicures, body wraps, aromatherapy, massage, and maybe more obscure treatments. Want a new look? The city has scores of high-end salons where you can have your nails buffed, skin cleansed, and hair coiffed. And for those who are searching for a makeover of a more ethereal nature, there are numerous meditation centers and schools of holistic studies where you can seek serenity and wellness. For beauty products, *see also Shopping, p.141–2.*

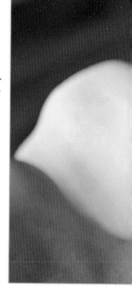

Midtown

Allure Day Spa and Hair Design
139 East 55th Street/Lexington Avenue; tel: 212-644-5500; Mon–Fri 10.30am–7.30pm, Sat–Sun 10am–6pm; map p.153 E4
The emphasis at this tranquil hideaway is more on beauty than wellness, but you will still feel pampered. Services include hairstyling, wraps, waxes, and massage.

Elizabeth Arden Red Door Spa
691 Fifth Avenue/East 54th Street; tel: 212-546-0200; Mon–Tue and Sat 8am–7pm, Wed–Thur 8am–9pm, Fri 8am–8pm, Sun 9am–6pm; map p.153 D4
Elizabeth Arden's spa and salon offers a full menu of services (hairstyling, make-up, waxing, manicures, facials, massage, and more) and is a longtime favorite of an Upper East Side clientele.
SEE ALSO SHOPPING, P.141

Frederic Fekkai Beauty Salon
712 Fifth Avenue, 4th Floor/East 56th Street; tel: 212-753-9500; Mon–Fri 8am–8pm, Sat 8am–7pm, Sun noon–7pm; map p.153 D4

A high-end hair salon with facials and other spa services.

Uptown

Féline Day Spa
235 West 75th Street/Broadway; tel: 212-496-7415; Mon–Fri 9am–8.30pm, Sat 9am–7pm, Sun 10.30am–5.30pm; map p.150 C4
A high-end spa that offers a comprehensive range of luxury services, including facials, skin treatments, seaweed wraps, mud baths, massage, and reflexology.

Glow Skin Spa
30 East 60th Street/Madison and Park avenues; tel: 212-319-6654; daily 10am–8pm; map p.151 D1
Skin care is the specialty at this diminutive spa, where clients enjoy expert facials, scrubs, wraps, acupuncture, and massages.

Chelsea, Union Square, Flatiron, and Gramercy

Essential Therapy
122 East 25th Street/Park and Lexington avenues; tel: 212-777-2325; Mon–Fri 10am–10pm, Sat 10am–8pm; map p.153 C1

Achieving inner peace in a hyperactive town like New York isn't easy. These meditation centers offer classes, meditation rooms, and the company of fellow practitioners: Chakrasambara Buddhist Center (322 Eighth Avenue/West 26th Street; tel: 212-924-6706) and Shambhala Meditation Center (118 West 22nd Street/Sixth Avenue; tel: 212-675-6544). Meditation is only one of dozens of classes and workshops at the Open Center (83 Spring Street/Crosby Street; tel: 212-219-2527), which offers instruction in the arts, yoga, world spirituality, holistic health and nutrition, massage, and bodywork.

Massage and bodywork in a variety of traditions – Swedish, shiatsu, deep tissue, hot stone, and more – for healing, serenity, and wellness.

Ohm Spa
260 Fifth Avenue, 7th Floor/East 28th Street; tel: 212-481-7892; Mon–Sat 10am–8pm, Sun 11am–7pm; map p.153 C1
Therapeutic massage is the specialty at this serene spot,

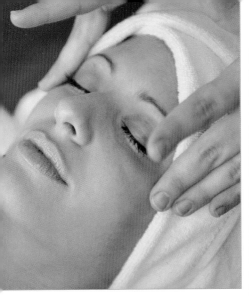

Left: become radiant and relaxed at a Manhattan day spa.

Fri 11am–7pm, Sat–Sun 10am–6pm; map p.156 B4
Treat yourself to any number of massages, facials, waxings, or a manicure, just to soak up the atmosphere at this calming and unpretentious spot.

Brooklyn

119 Smith St Spa

119 Smith Street/Dean and Pacific streets, Brooklyn; tel: 718-643-0087; Mon 10am–8pm, Wed–Sat 10am–8pm, Sun 11am–6pm
Services include body scrubs and massage, and exceptional, meticulous facials.

Area

281 Smith Street/Douglass Street, Brooklyn; tel: 718-624-3157; daily 10am–7pm
A holistic approach to wellness, with massage, wraps, and facials using organic products, and a yoga center.

D'mai Urban Spa

157 Fifth Avenue/Park Slope, Brooklyn; tel: 718-398-2100; Mon 11am-9pm, Tue–Fri 11am–7.30pm, Sat–Sun 10am–7pm
A lavish, soothing Asian ambience enhances relaxation at this full-service spa.

where clients can choose from shiatsu, hot stone, Swedish, acupressure, or sports massage. Facials and manicures are also offered.

SoHo and TriBeCa

Aveda

233 Spring Street/Sixth Avenue; tel: 212-807-1492; Tue–Sat; call in advance for appointment; map p.154 B2
Aveda's salons offer a complete range of services – hairdressing, facials, stress-relievers. This is the location of the Aveda Institute that trains salon professionals. There are several Manhattan branches.
SEE ALSO SHOPPING, P.142

Bliss Spa Soho

568 Broadway, 2nd Floor/Prince Street; tel: 212-219-8970; Mon–Fri 9am–9pm, Sat 9.30am–6.30pm, Sun 10am–6pm; map p.154 B1
Choose from an extensive à la carte menu of skin-care and body-care treatments, including massage, scrubs, waxing, manicures, and pedicures. All are indeed blissfully relaxing – but make sure to book ahead,

and be ready to flex the plastic.

Soho Sanctuary

119 Mercer Street, 3rd Floor/Prince Street; tel: 212-334-5550; Mon 3pm–9pm, Tue–Fri 10am–9pm, Sat 10am–8pm, Sun noon–6pm; map p.154 B1
This women-only spa offers the full range of spa services in a relaxing space above the hustle-and-bustle of SoHo.

Tribeca Day Spa

8 Harrison Street/Staple Street; tel: 212-343-2376; Tue–Wed 11am–8pm, Thur 10am–9pm,

Below: soak away your weariness in exotic bath salts.

Below: most city salons offer make-up sessions.

Parks and Gardens

A tree grows in Brooklyn – quite a few, in fact – and in the other four boroughs, too. From the ocean breezes of Battery Park and salt marshes of Pelham Bay Park to the rocky bluffs of the Hudson highlands and sculpted landscapes of Central Park or Brooklyn's Prospect Park, New York City encompasses a surprising number of green spaces, including a world-class zoo, several well-regarded botanical gardens, and a national wildlife refuge teeming with migratory birds and other species.

Central Park

Central Park Conservancy; tel: 212-310-6600; www.central parknyc.org; Dairy visitor center Tue–Sun 10am–5pm; map p.151

The heart (some say the lungs) of Manhattan, running up 51 blocks from 59th to 110th streets between Fifth Avenue and Central Park West. This vast green space is half a mile (0.8km) wide and 2½ miles (4km) long, and is one of the essential places where New Yorkers go to play. On summer weekends, residents and visitors come in thousands to play ball, skate, stroll, picnic, or listen to a concert.

Central Park's designers were Frederick Law Olmsted and Calvert Vaux, and the project, begun in 1858, took almost 20 years to complete. Creating a usable public space and gardens from a sparse, rocky landscape was a remarkable achievement, and revolutionized landscape architecture. Amazingly, almost everything here, from the Great Lawn and lakes to the apparently natural meadows and forest at the north end, had to be constructed.

Above: take a break from shopping and visit Central Park.

HIGHLIGHTS OF THE PARK

Attractions in the southern part of Central Park include the **Wollman Rink**, used for ice-skating in winter and hosting Victorian Gardens Amusement Park in summer. Closer to Fifth Avenue is **Central Park Zoo**, an endearing collection with a sea-lion pool, penguin house, polar bears, a children's zoo, and much else. Another favorite nearby is the historic **Carousel**, built in 1908 and still in use. You might want to drop in at the **Dairy**, a visitor center with information on events in the park and a small historical exhibit. On the west side, by 66th Street, is the **Tavern on the Green**, one of two restaurants in Central Park (the other is the Loeb Boathouse). Nearby is **Sheep Meadow**, a favorite spot for sunbathing, picnicking and Frisbee tossing.

In the middle of the park, beginning at 66th Street, is the **Literary Walk**, lined with statues of notable authors. The path leads to **Bethesda Fountain**, familiar from countless movies. A short walk away is the **Loeb Boathouse** on the lake, with a café and restaurant. Boat and bike rentals are available nearby. To the east is **Conservatory Water**, favored by model boaters, while to the west is **Strawberry Fields**, a memorial to John Lennon, who was killed outside the Dakota apartment building across Central Park West.

Farther north are the **Delacorte Theatre**, where you can see free plays in summer, and **Belvedere Castle**, which has a nature center and views

Left: Central Park from the Rockfeller Center observatory.

transfer to S57)
It's hard to imagine you're still in New York City in this 2,800-acre (1,120-hectare) stretch of connected parks, meadows, woodlands, and wetlands. At the heart of it all is **High Rock Park**, which is linked by some 28 miles (45km) of trails through tangled woods and rocky outcrops to Staten Island's green spaces.

Snug Harbor Cultural Center and Botanical Garden
1000 Richmond Terrace; tel: 718-448-2500; www.sibg.org; daily sunrise–sunset; entrance charge; bus S40 from Staten Island Ferry
The grounds contain several theme gardens, including a Chinese Scholars Garden, Tuscan Garden, Butterfly Garden, and Pond Garden.

Brooklyn

Brooklyn Botanic Garden
1000 Washington Avenue; tel: 718-623-7200; www.bbg.org; Tue–Fri 8am–6pm, Sat–Sun 10am–6pm, Oct–Mar closing time 4.30pm; subway: Eastern Parkway-Brooklyn Museum
Vegetation takes the spotlight at this urban oasis alongside

of the Great Lawn. The only big building in the park is the **Metropolitan Museum** on the east side at 82nd Street. Farther north, the park is divided by **Jacqueline Kennedy Onassis Reservoir**, beyond which are the **North Meadow**, a **Conservatory Garden**, and another lake, the **Harlem Meer**.
SEE ALSO CHILDREN, P.42; MUSEUMS, P.95; SPORTS, P.145

Elsewhere in Manhattan

Battery Park
Battery Conservancy, 1 New York Plaza; tel: 212-344-3491; www.thebattery.org; map p.156 A1
At the island's tip, harborside Battery Park is where New Amsterdam was first settled by Europeans, and has some of the best views of any New York park. Named for the battery of protective cannons that once stood here, the area includes **Castle Clinton**, a reddish-stone former fort built as a defense against the British in the War of 1812, which is now a museum and ticket office for the Statue of Liberty and Ellis Island ferries. The fort originally stood some

200ft (61m)offshore, but New York has grown around it. Big efforts are ongoing to revitalize Battery Park, with charming new gardens and a **Garden of Remembrance**, dedicated to the survivors of the 9/11 terrorist attack.

Inwood Hill Park
Dyckman Street and Payson Avenue; tel: 212-304-2365; www.nycgovparks.org; subway: Inwood-207th St
At the opposite end of Manhattan, its northern point, this 196-acre (78-hectare) expanse of trees and meadows is one of the most isolated places on the island. About half the park is occupied by Manhattan's last native forest. Flying squirrels and screech owls nest in a grove of 100ft (30m) tulip trees in the Shorakapok Natural Area, named for an Indian village that stood between what is now 204th to 207th streets.

Staten Island

The Greenbelt
Greenbelt Nature Center; Brielle Avenue/Rockland Avenue; tel: 718-351-3450; www.sigreenbelt.org; bus S62 from the Staten Island Ferry (then

Below: green leaves among the Lower Manhattan skyscrapers.

Above: New York City has several botanical gardens.

Prospect Park, with over 12,000 carefully nurtured plants and flowers. The site is renowned for its many specialty gardens, extensive research and educational programs, and the spring rite of Hanami, the Japanese cultural tradition of celebrating the cherry blossom season. Plants and trees from around the world are displayed in the grounds and also in the **Steinhardt Conservatory**. With concerts, festivals, and special events, the garden is also a mainstay of the city's cultural landscape, a place to stop, unwind, and 'smell the roses.'

Prospect Park
Grand Army Plaza; tel: 718-965-8951; www.prospectpark.org; subway: Prospect Park or Grand Army Plaza

Designed by Frederick Law Olmsted and Calvert Vaux, the same team responsible for Central Park, Prospect Park occupies 585 acres (234 hectares) in Brooklyn, and is lusher, denser, and greener than its Manhattan counterpart. From the main entrance at **Grand Army Plaza**, a path leads to the expanse of **Long Meadow**, stretching to a ridge of distant trees, part of the **Ravine** at the park's wild heart. There's also a small zoo (entrance on Flatbush Avenue).

Queens
Cunningham Park and Alley Park
Grand Central Parkway; www.nycgovparks.org; subway: lines E, F to Union Turnpike, then Q46 bus

Wedged between Long Island Expressway and Grand Central Parkway in northeastern Queens, two-thirds of Cunningham Park is forest, ponds, and fields. To the north, **Alley Park** borders the marshlands of Little Neck Bay, with woods (even if interrupted by highways) totaling 600 acres (240 hectares).

Flushing Meadows Corona Park
Long Island Expressway; tel: 718-760-6565; www.nycgovparks.org; subway: line 7 to Mets-Willets Point

Created for the World's Fair in 1939, this 1,255-acre (502-

Riders will find bridle paths in several city parks. Horses can be rented at the following locations: Pelham Bay Park (Bronx Equestrian Center, 9 Shore Road, tel: 718-885-0551); Van Cortlandt Park (Riverdale Equestrian Centre, Broadway/West 254th Street, tel: 718-548-4848); Prospect Park (Kensington Stables, 51 Caton Place, Brooklyn, tel: 718-972-4588); and Forest Park, Queens (Forest Equine Center, 88-11 70th Road, tel: 718-263-3500).

hectare) park now serves as the base for museums, sports facilities, and gardens.

There are paths for cycling and strolling, an indoor skating rink and a children's playground. Just outside the park on the north side is **Citi Field**, the new home of baseball's New York Mets. Citi Field seats 42,000 frenzied and loyal Met fans and offers them not just hot dogs and cotton candy, but a variety of food options.

SEE ALSO SPORTS, P.144

Jamaica Bay Wildlife Refuge
Visitor Center, Cross Bay Boulevard; tel: 718-318-4340; www.nps.gov; daily sunrise–sunset; subway: line A (Far Rockaway train) to Broad Channel

This wildlife refuge in the bay west of Kennedy Airport is home to more than 300 species of birds, as well as raccoons, chipmunks, and turtles. Trail maps, available from rangers at the visitor center, guide visitors to beautiful hiking routes through groves of red cedar and Japanese pine trees. Birding workshops are offered year-round. The birds avoid passing jets thanks to the use of

Below: the site of two World's Fairs and the current US Open.

Right: wintertime in Van Cortlandt Park, The Bronx.

falcons to keep them away from dangerous areas.

Queens Botanical Garden
43–50 Main Street, Flushing; tel: 718-886-3800; www.queens botanical.org; Apr–Oct Tue–Fri 8am–6pm, Sat–Sun 8am–6pm, Nov–Mar Tue–Sun 8am–4.30pm; free; subway: line 7 to Flushing Main Street

This lovely 39-acre (16-hectare) garden, alongside Flushing Meadows-Corona Park, has the largest rose garden in the Northeast. It's a colorful, very popular wedding venue.

The Bronx

Bronx Zoo
Bronx River Parkway; tel: 718-367-1010; www.bronxzoo.org; Apr–Oct Mon–Fri 10am–5pm, Sat–Sun 10am–5.30pm, Nov–Mar daily 10am–4.30pm; entrance charge; subway: East Tremont Ave/West Farms Square

This 265-acre (106 hectare) zoo shares **Bronx Park** with the New York Botanical Garden and is the country's largest city zoo. Popular exhibits include the World of Darkness (nocturnal animals), the Himalayan Highlands Habitat and the Butterfly Zone. There's a Children's Zoo, a monorail ride through Wild Asia, and a 40-acre (16-hectare) big cats habitat. The

Congo Gorilla Forest has acres of trees, bamboo thickets, and baby lowland gorillas.

New York Botanical Garden
Bronx River Parkway at Fordham Road; tel: 718-817-8700; www. nybg.org; Tue–Sun 10am–6pm; entrance charge; subway: Bedford Park Boulevard, or Metro-North train to Botanical Gardens

One of the world's premier botanical centers features idyllic pathways, an array of 50 different gardens, and the magnificent 'crystal palace' of the **Enid A. Haupt Conservatory**, with exquisite specimens from every one of the world's habitats. The **Everett Children's Adventure Garden** is a 12-acre (5-hectare) discovery experience, with a kids' herbarium and lab, a waterfall to splash around in and two mazes, of boulders and hedges and ivy-clad arches. Adventure of a different sort awaits in the 50-acre (20-hectare) **Forest**, where raccoons and skunks might be spotted in the underbrush, as red-tailed hawks swoop overhead. The majestic oaks, beech, and hemlocks are among the last remnants of the wilderness that once blanketed the New York area. Below well-marked paths,

the Bronx River tumbles through a deep gorge.

Pelham Bay Park
Bruckner Boulevard/Wilkinson Avenue; tel: 718-430-1890; www.nycparks.org; subway: Pelham Bay Park

The city's largest park is on Long Island Sound in the Bronx. Pelham Bay's 2,764 acres (1,106 hectares) encompass a public beach, two golf courses, a riding stable, and the city's police riding school, as well as impressive rock formations, forest, salt marshes, and meadows. Past **Goose Creek Marsh** is a wildlife sanctuary for herons, sandpipers, and other birds.

Van Cortlandt Park
Broadway/West 246th Street; tel: 718-430-1890; www.nycgov parks.org; subway: Van Cortlandt Park-242nd Street

Despite being crossed by major roads, much of this park feels remote: one trail passes through a centuries-old hardwood forest with skunks, pheasant, and raccoons; another meanders along Van Cortlandt Lake into a freshwater marsh with swans, egrets, and turtles; and the pièce de résistance is the route along the Old Putnam train line. Also in the park is **Van Cortlandt House Museum**, an elegant Colonial mansion from 1748.

Restaurants

New York has always been a culinary melting pot. From Jewish delis and Texas barbecue to falafel stands, sushi bars, French bistros, Italian trattorias, and Chinese noodle houses, diners can sample the cuisine of virtually every ethnic style and in every price range. Order a $1.50 hot dog at Gray's Papaya, or a hamburger with white truffles for 10 times that price at DB Bistro Moderne. Never content to sit on their laurels, the city's chefs – many celebrities in their own right – are constantly introducing fresh flavors and new trends to the fashionable Manhattan dining scene. *See also Cafés, p.38–41.*

Midtown

AMERICAN

21
21 West 52nd Street/Fifth and Sixth avenues; tel: 212-582-7200; L and D Tue–Fri, D Mon, Sat; $$$$; map p.153 D4
A New York enclave of the wealthy and powerful. The classic dishes (steak, oysters, rack of lamb) are superbly executed, and the wine cellars legendary. A plaque over Table 30 reads 'Bogie's Corner.' Sip his favorite tipple, Ramos gin fizz, and order the chicken hash.

Bryant Park Café and Grill
25 West 40th Street/Fifth and Sixth avenues; tel: 212-840-6500; L Wed, Sat–Sun, D Tue–Sun; $$$; map p.153 C3
A wall of glass and an enormous terrace make the most of one of New York's most idyllic dining venues, the leafy Bryant Square Park. A menu of expertly grilled and roasted fish and meats shows that food is more than an afterthought in this bucolic setting.

Carnegie Deli
854 Seventh Avenue/West 54th Street; tel: 212-757-2245; B, L,

and D daily; $–$$; map p.150 C1
You won't find a more authentic deli experience than this New York institution. The lines are long, but the sandwiches are worth walking a few blocks.

The Oyster Bar
Grand Central Terminal, Lower Level; tel: 212-490-6650; L and D Mon–Sat; $$–$$$; map p.153 D3
Bivalves rule at this arched-and-tiled 1913 landmark in the bowels of Grand Central Terminal – they show up on

Left: marinated fruits at Aquavit.

the half-shell, in several kinds of chowder, in pan roasts, and even in po'boys (a kind of sandwich). A seat at the lunch counter ensures an entertaining bird's-eye view of the comings and goings.

Smith and Wollensky
797 Third Avenue/East 49th Street; tel: 212-753-1530; L and D daily; $$$$; map p.153 E3
This New York institution is usually packed with braying executives and stock brokers. The steaks are huge, and the extensive wine list features only North American wine. For a less expensive option, try the adjacent Wollensky's Grill.

Virgil's Real BBQ
152 West 44th Street/Broadway and Sixth Avenue; tel: 212-921-9494; L and D daily; $$; map p.153 C4
Forget the diet at this fun southern restaurant serving delicious piles of ribs, biscuits and gravy, Texas red chili, and some of the best brisket in NYC. The hickory smoke from the grill hanging

Left: The Oyster Bar at Grand Central Terminal.

courtyard of the new Bloomberg building. Sample sumptuous versions of classic dishes like rack of lamb or sauteed veal.

INTERNATIONAL
Delegates' Dining Room
United Nations, First Avenue/ East 46th Street, 4th Floor; tel: 212-963-7626; L Mon–Fri; $$$; map p.153 E3

Enjoy spectacular views of the East River and a taste of UN living in this sparsely decorated dining room. The buffet-style menu changes biweekly and features international cuisines, from Swedish to Mongolian. You enter through a security checkpoint (bring photo ID). Men must wear jackets.

Le Bernardin
155 West 55th Street/Sixth and Seventh avenues; tel: 212-554-1515; L and D Mon–Fri, D Sat; $$$$; map p.150 C1

Le Bernardin's seafood menu will grab you hook, line, and sinker. The deceptively subtle preparations of anything that swims, from fried calamari to poached salmon to oven-roasted sea bass, are expertly served in simple surroundings. Arrive hungry.

in the air adds to the barbecue experience.

EUROPEAN
Aquavit
65 East 55th Street/Park and Madison avenues; tel: 212-307-7311; L and D Mon–Fri, D Sat, Br and D Sun; $$$; map p.153 E4

A new location, but it's the same sublime Scandinavian cuisine of Marcus Samuelsson. Sweden's beloved herring shows up as a work of art, as do all other manner of fish, venison, and game. Meatballs, smorgasbords, and, of course, aquavit, are also on hand, offered on *prix fixe* menus.

FRENCH
DB Bistro Moderne
55 West 44th Street/Fifth and Sixth avenues; tel: 212-391-2400; L and D Mon–Sun; $$$$; map p.153 D3

So *moderne* that the menu is organized by ingredients (check out the arugula section), chef Daniel Boulud's bistro is awash with Art Deco glitz and well-heeled publishing types and trendy tourists. The foie gras and truffle

Prices for an average three-course meal with house wine:	
$	under $25
$$	$25–$40
$$$	$40–$65
$$$$	over $65

burger is typical of the kitchen's culinary surprises.

La Grenouille
3 East 52nd Street/Fifth and Madison avenues; tel: 212-752-1495; L and D Tue–Fri, D Mon, Sat; $$$$; map p.153 D4

This 47-year-old classic is still one of New York's most important restaurants, serving impeccably prepared Gallic dishes such as grilled Dover sole, queenelles, and soufflés. The floral displays are stunning, the lighting flattering, and the clientele discerning and high-powered.

Le Cirque
One Beacon Court, 151 East 58th Street/Lexington and Third avenues; tel: 212-644-0202; L and D Mon–Fri, D Sat–Sun; $$$$; map p.153 E4

This legendary restaurant reopened to great acclaim in a new, sleek location, complete with entrance in the

Below: DB Bistro Moderne is full of culinary surprises.

Prices for an average three-course meal with house wine:	
$	under $25
$$	$25–$40
$$$	$40–$65
$$$$	over $65

Uptown

AMERICAN

Barney Greengrass
541 Amsterdam Avenue/West 86th and 87th streets; tel: 212-724-4707; B and L Tue–Sun; $$
The faded murals and Formica tables are deceptively downbeat, but New Yorkers continue to herald this institution as the best place in town for lox, smoked sturgeon, chopped liver, and other Jewish fare.

Boathouse
Central Park/East 72nd Street; tel: 212-517-2233; L daily, D daily Apr–Nov, Br Sat–Sun; $$$–$$$$; map p.151 D2
The lake and greenery of Central Park are the most memorable part of a meal in this airy, glass-fronted dining room and waterside terrace (the perfect spot for brunch). Expect sea urchin and caviar in a scallop shell, pan-roasted monkfish, and seared wild striped sea bass. Brunchtime hits are of the French toast and omelet variety.

Gray's Papaya
2090 Broadway/West 72nd Street; tel: 212-799-0243; daily 24 hours; $; map p.150 C3
A two hot-dog dinner with a soft-drink chaser. Stand-up only. Whaddya expect for less than five bucks? A good way to offset the cost of a ticket at nearby Lincoln Center.

Sarabeth's
1295 Madison Avenue/East 92nd and 93rd streets; tel: 212-410-7335; B, L, and D Mon–Fri, Br and D Sun; $$
Waffles, fluffy eggs, and other brunch favorites keep the punters lining up, while succulent roasts and other well-prepared dishes come out at dinner time. Child-friendly environs and homey decor.

Serendipity
225 East 60th Street/Second and Third avenues; tel: 212-838-3531; L and D daily; $$; map p.151 E1
The frozen hot chocolate and huge banana splits are legendary, and soups, sandwiches, and pasta add to the mix. Kids and shoppers from nearby Bloomingdale's crowd in by day, clubbers stop by at night; and no one seems to mind the cranky service.

EUROPEAN

Café Sabarsky
1048 Fifth Avenue/East 86th Street; tel: 212-288-0665; L and D Thur–Sun, L Mon, Wed; $$$
A wood-paneled salon of the Beaux Arts mansion that houses the Neue Galerie of German and Austrian art. Chef Kurt Gutenbrunner lives up to the surroundings, and the beef goulash, cod strudel, *linzer torte*, and other fare from the banks of the Danube take museum food to new heights.

Luzia's
429 Amsterdam Avenue/West 80th and 81st streets; tel: 212-595-2000; L and D daily; $–$$; map p.151 C4
A little piece of Portugal on busy Amsterdam Avenue. Exotic shrimp and pork dishes emerge from the kitchen best washed down with a few glasses of *vinho verde*.

FRENCH

Café des Artistes
1 West 67th Street/Central Park West and Columbus Avenue; tel: 212-877-3500; D Mon–Sat, Br Sat–Sun; $$$$; map p.150 C3
It's been a long time since these rooms with 'naïve nude' murals by Howard Christy Chandler were a home away from home for the bohemians who lived and worked in the studios – now posh apartments – upstairs. You'll find better French fare in the neighborhood, but not in surroundings as appealing as these.

Daniel
60 East 65th Street/Park Avenue; tel: 212-288-0033; D Mon–Sat; $$$$; map p.151 D1
Welcome to the magical world of Daniel Boulud – the flower arrangements and candlelit table settings are

Right: the packed and popular Barney Greengrass.

sumptuous, the service unhurried and pampering, the food, from the caviar to the cheese course, an absolute work of art. The price tag will bring you back to the real world, but you can't do any better. Reserve well ahead.

Jean-Georges
Trump International Hotel, 1 Central Park West; tel: 212-299-3900; L and D Mon–Fri, D Sat, Br Sun; $$–$$$$; map p.150 C2
The skyscraper on chaotic Columbus Circle is an unlikely location for one of the city's most sophisticated retreats. Here, chef Jean-Georges Vongerichten surprises diners with dazzling versions of French classics. While the bill can soar as high as the building in which the restaurant is housed, the $20 lunchtime *prix-fixe* in the less formal Nougatine Room brings it within reach. Reservations essential.

L'Absinthe
227 East 67th Street/Second and Third avenues; tel: 212-794-4950; L and D Tue–Sat, D Sun–Mon, closed Sun July–Aug; $$$; map p.151 E1
The etched mirrors, polished brass, and French waiters in white aprons are as authentic as the classic brasserie fare, such as poached sausages with lentils and potatoes.

INTERNATIONAL
Candle Café
1307 Third Avenue/East 74th and 75th streets; tel: 212-472-0970l L and D daily; $–$$; map p.151 E2
The staff at this small bastion of health serve up innovative, tasty vegan fare. Even carnivores might be tempted by the stir-fried tempeh with peanut sauce and casseroles of sweet potatoes and steamed

greens, not to mention the carrot cake with tofu frosting.

ITALIAN
Sfoglia Trattoria
1402 Lexington Avenue/East 92nd Street; tel: 212-831-1402; L and D Tue–Sat, D Sun; $$$
This rustic and hugely popular little northern Italian eatery serves up delectable dishes such as fusilli in *vin santo* cream sauce or *orata* in *tartufo nero* – they almost sound like operas! Finish off a meal with the yummy, handmade Sfoglia cookie plate. Be sure to book well in advance for dinner, or come here for lunch instead.

MIDDLE EASTERN
Beyoglu
1431 Third Avenue/East 81st Street, 2nd floor; tel: 212-650-0850; D daily; $$
All the flavors of the Middle East seem to explode from the array of dishes on offer, from minty yogurt rice soup, to the lamb or beef kebabs, and experiencing them can be as exciting as a walk through the Istanbul neighborhood for which this Turkish meze house is named. Since the portions are ideal for sharing, come with a group and explore the entire menu.

Harlem and Beyond

AMERICAN
Amy Ruth's
113 West 116th Street/Lenox and Seventh avenues; tel: 212-

Upper West Siders are divided on the contentious issue of where to find the best **bagels**, splitting their loyalties between H & H, at Broadway and 80th Street, and Absolute, Broadway between 107th and 108th streets.

Above: yummy pastries from Café Sabarsky, Neue Gallerie.

280-8779; B Tue–Sun, L and D daily; $
The owner was driver to local politician, the Reverend Al Sharpton (memorably portrayed in *The Bonfire of the Vanities*) for eight years, before opening Amy Ruth's. Partly because of that, the restaurant attracts political, sporting, and entertainment luminaries. However, the big attraction is mostly the fantastic southern food available here – from crispy yet fluffy waffles to tender short ribs, smoked ham hocks, and delicious pineapple-coconut cake.

La Fonda Boricua
169 East 106th Street/Lexington and Third avenues; tel: 212-410-7292; L and D daily
A vibrant local favorite, this East Harlem icon serves hearty traditional Latin and Puerto Rican dishes. Expect a unique, welcoming cultural experience.

Sylvia's
328 Malcolm X Boulevard (Lenox Avenue)/126th and 127th streets; tel: 212-996-0660; D Mon–Sat; $$

123

Above: try the traditional grub at the Empire Diner.

In 1962 Sylvia's was a lunch counter with 35 seats; nowadays it can seat 450, and tour buses arrive almost hourly – it's a must for politicians courting the Harlem vote. Miss Sylvia Woods still labors over the stove, but the southern cooking has inevitably lost that personal touch. The cakes and banana pudding, however, are still wonderful.

Chelsea, Union Square, Flatiron, and Gramercy

AMERICAN

Barbuto
775 Washington Street/West 12th Street; tel: 212-924-9700; L and D daily; $$; map p.154 A4
Another wonderful restaurateur, Jonathan Waxman, forges into the Meatpacking District at – what's this? – reasonable prices. Waxman presents imaginative American cuisine using first-class, seasonal ingredients.

Blue Smoke
116 East 27th Street/Park and Lexington avenues; tel: 212-447 7733; L and D daily; $$–$$$; map p.153 C1
Restaurateur Danny Meyer does down-home barbecue dog-gone good. His huge portions of ribs and Texas-style beef brisket make this a meat-eaters' paradise. The decor is casual but sophisticated, and the ceiling soaring. Food is also served in the downstairs Jazz Standards club.

Cookshop
156 Tenth Avenue/West 20th Street; tel: 212-924-4440; B, L, and D Mon–Fr, Br and D Sat–Sun; $$$; map p.152 A1
Featuring locally sourced ingredients on the market menu, this local favorite has a warm and comfortable atmosphere. In warm weather you can enjoy your meal at the sidewalk café.

Craft
43 East 19th Street/Broadway and Park Avenue South; tel: 212-780-0880; D daily; $$$$; map p.155 C4
The menu is split into sections (vegetables, sides, meat, and fish), and you concoct your own meal. This is a nightmare for the indecisive, but wildly popular with others. Craftbar, the informal sister-restaurant, offers a lunch menu and brunch on Sundays (at 900 Broadway/West 20th Street, tel: 212-461-4300).

Empire Diner
210 Tenth Avenue/West 22nd Street; tel: 212-243-2736; 24 hours daily; map p.152 A2
A slick, stainless-steel version of the roadside eateries that once lined US byways, this diner is open around the clock to feed clubbers with eggs, burgers, and other lunch-counter standards. Before the night crew arrives, a dinner crowd can enjoy pasta and other dishes.

Friend of a Farmer
77 Irving Place/East 18th and 19th streets; tel: 212-477-2188; B, L, and D Mon–Fri, Br and D Sat–Sun; $$; map p.155 D4
It feels like a Vermont bed and breakfast in this cozy and casual restaurant that serves hearty portions of American fare. Great for family eating and brunches, and for basic dishes such as lasagne, meatloaf, banana bread, and apple pie.

Gramercy Tavern
42 East 20th Street/Broadway and Park Avenue; tel: 212-477-0777; L Mon–Fri, D daily; $$$$; map p.155 C4
The 'new American' food here has been a triumph since it opened in the early 1990s, and it still draws in crowds to the large bar area up front, or the more formal back room. Comfortable and sophisticated, the cooking is always top-notch; such as

The nation's largest cooking school, the **Institute of Culinary Education**, is on West 23rd Street between Sixth and Seventh avenues. It offers several half-day classes most days. Go to www.iceculinary.com.

braised veal cheeks with gnocchi and morels, seafood stew, and rack of lamb. To follow, there is an impressive selection of cheeses.

Half King
505 West 23rd Street/Tenth Avenue; tel: 212-462-4300; L, and D Mon–Fri, Br and D Sat–Sun; $–$$; map p.152 A2

Just the sort of easygoing place that Chelsea could use more of. The bar room and lounge-like dining room serve as a gallery for artists and photojournalists; the garden is a snug retreat; and the fish and chips, shepherd's pie, burgers, and other pub fare are good and fairly priced. On Monday evenings there are readings by authors.

Mesa Grill
102 Fifth Avenue/West 15th and 16th streets; tel: 212-807-7400; L Mon–Fri, D daily, Br Sat–Sun; $$$; map p.154 C4

Very popular and delicious Southwestern dishes mixing sweet and sour flavors, and smoke and spice, in dishes such as wild-boar satay with a maple glaze, or 16-spice chicken. Everything here, from the eclectic menu to the fabulous lofty ceilings, is bold and imaginative.

Red Cat
227 Tenth Avenue/West 23rd and 24th streets; tel: 212-242-1122; L Tue–Sat, D daily; $$$; map p.152 A2

One of Chelsea's more grown-up eateries, as much a work of art as the pieces hanging in the galleries surrounding it. In a warm, wood-paneled room, classic American fish and

meat dishes are transformed into delicious, elegantly flavored, elaborate creations.

Union Square Café
21 East 16th Street/Fifth Avenue and Union Square; tel: 212-243-4020; L and D daily; $$$$; map p.155 C3

After 24 years in business, this 'new American' restaurant remains a firm favorite. This is largely down to the consistently good daily specials, ranging from lobster shepherd's pie and red-wine-braised prime rib of beef, to monkfish, Manila clams, and rock shrimp in Catalan garlic, almond, and tomato sauce. The casually elegant surroundings and the informed waiting staff keep it at the top.

ASIAN
Pongal
110 Lexington Avenue/East 26th and 27th streets; tel: 212-696-9458; L and D daily; $$; map p.155 D4

This Kosher vegetarian restaurant, with dishes from Gujarat, Punjab, and South India, is a good choice on this block filled with Indian eater-

Below: many cafés in the Meatpacking District are open 24/7.

ies and grocery stores. There's a wide choice of *dosai* (thin crisp crêpes with fillings of potatoes, onions, and cilantro), and the *kala chana* (black chickpeas in a creamy tomato and onion sauce) and *iddli* (steamed lentil and rice cakes) are excellent.

Spice Market
403 West 13th Street/Ninth Avenue; tel: 212-675-2322; L and D daily; $$–$$$; map p.154 B4

Step into this vast, 2-floor warehouse space and you'll be transported into another world that is exotic and fun. Chef Jean-Georges Vongerichten oversees a spicy menu inspired by Asian street fare that includes samosas, sushi, and fish and meat dishes that are as exciting as the surroundings.

EUROPEAN
El Quijote
226 West 23rd Street/Seventh and Eighth avenues; tel: 212-929-1855; L and D daily; $$; map p.152 B1

This worn but cheerful bastion of bohemia beneath the Hotel Chelsea has introduced generations of New Yorkers to the pleasures of Spanish cuisine – and continues to do so. The crowd is mostly young, but the meat and seafood dishes are strictly old-world, and, invariably, delicious.

FRENCH
Pastis
9 Ninth Avenue/Little West 12th Street; tel: 212-929-4844; B, L, and D daily; $$$; map p.154 A4

It seems like French bistro fare is available on almost every corner in Manhattan, so cuisine alone can't explain the unflagging appeal of this Meatpacking District warhorse. The steak frites and other standards are excellent, as is the breakfast fare, but the real draw is the young, beautiful clientele.

INTERNATIONAL
Socarrat Paella Bar
259 West 19th Street/Seventh and Eighth avenues; tel: 212-462-1000; L and D Mon–Fri, D Sat–Sun; $$; map p.154 B4
Named after the delicious crust that forms at the bottom of a paella pan, the focus here is all on paella. They also serve tapas at the large communal table. It's a cozy modern space, but don't plan on lingering too long, as there is usually someone waiting for your space at the table.

ITALIAN
Macelleria
48 Gansevoort Street/Ninth Avenue; tel: 212-741-2555; L and D Mon–Fri, Br and D Sat–Sun; $$$; map p.154 A4
The name is Italian for 'butcher shop,' as befits the simple but chic dining room in a former meat warehouse. Salads, pasta, antipasti, and wines are decidedly Italian, while steaks and chops are prime American cuts. Reservations are essential at the weekend.
Novità
102 East 22nd Street/Park and Lexington avenues; tel: 212-

Above: raw oysters on the half shell are a specialty at the Pearl Oyster Bar in Greenwich Village.

677-2222; L and D Mon–Fri, D Sat–Sun; $$$; map p.155 D4
This north Italian restaurant is much appreciated by its regulars. What makes it so successful are the delicious, freshly prepared dishes such as pappardelle with lamb ragu and porcini mushrooms, red snapper in tomato broth, or rack of lamb roasted with mustard and rosemary. Add the sophisticated decor, gracious service, and reasonable prices, and you have a winner.

Greenwich Village
AMERICAN
Blue Hill
West 75 Washington Place/Sixth Avenue and Washington Square West; tel: 212-539-1776; D only daily; $$$$; map p.154 B3
A mellow spot in a Village brownstone that gets rave reviews for its pretty main room (and small garden out back) and beautifully conceived American dishes the chef creates using ingredients from his family's farm, such as poached duck with a stew of organic carrots and toasted spices, crabmeat

lasagne, or grass-fed lamb loin. A find that many say is underrated.
Mexicana Mama
525 Hudson Street/Charles and West 10th streets; tel: 212-924-4119; L and D Tue–Sun; $$; map p.154 A3
This tiny Mexican spot is worth the wait to get in. The menu is limited, but the boldly flavored dishes are a far cry from average Tex-Mex fare. Things can get hectic inside, but the food and the price can't be beat. A taco here is a culinary masterpiece. Cash only.
One If By Land, Two If By Sea
17 Barrow Street/Seventh Avenue South; tel: 212-228-0822; D daily, Br Sun; $$$$; map p.154 B3
Located in historic Village townhouse, this elegant restaurant is considered one of the city's most romantic. The house specialties of beef Wellington and rack of lamb are impeccable; so is the service and the selection of wines, but it isn't cheap.
Pearl Oyster Bar
18 Cornelia Street/Bleecker and West 4th streets; tel: 212-691-

Prices for an average three-course meal with house wine:	
$	under $25
$$	$25–$40
$$$	$40–$65
$$$$	over $65

8211; L and D Mon–Fri, D Sat; $$–$$$; map p.154 B3

This little gem is considered by many to be the best seafood restaurant in town. Lines of hopeful diners wait patiently outside, and its popularity is entirely justified. The Maine specialties of lobster rolls, bouillabaisse, and oysters are fresh and delicious.

ASIAN
Café Asean
117 West 10th Street/Greenwich and Sixth avenues; tel: 212-633-0348; L and D daily; $–$$; map p.154 B3

This inviting place with a small garden serves an eclectic choice of Vietnamese, Thai, and Malaysian dishes at very fair prices. Chive and shrimp dumplings, Malaysian coconut curry chicken, and sirloin steak and green onions marinated in a soy-based sauce are among the many offerings.

FRENCH
AOC
314 Bleecker Street/Grove Street; tel: 212-675-9463; B, L, and D daily; $$–$$$; map p.154 B3

The waiters are French, conversations around you are in

French, and most of all, the duck *confit*, lamb chops, endive salad, and lamb shank are served as simply and perfectly as in a bistro. Unlike other hurried spots, you can linger as long as you like if no one needs your table. The garden out back is a bonus.

CamaJe
85 Macdougal Street/Bleecker and West Houston streets; tel: 212-673-8184; L and D daily; $–$$; map p.154 B2

The atmosphere may be casual, but this small restaurant is anything but casual about its food. Chef Abigail Hitchcock prepares top-notch French bistro dishes with imagination and heart (cilantro-crusted tuna or scallops cooked with Thai green curry). The reasonable prices make this a real find for foodies.

ITALIAN
Babbo
110 Waverly Place/Sixth Avenue and Washington Square West; tel: 212-777-0303; D daily; $$$$; map p.154 B3

The place pushes the culinary envelope with adventurous concoctions such as ravioli with beef cheeks, or pasta with calf's brain. If

The **James Beard House** at 167 W. 12th St (at Seventh Avenue) is now a club for food enthusiasts who enjoy meals cooked by established and emerging chefs from around the world. Beard, considered the father of American gastronomy, died in 1985.

you're too squeamish to be tempted by such unorthodox ingredients, there are more mainstream, but equally inspired, dishes like duck with chanterelle mushrooms and chicory, or goat's-cheese tortellini with dried orange and wild fennel pollen. Sensational wines, too.

Da Silvano
260 Sixth Avenue/Bleecker and West Houston streets; tel: 212-982 2343; L and D daily; $$$; map p.154 B2

The outdoor patio guarantees great people-watching, with frequent celebrity sightings both inside and out. Braised veal shank with saffron risotto, fresh spinach and ricotta-filled ravioli, and other Tuscan-inspired dishes rarely disappoint. Owner Silvano Marchetto's café-restaurant next door is a less expensive, more informal option.

Risotteria
270 Bleecker Street/Morton Street; tel: 212-924-6664; L and D daily; $; map p.154 B3

This casual restaurant knows its arborio from its canaroli; this is the place to come for expertly prepared risotto. Asparagus and saffron; gruyère and green onions; or lamb, spinach, and gorgonzola, are just three of the 35 tempting combinations on offer. Lucky patrons wangle a seat at one of the few tables; others perch on stools by the window. Pizzas and sandwiches also available.

Below: chef David Bouley at work in his kitchen at Bouley, *p.130*.

Left: Katz's Deli is a Lower East Side classic. **Right:** try Rice for something inexpensive, casual, and nice.

Street; tel: 212-254-2246; B, L, and D daily; $–$$; map p.155 D1

Founded in 1888, this old-style Jewish deli is a New York institution. The huge space is often filled to capacity, especially on Sunday mornings when a line forms out the door and around the block of people hungry for the deli's pastrami on rye or warm beef brisket. The portions are huge, and the service is friendly though brusque. A must for any first-time visitor to the city.

Tanti Baci
163 West 10th Street/Seventh Avenue South and Waverly Place; tel: 212-647-9651; L and D daily; $$; map p.154 B3

More of a café than a restaurant, but regulars like its coziness and simple but reliable pasta – you choose your own sauce – and salads. The front patio opens up in good weather to let in the breeze.

INTERNATIONAL
The Spotted Pig
314 West 11th Street/Greenwich Street; tel: 212-620-0393; L and D daily; $$–$$$; map p.154 B4

This tiny, casual restaurant was a hit even before it opened its doors, elevating pub food to gourmet status. Sit on plump cushions at small tables or perch on a stool and dig into chicken-liver parfait, squid and mussel salad, pork sausage with lentils, or slow-braised beef shin with risotto. Wash it all down with a beer or a glass of wine from the substantial list.

East Village to Chinatown

AMERICAN
Katz's Delicatessen
205 East Houston Street/Ludlow

Prune
54 East 1st Street/First and Second avenues; tel: 212-677-6221; L and D Mon–Fri, Br and D Sat–Sun; $$$; map p.155 C1

This small restaurant is a destination for foodies looking for a fix of excellent and unusual meat dishes. Salivate over the roasted marrow bones and parsley salad, fried chicken with cold buttermilk dressing, stewed chestnuts with fresh ricotta, or lentils with fried chicken livers, and Dutch chocolate cake for dessert.

WD-50
50 Clinton Street/Rivington and Stanton streets; tel: 212-477-2900; D Wed–Sun; $$$$; map p.157 E4

Star chef Wally Dufresne creates eclectic American cuisine. Oysters flattened into squares perched on granny smith apple slices with a dab of pistachio

Prices for an average three-course meal with house wine:	
$	under $25
$$	$25–$40
$$$	$40–$65
$$$$	over $65

puree, or skate curled next to a pile of lemon-flavored gnocchi garnished with hazelnut shavings are examples of his more mannered creations.

ASIAN
Jewel Bako
239 East 5th Street/Second and Third avenues; tel: 212-979-1012; D Mon–Sat; $$$$; map p.155 C2

Husband-and-wife team Jack and Grace Lamb have a well-deserved reputation for their uncommon but first-rate sushi choices, and imported rarities such as Japanese spotted sardines and needle-fish. Charming, knowledgeable service. Very popular, so reserve well in advance.

Rice
292 Elizabeth Street/East Houston and Bleecker streets; tel: 212-226-5775; L and D daily; $; map p.154 C2

The menu at Rice consists of around 10 varieties of the grain (including Bhutanese red, Thai black, and Japanese short), which are topped with a variety of accompaniments, from ratatouille to curries and Vietnamese lemongrass-

For dinner and a movie, go to the **Angelika Film Center** (18 West Houston Street), an art-house cinema with a fine café. The wraps and sandwiches are good, and the carrot cake and chocolate brownies are delicious.

chicken salad. There are also occasional specials such as a great paella. Finish with rice-crispy treats or rice pudding.

ITALIAN
I Coppi
432 East 9th Street/First Avenue and Avenue A; tel: 212-254-2263; D Mon–Sat, Br Sun; $$$; map p.155 D2

This Tuscan restaurant oozes authenticity thanks to its brick walls, terracotta floors, wood-burning oven, and pretty back garden. The dishes are rustic yet sophisticated (salad of pears with gorgonzola and stracchino cheese, pan-seared duck with Italian bacon, and onions roasted in balsamic vinegar). Pricey, but very romantic.

INTERNATIONAL
Angelica Kitchen
300 East 12th Street/First and Second avenues; tel: 212-228-2909; L and D daily; $$–$$$; map p.155 D2

This large, bright, warm space with oak picnic-style tables is thought to be the best vegetarian restaurant in the city. The pull – inventive cuisine like marinated tofu and tempeh reuben sandwiches, cornbread, and the fiery three-bean chili with tofu sour cream.
Indochine
430 Lafayette Street/Astor Place and East 4th Street; tel: 212-505-5111; D daily; $$$; map p.154 C2

This French-Vietnamese restaurant with trendy, tropical decor is still sexy after all these years. It's located across from the Public Theater, with a decent pre-theater menu and price deal.

SoHo
AMERICAN
Delicatessen
54 Prince Street/Lafayette Street; tel: 212-226-0211; L and D Mon–Fri, Br and D Sat–Sun; $$–$$$; map p.155 C1

This is a spinoff of the popular Cafeteria in Chelsea. Settle into the modern interior for comfort food in a lively environment. Large glass garage doors, which are great for people-watching, open up in warmer weather. A good option for a late evening craving for fried chicken in a bucket.
Jane
100 West Houston Street/Thompson Street; tel: 212-254-7000; L and D daily; $$$; map p.154 B2

Huge photographs of cornfields complement the creative dishes crafted from hearty American ingredients. Appetizers and puddings are reliably good, and the

cumin-flavored flatbread is addictive. Main courses can be unpredictable, except for a few standouts such as the steak and the honey-braised pork.
Mercer Kitchen
Mercer Hotel, 99 Prince Street/Mercer Street; tel: 212-966-5454; B, L, and D daily; $$$$; map p.154 B1

If you want a celebrity sighting during your stay in the city, invest in a meal at the Mercer – it's a magnet for models, movie stars, and musicians. The real star is the food. This is where celebrity chef Jean-Georges Vongerichten produces his 'everyday food.' Few eat black truffles, Maine lobster, and warm almond cake on a daily basis, but they probably would if they could afford it.
Zoë
90 Prince Street/Broadway and Mercer Street; tel: 212-966-6722; L daily, D Tue–Sun; $$$; map p.154 B1

You might not think it to look at it, but this elegant SoHo bistro is especially good if you have kids. There's a counter next to the exposed kitchen where children are encouraged to sit to be

Below: chef Wylie Dufresne's WD-50 remains a hotspot.

Above: start the day the American way – with pancakes.

given little tastes or demonstrations by the chef. Grown-ups, meanwhile, can get stuck in to some seriously smart variations on American classics.

FRENCH
Balthazar
80 Spring Street/Broadway and Crosby Street; tel: 212-965-1414; B, L, and D daily; $$$; map p.154 B1
Dinner reservations can be tricky to secure at this gorgeous, glittering Parisian bistro, so at least plump for breakfast, lunch, or a drink at the bar. Delicious daily specials – such as Friday's bouillabaisse and Saturday's braised short ribs – are added to the list of bistro standards, and there's a fabulous three-tiered seafood platter. One of Manhattan's best restaurants.

Raoul's
180 Prince Street/Sullivan and Thompson streets; tel: 212-966-3518; D daily; $$$; map p.154 B2
There's something enormously sexy about Raoul's, with its dark red banquettes. Ask for a table in the back room, if only for the hot walk through the middle of the kitchen. Raoul's is pricey, but

worth it for the great food, buzz, and chance of being seated near a celebrity.

TriBeCa

AMERICAN
Odeon
145 West Broadway/Duane and Thomas streets; tel: 212-233-0507; L and D daily; $$$; map p.156 B3
Odeon is the archetypal New York restaurant – a beautiful, big, glittering room, full to bursting with beautiful, thin, glitterati. The place is a marvel: it's managed to maintain high heat and hipness levels for over two decades while not changing a thing and remaining totally unpretentious. You may have to wait, but it's open late and the bar serves excellent Martinis.

Tribeca Grill
375 Greenwich Street; tel: 212-941-3900; L and D Sun–Fri, D Sat; $$$; map p.156 B4
Many people come here to see co-owner Robert De Niro and showbiz pals from his Tribeca Film Center upstairs. Chances are the closest you'll get is De Niro's dad's paintings on the walls, and while you do see people reading scripts, most of the clientele are business types or starstruck tourists. But the food rarely disappoints.

ASIAN
Nobu
105 Hudson Street/Franklin and North Moore streets; tel: 212-219-0500; D daily, L Mon–Fri; $$$$; map p.156 B4
Nobuyiku Matsuhisa re-works traditional Japanese recipes to incorporate new ingredients and modern inflections. His tasting menu is widely thought to include the best sushi in the world – the chances are, you'll never know unless you're prepared to plan your visit years ahead, have the patience of a saint, or the notoriously difficult-to-obtain-hotline number. Thankfully, however, there's also no-reservations **Next Door Nobu** (105 Hudson Street/Franklin Street; tel: 212-334-4445; D daily; $$$$). It looks like Nobu, it tastes like Nobu but, unlike the real thing, you can get in.

FRENCH
Bouley
163 Duane Street/Hudson Street; tel: 212-964-2525; L and D daily; $$$$; map p.156 B3
Truly inspired cuisine from a chef universally praised as one of today's best, plus elegant surroundings and immaculate service. If Bouley is beginning to sound intimidating, don't despair – it may have four stars from the notoriously hard-to-please *New York Times*, but there is nothing elitist or forbidding about it. Yes, it costs a lot, but you'll leave feeling it was money extremely well spent.

Prices for an average three-course meal with house wine:	
$	under $25
$$	$25–$40
$$$	$40–$65
$$$$	over $65

For a treat on a hot summer's afternoon, go to **Ciao Bella Gelato** in the World Financial Center, where flavors range from the decadent Valrhona chocolate gelato to the award-winning Blood Orange sorbet. The all-natural ingredients are sure to please.

Lower Manhattan

AMERICAN
Bridge Café
279 Water Street/Dover Street; tel: 212-227-3344; L and D daily; $$$; map p.156 B2
The three most important things about this bistro? Location, location, location, and in order of importance they are: beneath the Brooklyn Bridge; in a former brothel; and in the oldest surviving wooden building on Manhattan. Despite the olden-days longshoreman feel about it, the Bridge Café does food that is upscale, light, creative, and modern.
Delmonico's
56 Beaver Street/William Street; tel: 212-509-1144; L and D Mon–Fri; $$$–$$$$; map p.156 B1
This is the place where the movers and shakers of Lower Manhattan come to have power lunches and launch deals and mergers. Delmonico's is a club-like steakhouse with premises in a fine old building. Befitting its corporate intentions, the restaurant is closed at weekends.

ITALIAN
Ecco
124 Chambers Street/Church Street; tel: 212-227-7074; L and D Mon–Fri, D Sat–Sun; $$$; map 156 B3
A neighborhood stalwart with old world charm serving consistent, classic Italian cuisine. On weekends enjoy the piano bar entertainment.

Staten Island

AMERICAN
Aesop's Tables
1233 Bay Street/Maryland Avenue; tel: 718-720-2005; D Wed–Sat, Br and D Sun; $$
The focus is on fresh seasonal food – even the ketchup is homemade – at this country-style restaurant. The garden, open in summer, is a delightful place for a brunch of Swedish pancakes.

ITALIAN
Lento's
289 New Dorp Lane/Clawson and Edison streets; tel: 718-980-7725; L and D daily; $$
This is the Staten Island outpost of an Italian mini-chain that started in Bay Ridge in 1933. It is now the last one standing, with good southern Italian cooking – most notably a subtle, spicy marinara sauce, homemade pasta, and delicious crisp-crust pizzas.

Brooklyn

AMERICAN
Blue Ribbon
280 Fifth Avenue/1st and Garfield Place, Park Slope; tel: 718-840-0404; D daily; $$$
Park Slope knew it arrived as a serious food location once the highly regarded Blue Ribbon chainlet arrived. Blue Ribbon Brooklyn tries to be all things to all men – saloon, oyster bar, deli, and bistro – and succeeds. Blue Ribbon Sushi is just next door.
The Grocery
288 Smith Street/Sackett and Union streets; tel: 718-596-3335; D Mon–Sat; $$$
In summer, you can sit in The Grocery's gracious garden. Otherwise, the fresh sage-green rooms are a touch of spring and a serene backdrop to American bistro food of the highest quality. Prices are slightly higher than at most of its neighbors, but the chowders, salads, and entrees are all imaginative

Below: diners are one of the delights of eating in New York.

and good. Carrot sorbet may sound a little too imaginative but is actually delicate and delicious.

Nathan's
1310 Surf Avenue, Coney Island; tel: 718-946-2202; B, L, and D daily; $

Eating a Nathan's hot dog is a very New York experience (they're served at most of the city's hot-dog stands). However, they taste better here, in the original Nathan's restaurant, with a breath of sea air added and the sounds of the nearby amusement park as garnish. On July 4th this is the stage for the Hot-Dog Eating contest – one of the nation's first eating competitions. A particular favorite with families and kids. Enjoy hot dogs for breakfast? You better if you show up at 8am for breakfast.

Peter Luger Steakhouse
178 Broadway/Driggs Avenue, Williamsburg; tel: 718-387-7400; L and D daily; $$$$

Brooklyn's most famous restaurant, and arguably New York's best-loved steakhouse, Peter Luger opened as a German beer hall in 1887. It's barely changed since, and of late its owners have been accused of resting on their laurels. Peter Luger doesn't go out of its way to please, with bare wooden tables, gruff wisecracking waiters, an uncompromising menu (they only have one cut of steak – the porterhouse), but still people come back again and again. Note that credit cards are not accepted.

Prices for an average three-course meal with house wine:	
$	under $25
$$	$25–$40
$$$	$40–$65
$$$$	over $65

Above: take your pick from one of New York's 2,750 pizzerias.

Rose Water
787 Union Street/Sixth Avenue; tel: 718-783-3800; D daily, Br Sat–Sun; $$–$$$

Rose Water is a local favorite serving seasonal American cooking sourced from local regional farms. Cozy, small space with friendly waitstaff.

MEXICAN
Alma
187 Columbia Street/Degraw Street, Carroll Gardens; tel: 718-643-5400; D daily, Br Sat–Sun; $$

Make a trek off the beaten path and you will be rewarded with unrivaled views of the Downtown Manhattan skyline from the rooftop patio. The twinkling evening lights are quite magical. Enjoy the view with upscale Mexican fare and some killer margaritas.

MIDDLE EASTERN
Zaytoons
283 Smith Street/Sackett Street; tel: 718-875-1880; L and D daily; $

A simple restaurant, where no attempt at design or decoration has been made. But that's fine, because once the fluffy pitta bread comes and the rest of the tangy, meticulously prepared food follows,

you won't have eyes for anything else. And when the check arrives, you'll be delighted it doesn't include the cost of swish decor. Basbousa, a semolina caked with honey and almonds, is a pleasing lighter alternative to the delicious baklava.

Queens

AMERICAN
Water's Edge
East River/44th Drive; tel: 718-482-0033; L and D Mon–Fri, D Sat; $$$

If approached from the road, this seafood restaurant looks more like 'Industrial Edge,' so canny diners ride the ferry from 34th Street. Approached this way, Water's Edge is a romantic riverside restaurant with breathtaking views of the Chrysler Building and an intriguing menu of seafood. The white-jacketed waiters give it a formal look, but it is a relaxed place to watch the lights of Manhattan twinkling.

ASIAN
Ping's Seafood
83-02 Queens Boulevard, Elmhurst; tel: 718-396-1238; 8am–2am daily; $

The Queens outpost of the more famous Ping's Seafood on Mott Street in Chinatown is actually the original. It's a quiet haven where you can get fresh fish and seafood with a delectably light touch. People who normally run screaming from gooey sweet-and-sour dishes should be forced to try them here.

EUROPEAN
Bohemian Hall and Beer Garden
29-19 24th Avenue, Astoria; tel: 718-274-4925; D Mon–Fri, L only Sat–Sun; $$
Reasonably priced goulash and kielbasa, washed down with plenty of good beer; something they've been doing here – and doing well – for close to 100 years.

Cornel's Garden
46-04 Skillman Avenue/46th Street; tel: 718-786-7894; L and D daily; $$
This is not a garden restaurant in that it doesn't have a garden; it does, however, have indoor trellises bedecked with plastic roses. And it is a magnet for New York's Romanians, who flock here for *mamaliga-brinza-smintina* – a mouthful of warm polenta covered with Romanian ewe's cheese and sour cream – as well as *mititei* (sausages), doughnuts smothered in sour cream and strawberry preserves, and vast quantities of Romanian wine.

Telly's Taverna
28-13 23rd Avenue, Astoria; tel: 718-728-9056; Mon–Sat 4pm–midnight, Sun noon–midnight; $$
Telly's is a very popular spot for Astoria's Greek community, who flock here to enjoy good, simple cooking. There are excellent fresh grilled meats and fish sprinkled with little more than a few drops of olive oil and a few grains of sea salt to surprisingly delicious effect.

FRENCH
Tournesol
50-12 Vernon Boulevard/50th Avenue; tel: 718-472-4355; L Tue–Fri, D daily, Br Sat–Sun; $$
This cheery French bistro is a splash of sunshine near the gray mouth of the Queens-Midtown tunnel. The chefs make their own terrines and pates. The *plats du jour*, such as cassoulet and coq au vin, are reliably good, and the prices are remarkably kind.

ITALIAN
Bella Via
47–6 Vernon Boulevard/Tenth Avenue; tel: 718-361-7510; L and D Mon–Sat, D Sun; $$
Vernon Boulevard is trying to reinvent itself as New York's Left Bank, which may seem far-fetched given that

The most historic restaurant in New York is the **Old Bermuda Inn**, 2512 Arthur Kill Road, Staten Island; tel: 718-948-7600. The building dates from 1716 and is a good place for dinner or Sunday brunch. Try the Bermuda Triangle – puff pastry with seafood cooked in sherry.

it isn't exactly the 'lovely way' its name might lead you to believe it is. However, a wood-burning oven and the delicious crispy pizzas that come out of it are the big attraction of Bella Via.

Bronx

AMERICAN
Johnny's Reef Restaurant
2 City Island Avenue; tel: 718-885-2086; L and D daily, closed Dec–Feb; $$
City Island's waterfront has many seafood restaurants; most are mediocre and overpriced. This one, though, is the real deal, where you can get a good, old-fashioned Long Island fish fry (deep-fried battered fish). As you make your way down the cafeteria line, make sure you get plenty of the homemade cocktail sauce to dip your fries into.

ITALIAN
Dominick's
2335 Arthur Avenue/187th Street; tel: 718-733-2807; L and D daily; $$
Fans of Dominick's, and they are legion, claim that this is the real Little Italy. There's no menu, so listen up, your waiter will tell you what you need to know. You sit at long benches, and the atmosphere is convivial. There's no check either – they just size you up and pronounce a figure, so don't dress too fancy.

Below: brunch options are many and varied in the city.

133

Shopping

For those who rate shopping among life's great pleasures, it's difficult to find a more intriguing place than this grand bazaar-on-the-Hudson. Here thousands of boutiques, bodegas, department stores, discount outlets, chain retailers, and well-stocked emporia of all stripes jostle for a piece of the sales action. Prices? They run the gamut, from astronomical down to rock bottom. What follows is a list of a few of the city's most notable shops – from pricey to cheap, well known to well-kept secrets. As they say, if you can't buy it in New York City, it probably doesn't exist. *See also Fashion, p.50–57.*

Books and Music

MIDTOWN

Bauman Rare Books
535 Madison Avenue/East 54th and 55th streets; tel: 212-751-0011; Mon–Sat 10am–6pm; map p.153 E4
Bauman's has the look of a traditional library of the kind you might find at an Ivy League college, with a fascinating collection of rare books on its shelves.

Borders
461 Park Avenue/East 57th Street; tel: 212-980-6785; Mon–Fri 9am–10pm, Sat 10am–8pm, Sun 11am–8pm; map p.153 E4
This flagship branch of the vast international chain is arranged over four floors, and has an excellent music department. (Also at: 100 Broadway, at Wall Street, tel: 212-964-1988; 2 Penn Plaza, tel: 212-244-1814; 10 Columbus Circle, tel: 212-823-9775; 576 Second Avenue, at East 32nd Street, tel: 212-685-3938.)

Colony Music Center
1619 Broadway/49th Street; tel: 212-265-2050; call for opening times; map p.153 C4
Comb through Colony's vast sheet music collection, so

Above: *it's in the bag.*

comprehensive it has been nominated the 'World's Largest Karaoke Dealer.' It is housed in the legendary Brill Building, where songwriters like Leiber and Stoller, Carole King, Neil Diamond, and Neil Sedaka penned countless hits in the 1950s and 1960s.

Rizzoli
31 West 57th Street/Fifth and Sixth avenues; tel: 212-759-2424; Mon–Fri 10am–7.30pm, Sat 10.30am–7pm, Sun 11am–7pm; map p.151 C1
This bookseller and publisher knows that its customers often judge a book by its cover – hence their wonderful display of the novels *du jour*

and of their own beautifully produced art books.

UPTOWN

Argosy Book Store
116 East 59th Street/Park and Lexington avenues; tel: 212-753-4455; Mon–Fri 10am–6pm, Sat (Sept–Apr only) 10am–5pm; map p.153 D4
Used, rare and old books and prints are Argosy's specialty. A place for the connoisseur, or for an unusual gift.

Hue-Man Bookstore and Cafe
2319 Frederick Douglass Boulevard/West 124th Street; tel: 212-665-7400; Mon–Sat 10am–8pm, Sun 11am–7pm
One of the largest and best-known independent African-American bookstores in the country. A cultural landmark in Harlem which hosts frequent book readings and other events.

CHELSEA, UNION SQUARE, FLATIRON, AND GRAMERCY

Barnes & Noble
33 East 17th Street/Union Square; tel: 212-253-0810; daily 10am–10pm; map p.155 C3
Of all the chain bookstore

Left: Macy's – the world's largest department store *(p.137)*.

are available at this Bleecker Street store. The very know-ledgeable staff are a great help, though they might be a little scornful if you ask for the latest Beyoncé CD.

Partners & Crime Mystery Booksellers
44 Greenwich Avenue/Charles Street; tel: 212-243-0440; Mon–Thur noon–9pm, Fri–Sat noon–10pm, Sun noon–7pm; map p.154 A3
A huge selection of crime and mystery books. If you've a mystery fanatic in your life, this is a great gift shop.

Shakespeare & Company
716 Broadway/Washington Place; tel: 212-529-1330; Mon–Fri 10am–11pm, Sat–Sun noon–9pm; map p.154 C2
This classy independent is one of the few general book-sellers to have survived the expansion of the superstores. (Also at: 137 East 23rd Street/Lexington Avenue, tel: 212-505-2021; 939 Lexington Avenue/East 69th Street, tel: 212-570-0201.)

Strand Book Store
828 Broadway/East 12th Street; tel: 212-473-1452; Mon–Sat 9.30am–10.30pm, Sun 11am–10.30pm; map p.155 C3
Umberto Eco's 'favorite

When the weather warms up, its time for **weekend flea markets**. You'll find estab-lished markets at the Annex/Hell's Kitchen Flea Mar-ket (West 39th between ninth and tenth avenues), Greenflea (Columbus Avenue between West 77th and 79th streets), and SoHo Antiques Fair (Grand Street and Broadway).

locations in Manhattan, this is the most pleasant to sit in. It's also one of the largest; in addition to books, it stocks cards and stationery and has an excellent music section. (Also eight other locations around Manhattan, including: 555 Fifth Avenue/East 45th and 46th streets, tel: 212-697-3048; 396 Sixth Avenue/West 8th Street, tel: 212-674-8780; Lincoln Center, 1972 Broadway/Warren Street/Greenwich Street, tel: 212-587-5389.)

Books of Wonder
18 West 18th Street/Fifth Avenue; tel: 212-989-3270; Mon–Sat 10am–7pm, Sun 11am–6pm; map p.155 C4
Row upon row of children's books; this large, independ-

ent bookstore also organizes guest appearances by renowned and local authors.

Idlewild
12 West 19th Street/Fifth Avenue; tel: 212-414-8888; Mon–Fri 11.30am–8pm, Sat–Sun noon–7pm; map p.154 C4
Independent bookstore near Union Square specializing in travel and international litera-ture, organized by country.

GREENWICH VILLAGE
Biography Bookshop
400 Bleecker Street/West 11th Street; tel: 212-807-8655; Mon–Sun 11am–10pm, Fri–Sat to 11pm; map p.154 B3
If you are looking for an obscure biography, this small independent store is a great place to search beyond the bestsellers. It also carries other genres, and the staff are helpful and well informed.

Bleecker Street Records
239 Bleecker Street/Carmine Street; tel: 212-255-7899; Mon–Thur 11am–10pm, Fri–Sat 11am–11pm, Sun 11am–10pm; map p.154 B2
Rock, jazz, alternative, and much more – new and used –

Below: fashion on Fifth – the original and the best *(see p.138)*.

135

place in America,' while Steven Spielberg gave it $30,000 to furnish him with a 4,000-title library. It has 2½ million books, from half-price review copies to $100,000 rarities. Open since 1927, it's a New York institution.

EAST VILLAGE TO CHINATOWN
Bluestockings
172 Allen Street/Stanton and Rivington streets; tel: 212-777-6028; daily 11am–11pm; map p.157 D4

Bluestockings functions as a café and a community space as well as a bookstore, headlining books with a feminist focus. It also hosts readings by well-known authors.

SOHO AND TRIBECA
Housing Works Used Book Café
126 Crosby Street/Jersey Street; tel: 212-334-3324; Mon–Fri 10am–9pm, Sat–Sun noon–7pm; map p.154 C1

You can feel good about shopping here, whether you buy a secondhand book or a latte in the café: proceeds go to helping the homeless.
McNally Jackson
52 Prince Street/Mulberry Street; tel: 212-274-1160; Mon–Sat 10am–10pm, Sun 10am–9pm; map p.154 C1

Large, welcoming independent bookstore in NoLita with very knowlegeable booksellers, regular author events, and an in-store café.
The Scholastic Store
557 Broadway/Prince Street; tel: 212-343-6166; Mon–Sat 10am–7pm, Sun noon–6pm; map p.154 B1

The success of Harry Potter gave this publisher the market share (and money) to turn the ground floor of its offices into a shop for books, educational games, and videos.

Above: kids go crazy for the toys in New York.

Above: learning the alphabet the retail way.

Children
MIDTOWN
FAO Schwarz
767 Fifth Avenue/East 58th Street; tel: 212-644-9400; Mon–Thur 10am–7pm, Fri–Sat 10am–8pm, Sun 11am–6pm; map p.151 D1

A New York classic, this cavernous toy store has had its financial problems in the last decade, but has reopened under new ownership. For a tooth-aching selection of sweets, visit FAO Schweetz.
Toys R Us
1514 Broadway/West 44th Street; tel: 646-366-8800; Mon–Thur 10am–10pm, Fri–Sat 10am–11pm, Sun 10am–9pm; map p.153 C4

The only thing that might be more chaotic than Times Square itself is this toy megastore right at its center. The young-at-heart can ride a Ferris wheel inside the store. (Also at: 34–30 Union Square, tel: 212-798-9905; 3540 48th Street, Queens, tel: 718-937-8697.)

UPTOWN
Flora and Henri
1023 Lexington Avenue/East 73rd Street; tel: 212-249-1695; Mon–Sat 10am–6pm; map p.151 E2

Children's clothes that you might wish came in adult sizes. Soft cottons and flannels match simple styles and natural color schemes.
Granny-Made
381 Amsterdam Avenue/West 79th Street; tel: 212-496-1222; Mon–Fri 10.30am–7pm, Sat 10am–6pm, Sun 12.30pm–5.30pm; map p.151 C4

Extensive collection of handmade sweaters, hats, gloves, and children's clothes. There's an adult range of home-knits too.
Mary Arnold Toys
1010 Lexington Avenue/East 72nd Street; tel: 212-744-8510; Mon–Fri 9am–6pm, Sat 10am–5pm, Sun 10am–5pm; map p.151 E2

You will find personal service, knowledgeable sales clerks, and numerous hand-picked items at one of the few remaining classic toy stores.
Petit Bateau
1094 Madison Avenue/East 82nd Street; tel: 212-988-8884; Mon–Fri 10am–7pm, Sat 10am–6pm, Sun 11am–6pm; map p.151 E3

Really a children's shop, but their T-shirts are popular with women and come in great colors.
Z'Baby Company
100 West 72nd Street/Columbus Avenue; tel: 212-579-2229;

The **Diamond District** – on West 47th Street between Fifth and Sixth avenues – is the place for bargains on diamond jewelry. Nearly $500 million in gems are traded on this block every day.

Mon–Sat 10.30am–7.30pm, Sun 11am–6pm; map p.150 C3
Trendy baby clothes and a selection of practical items are packed into this store. The mini designer styles may seem over the top for practical parents, but it's a great source of gifts for fashion-conscious moms and dads. (Also at: 996 Lexington Avenue, tel: 212-472-2229; 31 Greenwich Street/Reade Street, tel: 212-334-7980.)

GREENWICH VILLAGE
Kidding Around
60 West 15th Street/Sixth Avenue; tel: 212-645-6337; Mon–Sat 10am–7pm, Sun 11am–6pm; map p.154 C4
This kid-friendly store showcases a full range of toys for all ages.
Yo Ya
636 Hudson Street/Horatio Street; tel: 646-336-6844; Mon–Sat 11am–7pm, Sun noon–5pm; map p.154 B4
Irresistible clothes for trendy tots by Petit Bateau, Judith Lacroix, and other designers.

EAST VILLAGE TO CHINATOWN
Crembebé
68 Second Avenue/East 4th Street; tel: 212-979-6848; Mon–Sat 11am–7pm, Sun noon–6pm; map p.155 C2
Crembebé stocks clothes for infants and toddlers by several French designers; some look almost too precious to wear, while others will work for the most accident-prone child. The store itself is as cute as some of the clothes – an indoor space made to look like an outside yard.

Dinosaur Hill
306 East 9th Street/Second Avenue; tel: 212-473-5850; daily 11am–7pm; map p.155 D2
Dinosaur Hill is packed with children's toys, puzzles, and mobiles to keep kids busy while their parents shop.

SOHO AND TRIBECA
Boomerang Toys
173 West Broadway/Worth Street; tel: 212-226-7650; Mon–Fri 10.30am–6.30pm, Sun 10am–6.30pm; map p.156 B4
Toys galore, from educational scientific games to frivolous dolls, with a good selection for tiny tots.

Department Stores
MIDTOWN
Bergdorf Goodman
754 Fifth Avenue/East 57th Street; tel: 212-753-7300; Mon–Fri 10am–8pm, Sat 10am–7pm, Sun noon–6pm; map p.151 D1
The most upmarket of all New York's department stores, Bergdorf Goodman has seven floors of women's clothes, shoes, jewelry, and

beauty products. Gentlemen are catered to in the elegant store across the street.
Henri Bendel
712 Fifth Avenue/East 56th Street; tel: 212-247-1100; Mon–Sat 10am–8pm, Sun noon–7pm; map p.151 C1
Bendel carries women's fashion, including sassy designs by Luella Bartley and Vivienne Tam, plus their own line of clothes – inexpensive versions of the designer lines.
Lord & Taylor
424 Fifth Avenue/West 38th Street; tel: 212-391-3344; Mon–Sat 10am–9pm, Sun 11am–7pm; map p.153 D2
Lord & Taylor is home to fewer high-end designers than its competitors, focusing instead on more reasonably priced fashions in conservative styles.
Macy's
151 West 34th Street/Sixth and Seventh avenues; tel: 212-695-4400; Mon–Thur 10am–9.30pm, Fri 9am–9.30pm, Sat 9am–10pm, Sun 11am–8.30pm; map p.152 C2
Macy's bills itself as the

Below: Bloomingdale's *(see p.138)* is a New York institution. The original is on East 59th Street; a newer branch is in SoHo.

137

world's largest department store – for some this might be a warning to stay away, but for others it's an invitation to explore. It has a vast array of shoes and clothes, not to mention services including a post office and restaurant. If you're visiting for Thanksgiving, stay to watch the spectacular Macy's parade.

Saks Fifth Avenue
611 Fifth Avenue/East 49th Street; tel: 212-753-4000; Mon–Sat 10am–8pm, Sun noon–7pm; map p.153 D4
Upmarket Saks is the epitome of the New York department store. It has the greatest range of styles and prices, and stocks all the major designers in its make-up, jewelry, luggage, and fashion departments.

Takashimaya
693 Fifth Avenue/East 54th Street; tel: 212-350-0100; Mon–Sat 10am–7pm, Sun noon–5pm; map p.153 D4
This Japanese department store stands out among its American contemporaries for its choice merchandise.

UPTOWN
Bloomingdale's
1000 Third Avenue/East 59th Street; tel: 212-705-2000; Mon–Sat 10am–7pm, Sun 11am–7pm; map p.151 D1
This New York institution takes up an entire block and is full of clothes, household

A block north of the American Museum of Natural History is another spot favored by aficionados of stones and bones. **Maxilla & Mandible** (451 Columbus Avenue/West 81st Street; tel: 212-724-6173) carries museum-quality fossils, skulls, antlers and other animal bones, human skeletons, and various insects.

Above: everything you can ever need for your home (and more) is waiting in a New York store.

goods, luggage, toys, and china. Most of the top designers – Marc Jacobs, Calvin Klein, Donna Karan, Armani – have mini-boutiques here, as do more moderately priced designers such as Tahari, Theory, and BCBG. (Also at: 504 Broadway, tel: 212-729-5900.)

Design and Interiors

MIDTOWN
An American Craftsman
Rockefeller Center, 60 West 50th Street/Sixth Avenue; tel: 212-307-7161; Mon–Sat 11am–7pm, Sun 10am–6pm; map p.153 D4
An eclectic collection of handmade items, including furniture, kaleidoscopes, jewelry, and pieces for the home. Many make memorable gifts. (Also at: 790 Seventh Avenue, tel: 212-399-2555.)

American Folk Art Museum
45 West 53rd Street/Fifth and Sixth avenues; tel: 212-265-1040; Tue–Sun 10am–5.30pm, Fri 10am–7.30pm; map p.153 D4
This museum shop sells replicas of its exhibits and other folk art. Ideal if you love the real thing, but can't afford it. (Also at: Columbus

Avenue/West 66th Street, tel: 212-595-9533.)
SEE ALSO MUSEUMS, P.90

Conran Shop
407 East 59th Street/First Avenue (under 59th Street bridge); tel: 866-755-9079; Mon–Fri 11am–7pm, Sat 10am–7pm, Sun 11am–6pm
Very spacious home furnishing store located under the 59th Street bridge. The focus is on modern design.

MoMA Design Store
44 West 53rd Street/Fifth and Sixth avenues; tel: 212-767-1050; Sat–Thur 9.30am–6.30pm, Fri 9.30am–9pm; map p.153 D4
No ordinary museum gift shop: it sells the usual stuff – postcards, posters, art books, and art-themed novelties – but you'll find a range of unique modern furniture and fixtures, too. (Also at: 11 West 53rd Street, tel: 212-708-9700; 81 Spring Street, tel: 646-613-1367.)
SEE ALSO MUSEUMS, P.91

UPTOWN
Adrien Linford
927 Madison Avenue/East 74th Street; tel: 212-628-4500; Mon–Fri 11am–7pm, Sat–Sun 11am–6pm; map p.151 E2
When you want to treat your

home to something original, this is the place to come; stylish salt-and-pepper shakers, unusual bookends, or necklaces and handbags.

Crate & Barrel
650 Madison Avenue/East 59th Street; tel: 212-308-0011; Mon–Fri 10am–8pm, Sat 10am–7pm, Sun noon–6pm; map p.151 D1

Famous as a mail order catalog long before it had a presence in New York, Crate & Barrel caters to all your household needs from margarita glasses to measuring cups, with contemporary and traditional designs. (Also at: 611 Broadway, tel: 212-780-0004.)

Gracious Home
1201, 1217, and 1220 Third Avenue/East 70th Street; tel: 212-517-6300; Mon–Fri 8am–7pm, Sat 9am–7pm, Sun 10am–6pm; map p.151 E2

Whether you need a lamp, bed sheets, or hammer and nails, these stores carry every household accessory under the sun. Different departments are divided between the three shops at the junctions of Third and 70th. (Also at: 1992 Broadway/West 67th Street, tel: 212-231-7800.)

La Terrine
1024 Lexington Avenue/East 73rd Street; tel: 212-988-3366; Mon–Sat 10am–5.30pm; map p.151 E2

Warm-hued Italian ceramics and French tableware are crammed into this small shop.

Metropolitan Museum of Art Store
1000 Fifth Avenue/East 82nd Street; tel: 212-570-3894; Tue–Sun 9.30am–5.15pm, Fri–Sat to 8.45pm; map p.151 E3

The store carries reproductions, posters, jewelry, note cards, and an excellent selection of art books associated with the museum's

exhibits. (Also at: Rockefeller Center, 15 West 49th Street, tel: 212-332-1360; The Cloisters, 799 Fort Washington Avenue, tel: 212-650-2277.)

SEE ALSO MUSEUMS, P.95

Pottery Barn
1965 Broadway/West 67th Street; tel: 212-579-8477; Mon–Sat 10am–9pm, Sun 11am–7pm; map p.150 C3

Another large store with a comprehensive selection of household goods and furniture. (Also at: 117 East 59th Street/Lexington Avenue, tel: 917-369-0050.)

Sara
950 Lexington Avenue/East 69th and 70th streets; tel: 212-772-3243; Mon–Fri 11am–7pm, Sat noon–6pm; map p.151 E2

Japanese tableware, much of which is almost too pretty or delicate for actual use.

William Wayne & Company
850 Lexington Avenue/East 64th and 65th streets; tel: 212-288-9243; Mon–Sat 10.30am–6.30pm; map p.151 D1

Full of eccentric little finds – monkey-shaped candelabras,

intriguing cocktail napkins, and fancy footstools – all in traditional styles. (Also at: 40 University Place/East 9th Street, tel: 212-533-4711.)

Williams-Sonoma
121 East 59th Street/Lexington Avenue; tel: 917-369-1131; Mon–Fri 10am–8pm, Sat 10am–7pm, Sun 11am–6pm; map p.151 D1

Everything you will ever need, large or small, for the kitchen. (Also at: Time Warner Center, 10 Columbus Circle, tel: 212-823-9750; 110 Seventh Avenue/West 16th Street, tel: 212-633-2203; 1175 Madison Avenue/East 86th Street, tel: 212-289-6832.)

CHELSEA, UNION SQUARE, FLATIRON, AND GRAMERCY

ABC Carpet & Home
881 and 888 Broadway/East 19th Street; tel: 212-473-3000; Mon–Fri 10am–7pm, Sat 10am–7pm, Sun 11am–6.30pm; map p.155 C4

There are really two ABCs adjacent to each other: one is the world's largest carpet and rug store – with every imaginable variety, from every part

Below: buy unique gifts from the design store at MoMA.

Below: buy bath accessories from Zitomer *(p.142).*

of the world – while the 'Home' store has everything else you might need for your home, from furniture and home-entertainment systems to baby bassinets. Prices are high, but there's a permanent sale in the basement of the carpet store at number 881. (Also at: 1055 Bronx River Avenue, The Bronx, tel: 718-842-8772.)

Olde Good Things
124 West 24th Street/Sixth Avenue; tel: 212-989-8401; daily 9am–7pm; map p.152 B1
This store dubs itself the 'place of architecturologists.' Pretentious perhaps, but the furniture selection stretches beyond usual antique shop fare, and includes fireplace mantels, barbershop chairs, and other unusual pieces.

Restoration Hardware
935 Broadway/West 22nd Street; tel: 212-260-9479; Mon–Fri 10am–8pm, Sat 9am–8pm, Sun 11am–7pm; map p.152 C1
Traditional and retro styles are presented with modern flair at this store – one of a chain with branches across the US. On show is a complete range of household items, from Mission-style furniture and fabrics to bathroom accessories and glow-in-the-dark ceiling stars.

GREENWICH VILLAGE
Design Within Reach
408 West 14th Street/Ninth Avenue; tel: 212-242-9449; Mon–Sat 11am–7pm, Sun noon–6pm; map p.154 B4
Bold and exciting furniture by

Wait Here For Next Available Point & Shoot Agent

established and up-and-coming names in contemporary design. More affordable than your average designer showroom, but still fairly pricey. There are five other branches around Manhattan.

EAST VILLAGE TO CHINATOWN
La Sirena
27 East 3rd Street/Second Avenue; tel: 212-780-9113; Sun–Thur noon–7pm, Fri–Sat noon–7.30pm; map p.155 C1
A splash of Mexico in the heart of Manhattan. Ornate silver frames and crosses, bright ornaments, hand-painted pottery, carved figurines, and loads of handbags and baskets are just some of the traditional Mexican artifacts packed into the store.

Lancelotti Housewares
66 Avenue A/East 5th Street; tel: 212-475-6851; Mon–Fri noon–8pm, Sat 11am–8pm, Sun 11am–7pm; map p.155 D1
This store's 1950s-style logo is emblematic of the retro-inspired designer items it sells. Furry floor pillows, bed linens, plastic tables, rechargeable lamps – all typical of the things that grace hip East Village apartments.

SOHO AND TRIBECA
Michele Varian
35 Crosby Street/Broome and Grand streets; tel: 212-226-1076; Mon–Fri 11am–7pm, Sat 11am–6pm; map p.154 B1
Big comfy floor cushions with throws to match, gorgeous pillows (paisley, abstract, geometric), duvet covers, and bedspreads to suit every taste and setting – all made here by the designer herself. Also other designers' work.

Pearl River
477 Broadway/Grand Street; tel: 212-431-4770; daily 10am–7.30pm; map p.154 B1
Items you might otherwise find scattered around Chinatown are neatly organized here. While still reasonably priced, these Chinese lanterns, silk slippers, and teapots are more expensive, if better packaged, than the ones a few blocks northwest.

R 20th Century
82 Franklin Street/Church Street and Broadway; tel: 212-343-7979; Mon–Fri 11am–6pm, Sat noon–6pm; map p.156 B4
TriBeCa is littered with antique shops. This one focuses on the 20th century,

Department stores usually allow you to return merchandise up to 30 days after purchase for full credit. Small shops are less accommodating; some allow store credit only, no returns on sale items, and no returns or exchanges after seven days.

Left: for anything photographic, try B&H Photo-Video *(p.143).*

with designs from wooden chaises longues to three-legged chairs. Some are extremely expensive, but there are bargains to be had.

Urban Archaeology
143 Franklin Street/Hudson Street; tel: 212-431-4646; Mon–Thur 8am–6pm, Fri to 5pm; map p.156 B4
Once famous for salvaging furniture and fixtures from old houses, UA is now in the business of reproducing antique objects, but are still on the hunt for one-off original pieces, from pool tables to shower heads and faucets.

Gifts and Souvenirs

UPTOWN
Avventura
463 Amsterdam Avenue/West 82nd Street; tel: 212-769-2510; Mon–Thur 10.30am–7pm, Fri 10.30am–6pm, Sun 11am–6pm
Glass vases, stemware, and jewelry, much of it made by Venetian glass studios, fill this sparkling little shop.

E.A.T. Gifts
1062 Madison Avenue/East 80th Street; tel: 212-861-2544; Mon–Sat 10am–6pm, Sun 11am–5pm; map p.151 E3
This is a store for the child in all of us. Its cute candy necklaces and fanciful toys prove that frivolity is fun.

Roam
488 Amsterdam Avenue/West 84th Street; tel: 212-721-0155; Mon–Fri 11am–7.30pm, Sat 11am–7pm, Sun noon–7pm
Thoughtful and interesting selection of gifts including letterpress cards, children's gifts, and clothes.

Right: the Strand Book Store has miles of books *(p.135).*

GREENWICH VILLAGE
Alphaville
226 West Houston Street/Sixth Avenue; tel: 212-675-6850; Mon–Thur noon–8pm, Fri–Sat noon–9pm, Sun 1–7pm; map p.154 B2
The quirky items on sale at this West Village fixture – from old lunch boxes to obscure vinyl albums, and special stocks of old toys, movie posters, and vintage sunglasses – wouldn't look out of place at a garage sale, but the quality is usually pretty decent.

mxyplyzyk
125 Greenwich Avenue/West 13th Street; tel: 212-989-4300; Mon–Sat 11am–7pm, Sun noon–5pm; map p.154 B4
Quirky mix of well-designed but affordable items with lots of gift options.

EAST VILLAGE TO CHINATOWN
Alphabets
115 Avenue A/East 7th Street; tel: 212-475-7250; Mon–Sat noon–8pm, Sun noon–7pm; map p.155 D2
This store manages to make souvenirs – T-shirts, magnets, tote bags – look cute.

Health and Beauty

MIDTOWN
The Body Shop

Rockefeller Center, 1270 Sixth Avenue/West 50th and 51st streets; tel: 212-397-3007; Mon–Sat 10am–8pm, Sun 11am–6pm; map p.153 D4
What began as a small British business making cosmetics with all-natural ingredients became a global success, and won founder Anita Roddick a reputation as a businesswoman with a conscience. Eight more stores around town.

Crabtree & Evelyn
520 Madison Avenue/East 53rd Street; tel: 212-758-6419; Mon–Fri 10am–6pm, Thur to 6.30pm, Sat 11am–6pm; map p.153 D4
Floral-scented toiletries and elegantly packaged foodstuffs that look like English imports, but actually come from Connecticut. (Also at: 10 Columbus Circle, tel: 212-823-9584; 30 Rockefeller Center, tel: 212-582-0190.)

Elizabeth Arden
691 Fifth Avenue/East 54th Street; tel: 212-546-0200; Mon–Tue and Sat 8am–7pm, Wed–Thur 8am–9pm, Fri 8am–8pm, Sun 9am–6pm; map p.153 D4
Stock up on Arden make-up and beauty products, or indulge at the Red Door Spa.
SEE ALSO PAMPERING, P.114

141

UPTOWN

Clyde's
926 Madison Avenue/East 74th Street; tel: 212-744-5050; Mon–Fri 9am–7.30pm, Thur to 8pm, Sat 9am–7pm, Sun 10am–6pm; map p.151 E2
A trove of health and beauty products that does a roaring trade and does not appear to be making a dent in the popularity of its more established neighbor Zitomer (see below). It has an in-store pharmacy.

Origins
2327 Broadway/West 84th Street; tel: 212-769-0970; Mon–Sat 10am–9pm, Sun 11am–7pm
Origins offers a wide range of eco-friendly beauty products in a feel-good atmosphere. There are Origins concessions in Macy's and other big stores. (Also at: 402 West Broadway/Spring Street, tel: 212-219-9764; Flatiron Building, 175 Fifth Avenue/East 23rd Street, tel: 212-677-9100.)

Zitomer
969 Madison Avenue/East 76th Street; tel: 212-737-5560; Mon–Fri 9am–8pm, Sat 9am–7pm, Sun 10am–6pm; map p.151 E3
Three floors packed with every bath and beauty product imaginable. Also stocks toys and an overwhelming choice of fun and functional hair accessories.

CHELSEA, UNION SQUARE, FLATIRON, AND GRAMERCY

Sephora
45 East 17th Street/Union Square West; tel: 212-995-8833; Mon–Sat 10am–9pm, Sun 11am–7pm; map p.155 C4
This French megastore stocks practically every cosmetic line all under one roof, from Sephora's own high-quality products to funky brands such as Stila and Urban Decay, and the more conventional Estée Lauder and Yves St Laurent.

Above: Bluestockings (see p.136) hosts events as well as selling a good selection of feminist-themed books, among others.

(There are 11 more branches around Manhattan.)

GREENWICH VILLAGE

L'Occitane en Provence
247 Bleecker Street/Leroy Street; tel: 212-367-8428; Mon–Sat 11am–7pm; map p.154 B3
Beautifully packaged bath and beauty products with fragrances reminiscent of the south of France. All bags are made from seaweed, no products are tested on animals, and products are also labeled in Braille. Their sister store, Oliviers & Co., next door, has a variety of olive oils, plus several other products with olive oil as their essential ingredient. (10 more branches around Manhattan, including outlets at Rockefeller Center and Grand Central.)

EAST VILLAGE TO CHINATOWN

Fragrance Shop New York
21 East 7th Street/Second and Third avenues; tel: 212-254-8950; Tue–Thur and Sun noon–7pm, Wed noon–5pm, Fri–Sat noon–8pm; map p.155 C2
Perfumes for men, women, and the home, plus oils and bath products. Be prepared for olfactory overload –

there are so many fragrances they often clash with one another.

Kiehl's
109 Third Avenue/East 14th Street; tel: 212-677-3171; Mon–Sat 10am–8pm, Sun 11am–6pm; map p.155 D3
You get the feel of being in a traditional apothecary when wandering among the old-fashioned shampoos, soaps, shaving items, and other products in Kiehl's lines.

SOHO AND TRIBECA

Aveda
233 Spring Street/Sixth Avenue; tel: 212-807-1492; Mon–Fri 9am–9pm, Sat 9am–7pm, Sun 10am–6pm; map p.154 B2
Aveda's deliciously scented bodycare products are made with plant and flower extracts. The store doubles as a beauty salon.
SEE ALSO PAMPERING, P.115

MAC
113 Spring Street/Greene and Mercer streets; tel: 212-334-4641; Sun–Fri 11am–7pm, Sat 11am–8pm; map p.154 B1
Most of the big stores have a MAC counter, but this huge branch of the Canadian cosmetics company gives a wider selection, with experts on hand if you want a full-blown makeover.

> On weekends the streets of SoHo are packed not only with shoppers but with street vendors selling jewelry, incense, CDs, and knock off handbags.

Specialties

MIDTOWN

B&H Photo-Video
420 Ninth Avenue/West 34th Street; tel: 212-444-5000; Mon–Thur 9am–7pm, Fri 9am–2pm, Sun 10am–6pm; map p.152 B3
Professionals and amateurs alike are catered to here – from film and lenses to flash-guns and lighting equipment. The store is run by Orthodox Jews and thus adheres to a strict religious calendar – closed before sundown on Friday and all day Saturday.

Brookstone
Rockefeller Center, 16 West 50th Street; tel: 212-262-3237; Mon–Sat 10am–8pm, Sun 10am–7pm; map p.153 D4
From foot massagers to ergonomic gardening tools, unusual gadgets are this store's specialty. (Also at: South Street Seaport, 18 Fulton Street, tel: 212-344-8108.)

UPTOWN

Capezio
1776 Broadway/West 57th Street; tel: 212-586-5140; Mon–Sat 10am–7pm, Sun noon–5pm; map p.150 C1
Traditionally for dancers, Capezio now offers exercise and street clothes, but it's still the place to come for leotards, leg warmers, and ballet and tap shoes. (Also at: 1650 Broadway/West 51st Street, tel: 212-245-2130; 136 East 61st Street/Lexington Avenue, tel: 212-758-8833; 1651 Third Avenue/East 92nd Street, tel: 212-348-7210.)

Il Papiro
1021 Lexington Avenue/East 73rd Street; tel: 212-288-9330; Mon–Sat 10am–6pm; map p.151 E2

Although you can now find marbleized Italian paper else-where, going to the source ensures that you get better quality and a great selection.

Papyrus
1270 Third Avenue/East 73rd Street; tel: 212-717-1060; Mon–Fri 9am–8pm, Sat 11am–7pm, Sun noon–5pm; map p.151 E2
Lovers of fine stationery and paper products will have a field day at these attractive stores. There are 16 more branches around Manhattan, including two at Grand Central Station and one at the Rockefeller Center.

EAST VILLAGE TO CHINATOWN

Autumn Skateboard Shop
436 East 9th Street/Avenue A and First Avenue; tel: 212-677-6220; daily 12.30–7.30pm; map p.155 D2
Everything for the skate-boarder, from boards, many of which are works of art in their own right, to knee pads.

Utrech Art Supply
111 Fourth Avenue/East 11th and 12th streets; tel: 212-777-5353; Mon–Sat 9am–7pm, Sun 11am–6pm; map p.155 C3
Easels, brushes, paints, pen-cils – this store can supply all your artistic needs and has

been at this location for almost 30 years.

SOHO, TRIBECA, AND LOWER MANHATTAN

Eastern Mountain Sports
530 Broadway/Prince and West Houston streets; tel: 212-966-8730; Mon–Sat 10am–9pm, Sun 11am–7pm; map p.154 C2
EMS stocks all the gear and clothing you need for a climbing, hiking, backpack-ing, or skiing expedition – or just to look the type.

Kate's Paperie
72 Spring Street/Crosby Street; tel: 212-941-9816; Mon–Sat 10am–8pm, Sun 11am–7pm; map p.154 B1
Renowned design and paper store. You will be mesmerized by paper prod-ucts in all colors, shapes, and sizes, as well as photo frames and albums. (Also at: 8 West 13th Street/Fifth Avenue, tel: 212-633-0570; 140 West 57th Street/Sixth Avenue, tel: 212-459-0700; 1282 Third Avenue/East 74th Street, tel: 212-396-3670.)

Pearl Paint
308 Canal Street/Mercer Street; tel: 212-431-7932; Mon–Fri 9am–7pm, Sat 10am–7pm, Sun 10am–6pm; map p.154 B1
Artists flock to this art supply warehouse, with six packed floors of supplies.

Below: home furnishings at SoHo's Michele Varian *(p.140)*.

Below: dance to your own tune at Urban Archaeology *(p.141)*.

143

Sports

Tennis, anyone? How about ice-skating or maybe running, golf, or chasing after Frisbees? There are plenty of places where you can indulge, as spectator or participant. Some of the venues are legendary, such as Yankee Stadium up in the Bronx and, in Midtown, Madison Square Garden, a mecca for fans of basketball, ice hockey, and much more. Horse racing is just a subway ride away at the Aqueduct track in Queens, and tennis fans visiting in August may want to take in the US Open at Flushing Meadows. For plain old wholesome fun, it's hard to avoid Central Park, which attracts some 25 million visitors every year.

Spectator Sports

New York has professional teams in all the major American sports. Tickets can be purchased from Ticketmaster (www.ticketmaster.com) or, in most cases, from the team's box office.

BASEBALL
New York Mets
Citi Field, Flushing Meadows Corona Park, Flushing; tel: 718-507-8499; http://newyork. mets.mlb.com; subway: Mets-Willets Point
New York Yankees
Yankee Stadium, 161st Street/ River Avenue, The Bronx; tel: 718-293-6000; http://newyork.yankees.mlb.co m; subway: 161st St/Yankee Stadium

BASKETBALL
New Jersey Nets
Continental Airlines Arena, Meadowlands Sports Complex, East Rutherford, NJ; tel: 800-765-6387; www.nba.com/nets
New York Knicks
Madison Square Garden, Seventh Avenue/31st and 33rd streets; tel: 212-465-6073; www.nba.com/knicks; subway:

Above: future players for the New York Knicks.

34th Street Penn Station; map p.152 B2

FOOTBALL
New York Giants
Giants Stadium, Meadowlands Sports Complex, East Rutherford, NJ; tel: 201-935-8222; www.giants.com; NJ Transit day-of-game service from NYC Port Authority Bus Terminal
New York Jets
Giants Stadium, Meadowlands Sports Complex, East Rutherford, NJ; tel: 201-925-3900; www.newyorkjets.com; NJ Transit day-of-game service from NYC Port Authority Bus Terminal

HORSE RACING
Aqueduct Race Track
110-00 Rockaway Boulevard, Jamaica, Queens; tel: 718-641-4700; www.nyra.com; subway: Old Aqueduct Station
Belmont Park
2150 Hempstead Turnpike, Elmont, NY; tel: 516-488-6000; www.nyra.com
Meadowlands Racetrack
Meadowlands Sports Complex, East Rutherford, NJ; tel: 201-843-2446; www.thebigm.com

ICE HOCKEY
New York Islanders
Nassau Veterans Memorial Coliseum, 1255 Hempstead Turnpike, Uniondale; tel: 631-888-9000; http://islanders.nhl.com
New York Rangers
Madison Square Garden, Seventh Avenue/31st and 33rd streets; Ticketmaster, tel: 212-307-7171; http://rangers.nhl.com; subway: 34th Street Penn Station; map p.152 B2

SOCCER
New York Red Bulls
Giants Stadium, Meadowlands Sports Complex, East

Left: CitiField, the Mets new home from 2009.

Park or the **Rockefeller Center** (tel: 212-332-7654). **Sky Rink**, (Pier 61 at the Hudson River; tel: 212-336-6100), part of Chelsea Piers, has skating year-round.

RUNNING

City parks have miles of jogging paths. For information, contact the **New York Road Runners Club** (tel: 212-860-4455; www.nyrr.org) or visit the **Running Center** (461 Central Park West; www.therunningroom.com).

TENNIS

Tennis can be played in Central Park and other city parks, and at several private facilities:

Manhattan Plaza Racquet Club
450 West 43rd Street; tel: 212-594-0554

Midtown Tennis Club
341 Eighth Avenue/West 27th Street; tel: 212-989-8572

USTA Billie Jean King National Tennis Center
Flushing Meadows-Corona Park, Queens; tel: 718-760-6200
NY's largest public tennis facilitiy and home of the US Open.

For numerous sports in one place, try the **Chelsea Piers Sports and Entertainment Complex** (tel: 212-336-6666; www.chelseapiers.com), which stretches along the Hudson River between West 17th and 23rd streets. Facilities include a multi-tiered golf driving range, boating, bowling, and in-line skating; day passes are available at the sports center, which has an Olympic-size pool, running track, and rock-climbing wall.

Rutherford, NJ; tel: 877-727-6223; http://redbull.newyork.mlsnet.com; NJ Transit day-of-game service from NYC Port Authority Bus Terminal

Participant Sports

New York City offers a wide array of recreational facilities, many in the city's parks. Baseball diamonds and basketball courts are readily available. In Central Park, roads are closed to traffic on summer weekends for the benefit of cyclists and in-line skaters. For information, call 311 in New York or 212-NEW YORK outside the city.

SEE ALSO PARKS AND GARDENS, P.116

GOLF

You'll find public golf courses at **Pelham Bay Park**, **Van Cortlandt Park** (both in the Bronx), and at **Latourette Park** in Staten Island.

HORSEBACK RIDING

There are bridle paths in several city parks. Horses can be rented at these locations:

Forest Park
Forest Equine Center, 88-11 70th Road; tel: 718-263-3500

Pelham Bay Park
Bronx Equestrian Center, 9 Shore Road; tel: 718-885-0551

Prospect Park
Kensington Stables, 51 Caton Place; tel: 718-972-4588

Van Cortlandt Park
Riverdale Equestrian Center, Broadway/West 254th Street; tel: 718-548-4848

ICE-SKATING

In winter visit the **Wollman** (tel: 212-439-6900) and **Lasker** rinks in **Central**

The city is host to numerous sporting events, including:

• **US Open Tennis Championship**. USTA Billie Jean King National Tennis Center, Flushing Meadows Corona Park, Queens; tel: 718-760-6200; www.usopen.org. August.

• **New York City Marathon**. New York Road Runners Club; tel: 212-860-4455; www.nyrr.org. November.

• **Five Borough Bike Tour**. Bike New York, 891 Amsterdam Avenue. Tel: 212-932-2453. May.

Theater

Give your regards to Broadway, but don't overlook off-Broadway or, for that matter, off-off-Broadway. As the epicenter of American theater, New York has a broad range of shows and venues to choose from. And with the price of Broadway tickets at an all-time high, you may want to explore the offerings of lesser-known theaters, which often provide a far more intimate and affecting experience than the blockbusters around Times Square. Have a taste for the avant-garde? New and experimental works are staged in numerous tiny theaters, some no more than a darkened room with a few chairs.

Broadway

Of the 39 theaters known as 'Broadway,' only a handful are on the Great White Way itself. Most are on side streets around Times Square, from 41st Street to the mid-50s.

The New York theater has been going strong for a while now. Broadway's theaters sell more than 12 million tickets annually, earning $938 million dollars. Imported megahits – *Phantom of the Opera, Cats* – dominated the box office for more than a decade, but American dramas and comedies are also produced with reassuring regularity. In an average season of 36 new productions, roughly half are new plays.

The clean-up of Times Square in the 1990s made the Broadway experience more family-friendly. Gone are (most of) the porno shops and peep shows. Nowhere is the transformation more evi-

Go to **www.playbill.com** or **www.theatermania.com** for information and tickets.

Above: see experimental theater at La Mama in the East Village.

dent than in the spate of Disney shows such as *The Lion King, Beauty and the Beast, Tarzan,* and *Mary Poppins.*

Off-Broadway

Broadway may make the headlines, but off-Broadway is considered by many to be the true soul of New York theater. Some playwrights bypass Broadway altogether in favor of the smaller venues. The vast majority of off-Broadway theaters, and indeed, the more experimental off-off-Broadway theaters, are Downtown. A hit in an off-Broadway theater like Play-wrights Horizons or the Public Theater often provides the confidence backers need

to move Uptown. Among the most prominent off-Broadway theaters are:

Cherry Lane Theater
38 Commerce Street/Bedford Street; tel: 212-989-2020; www.cherrylanetheatre.org; subway: Christopher St; map p.154 B3
The list of playwrights and actors associated with the Cherry Lane reads like a Who's Who of American theater – F. Scott Fitzgerald, Eugene O'Neill, David Mamet, John Malkovich, Barbra Streisand and Kevin Bacon, among others.

La Mama e.t.c.
74A East 4th Street/Second Avenue and Bowery; tel: 212-475-7710; www.lamama.org; subway: 2nd Ave; map p.155 C2
La Mama has produced new and experimental theater for more than 45 years.

Lucille Lortel Theater
121 Christopher Street/Bedford Street; tel: 212-279-4200; www.lortel.org; subway: Christopher St; map p.154 B3
One of the city's most prominent off-Broadway theaters, known for crowd-pleasing productions featuring well-

Left: high-steppin' Broadway babes take to the stage.

year, many by emerging young playwrights.
Union Square Theatre
100 East 17th Street/Park Avenue South; tel: 212-505-0700; subway: Union Square; map p.155 D3
New and challenging drama, comedy, and musicals. This is also a good area for dinner before or after the show.

Tickets

The TKTS booth under the red steps in Father Duffy Square on Broadway (at 47th Street) has discounted tickts (25–50 percent off) for that night's performances. Open Mon–Sat 3pm–8pm for evening performances, Sat–Wed 10am–2pm for matinees, and Sun 11am–7.30pm. A booth at the corner of Front and John streets near the South Street Seaport sells tickets for the same-day evening and next-day matinee performances (Mon–Sat 11am–6pm).

Unsold tickets are often available at the box office an hour or so before show time. Numerous ticket brokers can be contacted via hotel concierges. Expect to pay top dollar.

The **Times Square Visitor Center** on Broadway between 46th and 47th streets also sells tickets.

In summer the Public Theater stages **Shakespeare in the Park** at Central Park's Delacorte Theater. Performances are free and, in the past, have featured such well-known actors as Philip Seymour Hoffman, Meryl Streep, Kevin Kline, and Denzel Washington.

known actors, directors, and playwrights.
Playwrights Horizons
416 West 42nd Street/Ninth and Tenth avenues; tel: 212-564-1235; www.playwrights horizons.org; subway: 42nd St; map p.152 B4
One of several venues on Theater Row, this theater is devoted to staging the work of developing playwrights with some of the hottest up-and-coming actors on the scene.
The Public Theater
425 Lafayette Street/Astor Place; tel: 212-539-8500; www.publictheater.org; subway: Astor Place; map p.155 C2
A highly regarded arts organization with a complex of theaters dedicated to innovative and avant-garde plays and

musicals, as well as Shakespeare and other classics.
SoHo Playhouse
15 Vandam Street/Sixth Avenue and Varick Street; tel: 212-691-1555; www.sohoplayhouse.com; subway: Spring St; map p.154 A2
Edward Albee, Lanford Wilson, Sam Shepherd, and Amiri Baraka are just a few of the playwrights whose early works were presented at this 199-seat venue.
Theater for the New City
155 First Avenue/9th and 10th streets; tel: 212-254-1109; www. theaterforthenewcity.net; subway: First Ave; map p.155 D2
More than 30 new American plays are staged here each

Below: New York's best-known off-Broadway theater.

Transportation

Traffic can be murder in New York, so do yourself a favor and leave the car at home. Public transportation (or your own two feet) can get you anywhere you want to go in the metropolitan area, and riding the subway or hopping a cab is a quintessential Big Apple experience. Although Downtown's jumbled streets can be confusing, getting around the rest of Manhattan is a snap. Just remember that avenues run north–south, and numbered streets run east–west. When in doubt, ask for directions. New Yorkers are sometimes rough around the edges, but most are happy to help.

Getting There

By Air
New York's two major airports, **John F. Kennedy** and **LaGuardia**, are respectively 15 and 8 miles (24 and 13km) from Manhattan. Driving time to the airports is just under one hour, although heavy traffic can easily double this. The metropolitan area's third major airport, **Newark Liberty International**, is actually across the Hudson in New Jersey, but for many New Yorkers can be more convenient than JFK and LaGuardia.

By Rail
Trains arrive and depart from Manhattan's two railroad terminals: Grand Central Terminal at Park Avenue and East 42nd Street, and Pennsylvania Station at Seventh Avenue and West 33rd Street. Amtrak information, tel: 800-872-7245.

By Bus
The main bus terminal is the Port Authority (Eighth Avenue at West 40th and 42nd streets). The station sits atop two subway lines and is

Above: taxis stack up at Grand Central Terminal.

serviced by bus companies and local commuter lines. City buses stop outside. Greyhound information, tel: 800-231-2222.

Getting Around

Airport Transportation
AirTrain is a rail system connecting JFK and Newark airports with the subway and the regional rail network. AirTrain JFK: tel: 877-535-2478; www.airtrainjfk.com. AirTrain Newark: tel: 888-397-4636; www.airtrainnewark.com.

New York Airport Service (tel: 212-875-8200; www.nyairportservice.com) operates **buses** to and from Manhattan and JFK and LaGuardia. Pick-up and drop-off points include: the Port Authority Bus Terminal, Penn Station, and Grand Central Terminal.

Newark Liberty Airport Express buses, operated by Olympia Trails (tel: 877-863-9275; www.coachusa.com), run regularly between Newark Airport and Manhattan, calling at the Port Authority Bus Terminal, Penn Station, Grand Central, and Fifth Avenue.

A door-to-door minibus service from all three airports to hotels and other destinations in Manhattan is provided by **Super Shuttle** (tel: 800-258-3826; www.supershuttle.com), offering a frequent service for about $20.

Subways and Buses
Subways and buses run 24 hours daily, less frequently after midnight. Fares must be paid by exact change (minimum $2), but it's much better to get a MetroCard, available at subway ticket booths. You

Left: New York subways run all day and all night long.

Download New York City subway and bus maps at www.mta.info.

is $2.50 upon entry plus 40¢ for every one-fifth of a mile (when the taxicab is traveling at 6 miles an hour or more) or 60 seconds (when not in motion). The flat rate for a taxi to or from JFK and Manhattan is $45 plus tolls.

One fare covers up to four passengers (five in a few of the larger cabs). There is a $1 surcharge on all taxi rides from 4pm to 8pm on weekdays, and a night surcharge of 50¢ from 8pm to 6am. Taxis now accept credit cards (with no minimum or fees). Always remember to take a receipt, just in case you leave something behind. If you do, call 311 and they can help you locate the taxi and your missing belongings.

Driving in New York

Driving is the least efficient way to get around New York. Drivers are aggressive, traffic is frequently snarled, street parking is scant, parking tickets are punitive, and commercial parking lots and garages can be extremely expensive.

If a car is necessary, rentals are available at all airports and numerous locations in the city. In order to rent a car, you must be at least 21, have a valid driver's license and a major credit card. Be sure that you are properly insured.

Generally, avenues in Manhattan run north to south; streets run east to west. Even-numbered streets tend to have one-way eastbound traffic; odd-numbered streets, westbound traffic. There are very few exceptions. Most avenues are one-way, either north or south, the major exception being Park Avenue, which has two-way traffic north of 44th Street.

---

charge it up as much as you want (minimum $4), and an amount is deducted each time you swipe the card entering the subway or boarding buses. This will be cheaper and more convenient than paying each time. Unlimited-ride passes good for seven or 30 days are also available, and a one-day 'Fun Pass' is sold at newsstands, hotels, and in subway stations.

Buses run on most avenues (except Park Avenue) as well as on the following major cross-streets: Houston, 14th, 23rd, 34th, 42nd, 57th, 66th, 86th, 116th, 125th, and a few

others. Subway trains cross town at 14th and 42nd streets, but there is no north–south line east of Lexington Avenue or west of Eighth Avenue and Broadway above 59th Street. Subway and bus information, tel: 718-330-1234; www.mta.info MetroCard information, tel: 212-638-7622.

PATH (Port Authority Trans Hudson) **trains** run from six stations in Manhattan to most parts of New Jersey. PATH information, tel: 800-234-7284.

Taxis

Taxis, all metered, cruise the streets and must be hailed, although there are designated taxi stands at places like Grand Central Terminal and Penn Station. Be sure to flag down an official yellow cab, not an unlicensed cab. The base rates on taxi fares

Right: a city bus speeds along.

Pedestrian area
Accommodation
Shopping

p150 | p151
p152 | p153
p154 | p155
p156 | p157

4

3

New Jersey
New York

Hudson

Circle Line Boat Tour

West Side Highway (Miller Highway)

Freedom Place

2

99
98
97
96
95
94
93
92
90
88

N.Y. City
Passenger
Ship Terminal

12th Ave

West End Avenue

West

DE WITT
CLINTON
PARK

Terminal 5

West Side Highway

Eleventh Avenue

Tenth Avenue

Ninth Avenue

Amsterdam Avenue

Columbus Avenue

Broadway

1

Intrepid
Sea, Air & Space
Museum

0   400 yds
0   400 m

West
West
West
West
West
West
West

61st
60th
59th
58th
57th
56th
55th
54th
53rd
52nd
51st
50th
49th
48th
47th   St

St Luke's
Roosevelt
Hospital

Fordham
University

Lincoln
Center

Metropolitan
Opera

New York
State Theater

Avery
Fisher
Hall

A. Tully
Hall

V. Beaumont
Theater

Julliard
School

Pottery Barn

Con-Edison   West 66th

Merkin
Concert
Hall

West 66th
West 67th

Lincoln
Square

ABC Studios

Broadway

W. 69th St
W. 68th St
W. 63rd St
W. 62nd St

Central Park

72ND ST

Verdi
Square

Beacon
Theatre

Beacon Hotel

The Milburn

McGinn
Cazale
Theatre

On the Ave

Zabar's

79'

West
West
West
West
West
West
West

Riverside Drive

West End Avenue

Eleanor
Roosevelt

59TH ST
COLUMBUS CIRCLE

Time
Warner
Center

Hudson

Mandarin
Oriental

Columbus
Circle

Maine
Memorial

Trump Internat'l
Hotel & Tower

Museum of
Arts & Design

Newsweek
Bldg

57TH ST

Carnegie Ha

Hearst
Tower

Alvin Ailey
Dance Theater

Wellington Hot

Ed
Sullivan
Theater

1700 B'way
Bldg

7TH AVE

50TH ST

7th Avenue

New Y
City Ce

Allian
Cap.
B.

New York
Hilton Towers

150

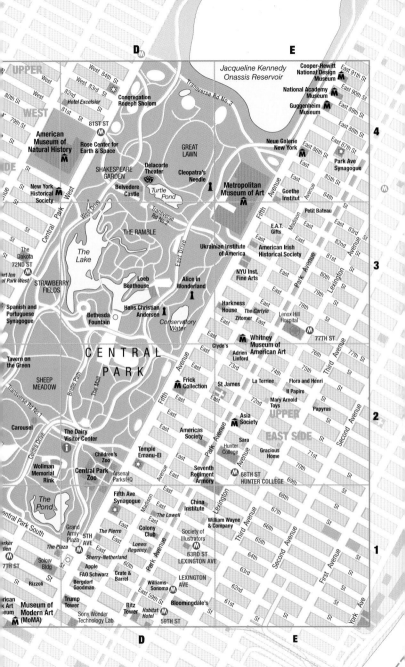

D

E

7TH AVE

West

Colony
Music
Center

Renaissance
New York
Times Sq.
nation Center
assy Theater)

Henri
Bendel

Trump
Tower

LEXINGTON AVE

American
Folk Art
Museum

Museum of
Modern Art
(MoMA)

50TH ST

Peninsula

Argosy
Book Store

Bloomingdale's

59TH ST

Seventh Avenue

West

CBS
Bldg

Takashimaya

Sony Wonder
Technology Lab

Borders

East

Third

Avenue

58th St

56th St

Rockefeller
Center

St Thomas

Elizabeth
Arden

Bauman
Rare Books

East 57th Street

Duffy
Square

Radio City
Music Hall

49TH
ST

Chase
Bldg

RADIO CITY
MUSIC HALL

Paley Center
for Media

Omni
Berkshire
Place

Lever
House

Central
Synagogue

Hotel 57

919
Third Ave

McGraw-Hill
Bldg

GE
Bldg

Olympic
Tower

Park Ave
Plaza

55th

The Hotel
at Times
Square

48th
ST

50TH ST
ROCKEF.
CENTER

St Patrick's
Cathedral

Crabtree &
Evelyn

Seagram
Bldg

Citigroup
Center

909 Third Ave

Fox News
Bldg

Rockefeller Plaza

Madison

Saks
Fifth Avenue

New York
Palace

345
Park Ave

LEXINGTON
AVE

54th

Manhattan
Arts & Antiques
Center

Toys R Us

Comfort Inn
Midtown

mes
are

MID-

DIAMOND
DISTRICT

(Sixth Avenue)

Mutual of
America Bldg

East 53rd

Times
Square

International
Center of
Photography

TOWN

St

Wardorf-
Astoria

51ST ST

52nd

asablanca

Algonquin

Barclay
New York

UBS

W New York

Pod
Hotel

51st

ND ST

42ND
ST

Iroquois

St

JP Morgan
Chase

800 Third Ave
Bldg

50th

Avenue

Verizon
Bldg

Royalton

St

East

Helmsley
Bldg

49th

Grace
Bldg

42ND ST
BRYANT
PARK

East

Vanderbilt

Prest

MetLife
Bldg

47th

First

Avenue

New York
Public Library

Fifth

East

Depew Pl.

Grand Central
Terminal

46th

Hammarskjöld
Plaza

1 Dag
Hammarskjöld
Plaza

Avenue

American
Standard
(Radiator) Bldg

Lincoln
Bldg

Graybar
Bldg

45th

Third

Beekman
Tower

Lord &
Taylor

Whitney Museum
of American Art
at Altria

42ND ST
GRAND
CENTRAL

Chrysler
Bldg

Chanin
Bldg

44th

Second

Millennium
UN
Plaza

Statue
of Peace

omfort Inn
anhattan

East
Morgans
East

101
Park Ave

Former
Mobil
Bldg

43rd

42nd

2 UN
Plaza
1 UN
Plaza

United Nations Plaza

United
Nations

MURRAY

Lutheran Church in
America

East

East

40th

Murray Hill
East Suites

Ford
Foundation
Bldg

St

Secretariat
Bldg

Empire
State Bldg

Morgan
Library

East

East

39th

Former
Daily News
Bldg

Tudor City Pl.

St

Hammarskjöld
Library

uinta
hattan

Church of the
Incarnation

East

38th

HILL

37th

Marriott
ExecuStay
Aurora

2

East

36th

St

33RD ST

35th

Exit Plaza

34th

33rd

Entrance

ST GABRIEL'S
PARK

Street

1

Hotel Roger
Williams

32nd

hwin

Ramada Inn
Eastside

31st

Avenue

East

New York
Life

28TH ST

Lexington

29th

Third

30th

St

E 34th St
Heliport

p150 p151

East

28th

Avenue

St

p152 p153

Park

East

27th

Second

p154 p155

opolitan Life
ance Tower

25th

26th

St

First

N.Y.U.
Medical
Center

Franklin D. Roosevelt Drive

East

p156 p157

23RD ST

24th

East

D

E

153

A | B

54
53 Bloomfield St
52
51
49
48
46
45
42
40
34

Holland Tunnel
(Toll)

4
3
2
1

Chelsea Market
Maritime Hotel
Joyce Theater
West 23RD
West West 20th
Design Within Reach
Ninth Ave West 19th
West West 18th
MEATPACKING DISTRICT
16th
West 14TH ST 8TH AVE
15th
Rubin Museum of Art
17th

Little W. 12th St
Hotel Gansevoort
Gansevoort
14th
Alegrias Flamenco Theater
Yivo Institute for Jewish Research
West Street

Fire Boat Station

Horatio
Jackson Square
13th
Greenwich Avenue
14TH ST
14TH ST

The Jane
Jane
Street
Yo Ya
Kidding Around

West
12th
Abingdon Guest House
Street Street
12th
mxyplyzyk

Bethune
Abingdon Square
Street
Street

Westbeth
Bank
Biography Bookshop
Village Vanguard
GREENWICH
St Vincent's Hospital
Forbes Magazine Galleries

West
11th
Avenue
W. 4th St
New School for Social Research
St W. 11th St

Perry
Hudson
Street
Bleecker
Street
Waverly Avenue
Patchin Pl
Jefferson Market Library
W. 10th St
Church of the Ascension

Charles
Street
10th
Sheridan Square
Waverly Pl
West 8th St
East

LOWER
Lucille Lortel Theater
CHRISTOPHER ST SHERIDAN SQ.
Washington Place
Washington Square Hotel
East
VILLA

West
Bedford
Christopher
Grove
W. 4th St
Jones St
Waverly
Washington Sq N
East
8th

Weehawken St
Barrow
Commerce St
Cornelia St
Provincetown Playhouse
WASHINGTON SQUARE PARK
Washington Sq E

WEST
St-Luke-in-the-Fields
Morton
Cherry Lane Theater
W 4TH ST
Bleecker St Records
Wash. Sq. S
Waverly

Our Lady of Pompeii
Minetta Lane Theater
Wash Sq S

Leroy
St Luke's Place
Seventh
Carmine St
Father Demo Square
Caffè Reggio
Judson Memorial Church
NY University
Shakespeare & Co

Clarkson
St
Downing St
Alphaville
Bleecker
LaGuardia Place
West 4th St
3rd

SIDE
WEST
W. Houston
King
St
Street
HOUSTON ST
West
Houston
Street
Mercer
Great

Washington
Charlton
Americas
Prince
Bond

VILLAGE
Vandam
Street
MacDougal
Dia Center for the Arts
University Plaza
BLEECKER ST

Spring
New York City Fire Museum
Street
SPRING ST
Joyce Soho
BROADWAY LAFAYETTE
NOLITA

Dominick
St
SoHo Playhouse
Spring
Aveda
Mercer
MAC
Apple Store
SOHO
Eas

Watts
Hudson
Broome
St
Sullivan
Thompson
PRINCE ST
Little Singer Bldg
Dean & DeLuca
Old St Patrick's Cathedral

Desbrosses St
Canal Street
the
Broome
SoHo Cast-Iron Historic District
Broadway
Eastern Mountain Sports
LITTLE
SPRING ST

Vestry St
of
Spring
Ohio Theater
Performing Garage
Bloomingdale's Soho
McNally Jackson
Mott
Prince

Laight
St
Americas
Grand St
Grunther Bldg
Pearl River Mart
Mulberry

Hubert
St
CANAL ST
Wooster
Greene
Haughwout Bldg
Children's Museum of the Arts
Cleveland Pl
Kenmare St

Beach St
Ericson Pl.
York St
John's La.
Mercer
Old Police Bldg

North
Moore
St
Tribeca Grand
Lispenard St
CANAL ST
Lafayette
Centre St
ITALY
BOWER

Manhattan Community College
Tribeca Film Center
Franklin St
Tribeca
Walker St
Howard St
Elizabeth

TRIBECA

A | B

154

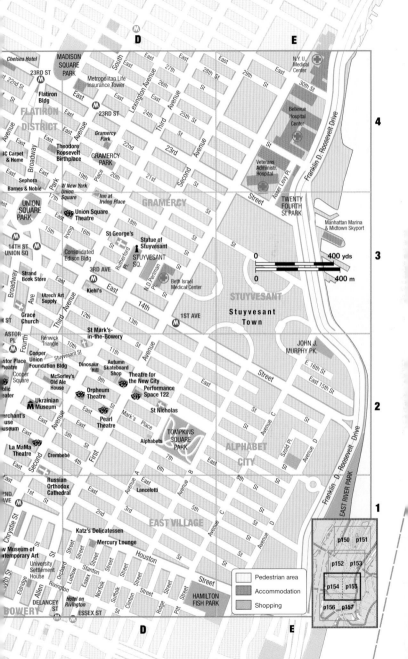

Chelsea Hotel

MADISON SQUARE PARK

23RD ST

Flatiron Bldg

FLATIRON DISTRICT

Metropolitan Life Insurance Tower

East 27th

East

East

East

East 28th St

East 29th

N.Y.U. Medical Center

East 30th St

East 22nd St

23RD ST

East

23rd

Bellevue Hospital Center

Franklin D. Roosevelt Drive

4

3C Carpet & Home

Theodore Roosevelt Birthplace

Gramercy Park

GRAMERCY PARK

Veterans Administ. Hospital

Sephora

Barnes & Noble

W 19th Union Square

20th Place

21st

Asser Levy Pl.

Street

Inn at Irving Place

GRAMERCY

TWENTY FOURTH St PARK

UNION SQUARE PARK

Union Square Theatre

18th

St

Manhattan Marina & Midtown Skyport

14TH ST UNION SQ

15th

St George's

Consolidated Edison Bldg

Statue of Stuyvesant

STUYVESANT SQ.

0   400 yds

3

Strand Book Store

3RD AVE

Beth Israel Medical Center

0   400 m

Utrecht Art Supply

Kiehl's

14th

STUYVESANT

Grace Church

12th

13th

1ST AVE

Stuyvesant Town

ASTOR PL

St Mark's-in-the-Bowery

Renwick Triangle

10th

11th

JOHN J. MURPHY PK.

Cooper Union Foundation Bldg

Stuyvesant St

Dinosaur Hill

Autumn Skateboard Shop

E. 16th St

stor Place heatre

Cooper Square

McSorley's Old Ale House

Orpheum Theatre

Theatre for the New City

Street

East 15th St

Ukrainian Museum

Performance Space 122

2

erchant's use useum

Pearl Theatre

St Mark's Place

St Nicholas

Avenue C

Avenue D

La MaMa Theatre

Alphabets

TOMPKINS SQUARE PARK

Scout Pl.

Crembebé

4th

7th

ALPHABET CITY

Russian Orthodox Cathedral

East

2nd

Lancelotti

6th

EAST VILLAGE

Avenue A

Avenue B

Avenue C

Avenue D

EAST RIVER PARK

1

Chrystie St

Katz's Delicatessen

Mercury Lounge

Houston

w Museum of temporary Art

University Settlement House

Stanton

Rivington

Essex Street

Street

DELANCEY ST

Hotel on Rivington

ESSEX ST

Ridge

Pitt

HAMILTON FISH PARK

Pedestrian area

Accommodation

Shopping

p150   p151

p152   p153

p154   p155

p156   p157

D   E

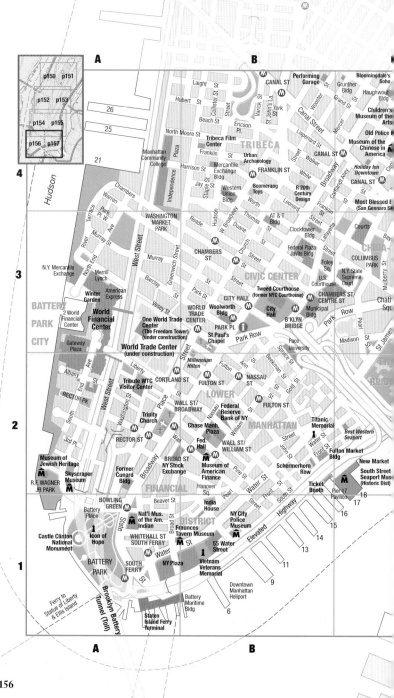

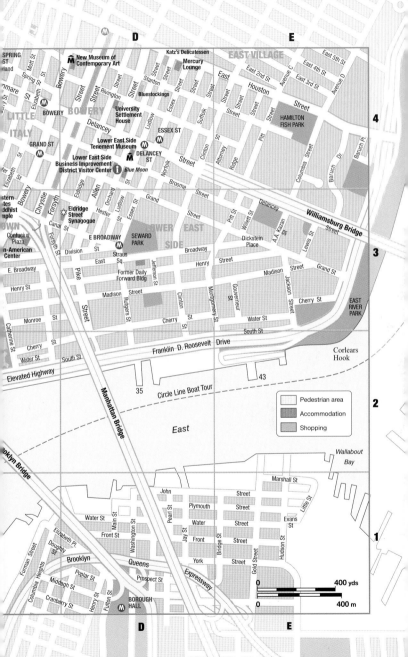

Atlas Index

SIGHTS OF INTEREST

158

Index

Insight Smart Guide: New York
Compiled by: John Gattuso
Updated by: Karen Farquhar
Cartography: James Macdonald
All photography by Britta Jaschinski/Apa except: akg-images, London 86C, 86/87T; Alamy 114/114T; Bronx Museum of Arts 105BL; Tom Caravaglia 47; Corbis 46C, 46/47T, 47B, 70T&CB, 71CT, 82C, 105BR, 109B; Getty Images 71T, 106C, 108T, 146/147T; Istock 5TL, 5TR, 149; Catherine Karnow 73B; Bob Krist 5TL&TR; Leonardo 73, 75; metsfan84 145; Anna Mockford & Nick Bonetti/Apa 2B, 4T&B, 5C&CR, 9T&B, 13T, 15B, 21B, 23T&B, 25B, 33B, 44/45T, 58/59T, 59B, 60C, 64B, 72/73T, 75B, 78B, 84C, 94BR, 95T, 98/99B, 99TL&TR, 102B, 102/103T, 103B, 106/107T, 118T, 120T, 144C; Museum of Modern Art 91B; National

Museum of the American Indian 100; PA/EPA 9, 58–9, 71CB&B; Tony Perrottet /Apa 146B; Mark Read/Apa 15T, 50C, 50/51T, 51B, 52TL&TR, 55BR, 57T&B, 60/61T, 68C, 115BL&BR, 134C, 135B, 136TL&TR, 137B, 138T, 139BR, 140T142T, 143BL&BR; Rex Features 46–7, 83B.
Picture Manager: Steven Lawrence
Series Editor: Jason Mitchell
First Edition 2008
Second Edition 2009
© 2009 Apa Publications GmbH & Co.
Verlag KG Singapore Branch, Singapore.
Worldwide distribution enquiries:
Apa Publications GmbH & Co. Verlag KG (Singapore Branch); apasin@signet.com.sg
Distributed in the UK and Ireland by:
GeoCenter International Ltd; sales@geocenter.co.uk

Distributed in the United States by:
Langenscheidt Publishers, Inc.;
orders@langenscheidt.com
Contacting the Editors
We would appreciate it if readers would alert us to errors in information by writing to:
Apa Publications, PO Box 7910, London SE1 1WE, UK; insight@apaguide.co.uk
No part of this book may be reproduced, stored in a retrieval system or transmitted in any form or by any means (electronic, mechanical, photocopying, recording or otherwise), without prior written permission of Apa Publications. Brief text quotations with use of photographs are exempted for book review purposes only. Information has been obtained from sources believed to be reliable, but its accuracy and completeness, and the opinions based thereon, are not guaranteed.